Praise for
Viral

"There are plenty of books on technology by writers who don't understand Christianity. And there are plenty of books on Christianity by people who are lost in the world of technology. The genius of Leonard Sweet is that he navigates both worlds, and his insight into living as a believer in today's media-driven culture is not just helpful, it's critical. *Viral* connects the dots between social media and our witness to the world."
—PHIL COOKE, PhD, filmmaker, media consultant, and author
    of *Jolt! Get the Jump on a World That's Constantly Changing*

"*Viral* is culturally astute, Christ centered, gospel focused, kingdom oriented. Tweet that! Leonard Sweet captures the zeitgeist of our age in a biblically subversive way that redeems our technoculture for Christ. He explores the promise and the peril of our brave new world of electronic connectivity, while showing Christians how to apply the gospel at the crossroads of modernity and postmodernity, individualism and community, rational and relational faith. If you are skeptical of TGIF (Twitter, Google, iPhone, Facebook) or want to learn more, you must read this book."
—BRIAN GODAWA, screenwriter of *To End All Wars* and author
    of *Hollywood Worldviews, Word Pictures,* and *Noah Primeval*

"Leonard Sweet has always been Patient Zero for Spiritually Transmitted Dis-ease, and *Viral* transmits the pathogen of the Paraclete better than any other work I know. Sweet connects the incarnation to the web, taking readers beyond the vapid and introducing us to the layers of meaning behind the pixels on the screen."
—DAVID MCDONALD, author of *The Undwellable City*

"In *Viral,* Leonard Sweet paints a fascinating picture of today's highly creative TGIF culture, while inviting the Gutenberg Generation into a new experience of Jesus's timeless campfire story. The Googler Generation's passion for spreading the divine viral epidemic through their passion for social media and narratives, as well as their longing for connectivity and participation, provides fascinating challenges for all followers of Jesus. Christians need to become part of God's viral revival. Sweet shows us how."
—STEPHAN JOUBERT, extraordinary professor in New Testament studies,
    University of Pretoria, South Africa; extraordinary professor of contemporary ecclesiology, University of the Free State, South Africa; research fellow at Radboud University, Nijmegen, The Netherlands; and editor of *Ekerk/Echurch*

"The church has never been more equipped to reach people with the gospel. With that opportunity comes a tremendous responsibility to communicate the unchanging message of the gospel in an ever-changing, hyper-connected culture. Leonard Sweet shares how Christ-followers can spread this life-changing message and bring about a revival unlike any we have seen before. He provides practical ideas and pastoral insight into leveraging the exponential opportunities available to share our faith through social media."

—TIM SCHRAEDER, co-director of the Center for Church Communication and editor of *Outspoken: Conversations on Church Communication*

LEONARD SWEET

VIRAL

How Social Networking
Is Poised to Ignite Revival

WATERBROOK
PRESS

VIRAL
PUBLISHED BY WATERBROOK PRESS
12265 Oracle Boulevard, Suite 200
Colorado Springs, Colorado 80921

All Scripture quotations, unless otherwise indicated, are taken from the Holy Bible, New International Version®, NIV®. Copyright © 1973, 1978, 1984 by Biblica Inc.™ Used by permission of Zondervan. All rights reserved worldwide. www.zondervan.com. Scripture quotations marked (DRB) are taken from the Douay-Rheims Bible. Scripture quotations marked (ESV) are taken from The Holy Bible, English Standard Version, copyright © 2001 by Crossway Bibles, a division of Good News Publishers. Used by permission. All rights reserved. Scripture quotations marked (JB) are taken from the Jerusalem Bible, © 1966, 1967 and 1968 by Darton, Longman & Todd Ltd. and Doubleday & Company Inc. Scripture quotations marked (KJV) are taken from the King James Version. Scripture quotations marked (MSG) are taken from The Message by Eugene H. Peterson. Copyright © 1993, 1994, 1995, 1996, 2000, 2001, 2002. Used by permission of NavPress Publishing Group. All rights reserved. Scripture quotations marked (NKJV) are taken from the New King James Version®. Copyright © 1982 by Thomas Nelson Inc. Used by permission. All rights reserved. Scripture quotations marked (NRSV) are from the New Revised Standard Version of the Bible, copyright © 1989 by the Division of Christian Education of the National Council of the Churches of Christ in the USA. Used by permission. All rights reserved.

Italics in Scripture quotations reflect the author's added emphasis.

ISBN 978-0-307-45915-2
ISBN 978-0-307-45916-9 (electronic)

Cover design by Mark D. Ford

Grateful acknowledgment is made for the use of "The Mysting," copyright © 2012, by Timothy Orton; "A Prayer for When We Limit God," copyright © 2012, by Craig Oldenburg; and the translation of Ephesians 2:10, copyright © 2012, by Jerrell Jobe.

Published in the United States by WaterBrook Multnomah, an imprint of the Crown Publishing Group, a division of Random House Inc., New York.

WATERBROOK and its deer colophon are registered trademarks of Random House Inc.

Library of Congress Cataloging-in-Publication Data
Sweet, Leonard I.
    Viral : how social networking is poised to ignite revival / Leonard Sweet. — 1st ed.
      p. cm.
    Includes bibliographical references (pp. 199–229).
    ISBN 978-0-307-45915-2 — ISBN 978-0-307-45916-9 (electronic)
  1. Online social networks—Religious aspects—Christianity. I. Title.
    BR99.74.S94 2012
    269'.202856754—dc23
                          2011039572

Printed in the United States of America
2012—First Edition

10 9 8 7 6 5 4 3 2 1

SPECIAL SALES
Most WaterBrook Multnomah books are available at special quantity discounts when purchased in bulk by corporations, organizations, and special-interest groups. Custom imprinting or excerpting can also be done to fit special needs. For information, please e-mail SpecialMarkets@WaterBrookMultnomah.com or call 1-800-603-7051.

To Aaron Linne,
who called me out and set me on the TGIF path.

CONTENTS

Acknowledgments

There is a little-known phenomenon called change blindness. When two similar but not identical pictures of a scene are shown in rapid succession, we can fail to notice quite substantial differences and changes. It is possible for us to still see the old picture even when we are looking at an almost totally new scene. More than we care to admit, perceptions are predictive hypotheses. Said another way: we see what we were looking for.

Certain people have helped me fight my change blindness. I dedicated this book to one of them. Aaron Linne solicited his followers on Twitter to nominate those authors/pastors/musicians who should be on Twitter, but weren't. When my name appeared, he e-mailed me and challenged me to take being called out by the Twitterati seriously. Not only that, he engaged me in a conversation about social networking that showcased my change blindness.

Don Heatley, church planter and videographer of my pioneering *AquaChurch* videos, reinforced what Aaron was telling me by introducing me to the concept of "persistence of vision." Our minds can fill in the blanks between the twenty-four frames per second, the threshold that changes photography into videography. Video/film captures reality as a series of stills, when the truth is that reality was never still in the first place. What if our notions of truth are indeed "24 fps" samples of reality, Heatley asked, and we sample parts of reality into easily manageable stills but never capture the infinite motion of the whole continuous stream?

The rest, as they say, is history.

Charlie Chaplin, when asked the secret of his success, replied that it was "sheer perseverance to the point of madness."[1] The people who shared my madness in writing this book were my agent, Mark Sweeney; my research assistant, Betty O'Brien; my editor, Ron Lee; and my coauthor on novels, Lori Wagner. All of them kept me believing in this project.

I almost dedicated this book to my brother John, a Presbyterian minister in the Philadelphia presbytery, who keeps arguing the Gutenberg case in my ear. You might say I wrote this book to change his mind.

It is the role of family not to allow our preconceptions to fill in the blanks and create the illusion that we have captured the whole of truth. Whenever I started to project my snippets of reality on them (whose minds, in turn, fill in those blanks again); whenever I started to mistake the optical illusion of my projected shadows to stand for the real thing without any checks and balances, Elizabeth, Thane, Soren, and Egil were quite willing to bust up my "persistence of vision." It's the greatest gift they could give me.

—Leonard Sweet
Orcas Island

THE ANATOMY OF HUMAN LONGING

The Christian life is neither Christian nor any kind of life unless we are living out our faith. And faith is not static or regimented. It is viral, and as dynamic and organic as life itself.

Your life and your experience of God will differ from mine in significant ways. But like every human on earth, we share the basic needs of nourishment, shelter, and a network of companions. These longings and pursuits shape us, even when we are not consciously aware of them. Incubating within us is the desire to reach out in order to fill our biological and relational needs. We gather food, find shelter, and do all we can to avoid being alone.

We may laugh at the Delbert McClinton song "If You Don't Leave Me Alone (I'll Find Somebody That Will)," but no one truly wants to be left alone. We sense that alone means lonely, and loners are losers in the lottery of life. Beyond that, something inside us pushes us to connect with others. We know that being alone means being miserable. The great poet W. H. Auden predicted the feared manner of his death: "alone at midnight, in a hotel, to the great annoyance of the management."[1] He died of a heart attack in a hotel in Vienna, on September 28, 1973. Alone.

Connection is one of the absolutes of life. We don't choose it; it is hard-wired within us. Just as neurons that are unable to connect with other neurons will die, so abandoned souls will atrophy and die. Our well-being depends on our ability to connect with other humans. This drive pushes us with as much force as the longing for self-expression, our attraction to stories and storytelling, and the core human urge to know others and to be known. These are not all the things that make us human, but taken together they go a long way toward defining a human being as God created us.

Nature and nurture, destiny and design, shape the way we approach God and the way we live our faith. But it is not only who we are that determines the default setting of our lives (the ways we act and react, how we think). Also shaping us is the culture in which we live. In fact, the theory of neuroplasticity argues that the structure of the human brain is somehow shaped by our experiences, technologies, and cultures.

Admittedly, the word *culture* is one of the most slippery terms used in the social sciences. In fact, a founder of the field of culture studies, Raymond Williams, called the word *culture* one of the two or three most complicated words in the English language. When I refer to culture, I mean primarily the unvarnished vernacular of a place or period. In the 1960s, when middle-class youth wanted to rebel, they grew beards and smashed stereos. When Amish youth wanted to protest in the 1960s, they shaved their beards and bought stereos. Culture shapes behavior and how we express our beliefs. Faith is not just a matter of logic and learning but of imagination and emotion and culture.

LIFE, FAITH, AND THE DIGITAL AGE

If you are reading this, you almost certainly are a holdover from the twentieth century. You were born toward the end of the last millennium and, without even trying, you bring into this new era some of the trappings of the previous era. For purposes of this discussion, we will refer to two families (or tribes, if you prefer) that populate the twenty-first century. Both arrived here from the last century, but one group is rooted in the past and the other is fully at home in the new world, which encompasses the present as well as what can be seen on the horizon.

We know time is constant, but in recent years it seems time started moving much more quickly. Here is a simple example from just a decade ago. Back then, when travelers were waiting for a flight, they would occupy themselves with people watching, talking, reading a book or magazine, staring into space, or relaxing. Now think about the last time you were waiting for a flight. What were other travelers doing to fill the time? They were watching Hulu, sending pictures to friends, perfecting PowerPoints, creating photoshopped photos, texting, tweeting, on Facebook, and checking e-mail.

The culture has gone digital, but as recently as 1979, the then-current edition of *The*

Chambers Dictionary (TCD) defined *digital* only as "pertaining to the fingers, or to arithmetical digits." If you are native to the Digital Age, think about this: the word *digital* had an entirely different meaning when your parents were in college, or getting married, or starting to think about adding you to the family.

The tribe that feels most at home in the twenty-first-century Digital Age is what we will call the Googlers—the digitized, globalized group that spends much of its life getting to know one another in a virtual world. The tribe that immediately precedes the Googlers we will refer to as the Gutenbergers—those who arrived from the twentieth century bringing with them influences and assumptions launched long before, in the fifteenth century. Gutenbergers believe they were shaped primarily by the space race, John Kennedy, the Cold War, and the Beatles. They are largely unaware of a more basic influence that determines their approach to life and faith. They are the product of the movable-type technology perfected by Johannes Gutenberg in the 1400s.[2]

If Gutenbergers still prefer to read a book that is printed on paper, rather than on an iPad, at least credit them with being loyal to the namesake.

WHY GUTENBERG IS SUCH A BIG ICEBERG

When the discovery of the Dead Sea Scrolls became widely known in the late 1940s, biblical scholars were eager to examine what grew to be a library of very early, hand-copied biblical texts. Comparisons of the scrolls' hand-lettered words with modern translations of the Hebrew Scriptures showed remarkable consistency. Painstaking copying by hand had preserved the integrity of the biblical text over millennia. Christians can be thankful that Essenes and others who honored the words of Scripture used more than just their thumbs in copying the texts.

For nearly fifteen hundred years the Scriptures (Jewish and Christian) were preserved by the time-consuming process of hand copying. This served to keep the sacred text in circulation, but it was a very limited circulation. The laborious copying process meant there simply were not enough scrolls or codex produced for mass distribution. The available copies were read aloud and listened to, a system well-suited to a largely illiterate population.

That began to change in the 1400s, when technology took a breathtaking leap. Johannes Gutenberg came up with a way to produce books by hand, but through a process that avoided hand copying. Instead, movable type was used to reproduce words, sentences, entire books. His printing press introduced a radical advance in the mass production of books.

The first book created on the first movable-type printing press was the Bible. Gutenberg's technology eventually resulted in the wide availability of affordable editions of the Scriptures. If any invention deserves the accolade "revolutionary," give it to the printing press of Johannes Gutenberg.

The first Bible came off press around the year 1439, and the Protestant Reformation followed some eighty years later. Launched by Augustinian monk Martin Luther's list of ninety-five points issued in Wittenburg, Germany, the Reformation owes more than a little of its success to printing and the technological advances of Gutenberg and the Italian printer Aldus Manutius, who in 1501 introduced the pocket-sized octavo format. This miniaturized the book and brought reading out of libraries into everyday lives.

Think how omnipresent printing has become. Just about every home has its own

Are You More Googler or Gutenberger?

We're all part of a tribe, and the two we'll be looking at in this book are Googlers and Gutenbergers. There is a loose tribal correlation to your age, but a much higher correlation between tribe and your worldview, daily habits and practices, assumptions, and values. Use these questions to determine which culture you're most comfortable in:

1. Have you sent a handwritten note to someone in the past six months?
2. Have you mastered enough acronyms for quick and efficient texting?
3. Have you written a check to pay a bill in the past two months?
4. Have you used a postage stamp in the last six months?
5. In the last month, have you written in cursive beyond just your signature?
6. If you misplaced your cell phone, could you still send e-mail and cruise the Internet?
7. When you're at home, does an incoming phone call require use of your cell?
8. Have you been listed in a phone book in the last three years?

printing press hooked up to a laptop or desktop computer. But with more and faster ways to circulate written data electronically, most of us don't bother to print documents. We still are wed to words, but we access them in ways we couldn't have imagined at the turn of the twenty-first century.

When Technology Changed the World

Why all the talk about text, printing, Gutenberg, and movable type? The first printing technology in the West is critical for one reason: the ability to print books on a mass scale reoriented the world, including the Christian world. And it wasn't just by producing pamphlets that advanced the teachings of Luther and Calvin and Zwingli, although that didn't hurt. But the impact was more far-reaching and sustained. Printing fueled

9. If the battery in your mobile device went dead, could you read the most recent book you purchased?
10. Do you watch television programs when they are first shown and on a conventional television set (not a laptop screen or mobile device)?
11. Have you looked up a number or address using a telephone book in the last three years?
12. Do you use a pencil or pen to keep a journal?

Scoring: Count your yes answers to questions 2 and 7 and your no answers to 1, 3, 4, 5, 6, 8, 9, 10, 11, 12. Multiply the sum by two. Total score A = _____.

Count your yes answers on questions 1, 3, 4, 5, 6, 8, 9, 10, 11, 12 and your no answers on 2 and 7. Divide the sum by two. Total score B = _____. Now add A and B. Combined score = _____.

The higher your score, the less Gutenberger you are in your everyday habits. And it is likely that changing your habits also is changing the way you think about life, faith, and relationships. So just how Googler or Gutenberger are you? A score of six rivals Johannes Gutenberg himself. A score between six and twelve puts you in transition mode, adopting some Googler practices. A score of thirteen to twenty-four is full-on Googler. You must be a Digital Age native.

the spread of Christianity and helped form its character and practice by underscoring the power and importance of words over images. Cartoonist James Thurber would complain of this dominance of word over image in these words: "A drawing is always dragged down to the level of its caption."

The Gutenberg tribe is unapologetically grounded in text, and I use *text* here as a noun. Long ago they accepted as a primary mission the task of getting the printed Word of God into the hands of members of every language group on the planet. Preachers love to hold a thick Bible aloft and shout that the words in this book are the source of life. Gutenbergers love words printed on paper and books bound between covers sitting on shelves. In Gutenberg Christianity, the text that backs up belief (the Bible) tends to receive as much emphasis (if not more) as the daily life of faith. Words are on a par with living out one's beliefs.

GOOGLERS OF THE WORLD, CONNECT

The other tribal culture, the Googlers, would be hard-pressed to pick Johannes Gutenberg out of a police lineup. But they have taken his invention and extended it to uses and applications that changed not only the way people read and access information but the way people relate to one another. I have far more friends whom I've never met than I have friends in face-to-face relationships. Googlers have rewritten the rules of forming networks, connections, and relationships. In the hands of Googlers, technology has been bent to the purposes of core human longings: knowing, being known, belonging, perception. A primary way these things happen in Googler Culture is through the use of metaphors for storytelling, story catching, and story sharing. The technology of Googler Culture, advancing at a faster rate than any other in history, takes its cues more from premodern times than from the movable-type technology that helped launch the modern era. Googlers harken back to the era of Jesus. And it's no accident that Jesus serves as the world's leading storyteller. He excelled at connecting people to one another, to himself, to creation, and to God.

We are all singing with Johnny Cash "I'm Bound for the Promised Land,"[3] but you can't be eternity bound without being earth based and time bound. And the bindings of our time are more Googler than Gutenberger. This transition to a new culture has created a myriad of problems. Gutenbergers criticize Googlers for being shallow, obsessed with games, narcissistic, and irresponsible. They like to characterize Digital Age natives as perpetual adolescents who confuse status updates with authentic, legitimate human relationships.

But is that an accurate assessment? As I look at the waning of Gutenberg Culture and the arrival of Google Culture, I have to wonder if Jesus wouldn't be more at home with the Googlers. In fact, as the Western church built by Gutenbergers continues to lose ground in a world of Googlers, I am convinced that Christians need to start taking cues from the Googlers. Even more, I sense a Googler inside many a Gutenberger, crying to get out and pursue relationship with others. But the inner Googler in too many cases is held back by fear and uncertainty.

Humans are driven to belong, find acceptance, connect with others, and share life. This is true of Gutenbergers and Googlers alike, but Googlers freely admit it. How many cultures in history have devoted so much effort, invention, time, and passion to building networks that offered no payoff beyond engaging with other people? This is getting pretty close to pure relationship, when connecting is its own reward. No one is trying to sell me a timeshare or recruit me into their multilevel marketing program.

Googlers talk about their day and ask others about their lives. Maybe they talk about music or ideas, or they play chess via the Internet. These things used to occur over the backyard fence or in the family rec room. Now they occur across national borders and create bonds among people who will never meet face to face. If "necessity knows no law" (Aquinas), desire for connection knows no bounds.

If "Google Is God," Is God Google?

I don't knock Gutenbergers; I was born into that culture. In many ways it still feels familiar and comfortable to me, like walking through an airport terminal and overhearing an accent that reminds me of home. I used to dream of what it would be like to have a collection of one hundred record albums (called LPs for "long playing"). Now Googlers have ten thousand "favorite" songs on an iPod. I'm still learning the language and links of Googler Culture: I was no sooner transported by the blue line of hyperheaven than I crashed from the blue screen of death. I am so Gutenberger in background that I still believe that to write well is to make a better world.

Gutenbergers have held sway in the world—and in the Christian world—for hundreds of years. They launched the modern missions movement and recast the Bible in more languages (and multiple versions of the English language) than ever before. They put the gospel on radio and television and in the movies. They built churches that resemble college campuses with an indoor minimall. The contributions of Gutenbergers to a global civilization? Religious tolerance, rule of law, freedom of speech and press. Humanity leaves these behind at its peril.

Gutenbergers figured out how to apply the practices of USAmerican business (the most advanced form of capitalism) to the operation of the church, and introduced an allegiance to bigger and better as the most reliable measure of effective ministry. Gutenberger churches became citadels of command and control. No one would accuse Gutenbergers of lacking resourcefulness, devotion to the cause, single-mindedness, or confidence. I could take you to fifty churches around USAmerica with which any community college would gladly trade facilities. You don't build a state-of-the-art church on 120 acres if you're not sold out to the vision of providing a niche for every person. A gym for the athletes, art classes for the artsy, a coffee bar for the Javalujahs!, kids' programs cradle roll through high school, singles, seniors, bikers, runners, crafters, skateboarders, and fans of Bible study.

In a niche-or-be-niched world, what better way to help people belong than to offer them multiple options tailor-made to fit their hobby, athletic inclination, taste in pastries, or yearning to scrapbook?

Googlers are doing a similar thing, but starting from the other end of the equation. They first create a community and invite everyone in. Once people are interacting in the community (most often online or by Twitter or text message), they are invited to share who and what they are. Passions, interests, areas of knowledge and expertise, likes and dislikes, questions, needs, joys. It all comes out as the longings of being human come to the fore. If you want to shoot a round of golf, you can do that too. But Googlers won't build a golf course just so you'll have a place to belong.

In my experience, Googlers lack the Gutenberger drive to make it on your own, to be dependent on no one else, to stand tall and make your own way in the world and succeed or fail completely on your own. The John Wayne gene doesn't seem to have carried over to the Googlers. Instead, they are drawn to 140-character updates from friends and strangers who talk about a great movie they saw, or present an idea worth considering, or toss out a question to ponder or a reason to celebrate. To Gutenbergers, this seems way too surfacey and even useless. Why waste time, technology, and your battery on such drivel?

God promised that anyone who seeks God with their whole heart will find God.[4] Gutenbergers are wholehearted about a lot of things, and history records their accomplishments. No one surpasses Gutenberg Culture when it comes to applying yourself and accomplishing goals. But somehow, relationships were relegated to a different category—the nice-to-have-but-not-crucial category. Building something or improving it or advertising it or promoting it took priority. In the words of Walter Gropius, in his *Bauhaus Manifesto,* "The ultimate aim of all creative activity is a building!" Creativity issues in artifacts and achievements, not relationships. Gutenbergers have been far more concerned about rectitude of thoughts about God than they have on rectitude of relationship with God.

Googlers, as well, are creative, innovative, passionate, committed, and productive. They are not against progress. Witness the iPad 2, full-color e-readers that link to video clips and sound effects, phones that do everything but wash your laundry. Technology is the holy handmaiden of Google Culture and they excel in it.

But the motivation and driving force for Googlers is not to build something huge and expensive that the masses will admire. Instead, they are driven to develop and use technology in ways that improve lives. A Googler would not think it wise to build a church that is so large it requires the installation of an escalator. They have no desire to bask in the reflected glory of a multimillion-dollar artifact. To them, artifactual is the artificial without more and better relationships, defined as networking, sharing, connecting, belonging, and letting others get to know you.

Is bigger really better, or is smaller and more convenient the way to go when it enhances relationships and connection? What lies at the core of our humanness—the grandiose or the simple? Don't we all long to return to the direct simplicity of God walking in the dew of the day with Adam and Eve? I'm not saying that all Googlers, or even most of them, pursue connections because they are pursuing God. For many, it is not intentional. But a wise Scripture writer mentioned that God put eternity into every person's heart.[5] Every culture bears the "seeds of the Word"—the Spirit of God keeps alive in humanity the innate desire to be united with God. That desire of union with God is true of Googlers and Gutenbergers alike.

Yet Googlers are the ones who have made relationships a life mission. Googlers are the ones more likely to trust that the common good in the long run is the personal good. And Googlers are most ready to take seriously what any scientist, when pinned to the wall to say what anything is—whether a gland or a galaxy, a lepton or a lemur—ends up saying: a system of relationships.

GOD AND RELATIONSHIPS AND BEING HUMAN

The teenage granddaughter of a minister friend reported to her grandparents that she'd prefer going to the traditional worship service with them because they sang out of books and she could see the music and not just the words. A hymnbook enabled her to sing notes other than the melody line. My research assistant, Betty O'Brien, was in conversation with the youthful praise team leader at her home church in California. A powerful organ offertory moved him profoundly. He is a fan of new sounds, and he wanted to hear more.

So what keeps Googlers and Gutenbergers from finding common ground? We have seen that being human means we share the same longings, and those longings drive us toward relationship with others and ultimately toward God. So why the disconnect between these two cultures?

Fear does its dishonorable work, creating maladaptive responses instead of metabolic ones. Never underestimate the power of fear geared up and egged on by ego to keep us from moving forward. There is an old saying that some people are so fearful of change, had they been present at creation they would have voted for chaos. Fear causes us to hide in the face of change, and it leads to living a reactive rather than constructive life. The choice is to be an active part of positive change, which already is upon us, or to passively and grudgingly tolerate inevitable change. This "such a time" moment has a right to expect that we won't be satisfied to sit on the sidelines but that we will initiate and participate in change. The future cannot afford an AWOL church. Jesus gave us a love we can trust, even in the face of our fears.

Al Caldwell is a friend of a friend. He was scheduled to preach one Sunday and called the church in advance to talk to someone about details. The person's cell phone kept cutting out. Finally, the person at the other end of the line apologized: "Sorry, sir, this is a dead zone!"

How many of us live in a dead zone? How many churches are dead zones to the future? Al's response was immediate: "Someone get me a trumpet, a bugle, an alarm clock, and an electronic Bible so we can move out of the dead zone and bring some life and energy to this place."[6]

This book is a tale of two tribes: Gutenbergers and Googlers. I will tell a bit about each tribe, both the pros and the cons, and will trace some tracks of how they intersect in our world. Each tribe has its promises, perils, potentials, and problems. Each tribe has some baggage we could lose and some we should hold on to. Clearly the future belongs to the Googlers, but not for long. The world of Google and its contemporary technologies will have its day, and then another culture will be born. But for the next two decades, the primary missional challenge of the church will be to incarnate the gospel in a Google world.

Of all the pictures in the National Gallery of London, more than one-third are religious, and more than half of them portray the face of Christ in various times and climes.[7] This is where we begin: imagining the face of Christ in the Digital Age, the world of the Googlers.

PART I

—

Where Are We?

LOGOS AND LOGO

Is the Gospel Personal Connection or Heated Argument? Your Answer Will Tell You Something

> All the mischief of the world is done by one thing; the
> inability to remain at rest within one's own room.
>
> —BLAISE PASCAL, *Pensées*

I entered the world as a Gutenberger, and I share a deep devotion to the written and spoken word. But I wrestle with the Gutenberger Culture's use of words, and sometimes even its use of the Word. Gutenbergers proceed from a fixed point, which helps explain why they are drawn to objective facts, unimpeachable research, and hard statistics. For them, words serve much the same purpose as a mathematical proof. There is a feeling of certainty that comes with precise words and piercing definitions.

Googlers also are big fans of words, but they approach them differently. To a Googler, words are important because they help a person express ideas, share news, and tell stories. Words can establish common ground and reveal shared interests. Instead of serving as a tether or anchor to a fixed point, for Googlers words are agents of change, experiments in conversation, small change in the coinage of the new realm of unmediated, interactive, unscripted connection.

Words can be signposts erected to mark the location of incontrovertible truths. They also can be messengers and emissaries. They can be mile markers to show you where you are or vehicles that take you to the place you've been striving to reach. Words can show you where you are or where you are going. They can tether you to an unvarying point of reference or move you into unmarked territory.

Googlers are not as interested in proving a point as they are in making connections. Trust me, 800 million-plus human beings from around the world do not log on to Facebook so they can get into an argument. They do it to be connected to other people.

Logos That Lead to *Logos*

I playfully date the origin of Googler Culture to 1973, the year the mobile phone was invented. I was an early adopter. My first mobile device was a bag phone, so named because it was so big it came with its own body bag. When I would meet someone for lunch, the phone required its own chair at the table. (*Mobile* was used loosely when it came to this monstrosity.) Still, the invention of a telephone that was not dependent on a wall plug, not fixed to a location, and small enough to be taken with you throughout the day accomplished much more than convenience in communicating. It ushered in a new era, what I am calling the TGIF era (more on this later). The connected generation was born when inventor Martin Cooper called up his AT&T rival on an unplugged telephone from the streets of New York City.

While I was an early adopter, I'm still an immigrant in Googler Culture. I earn my keep with words, hence I am logocentric. But Googler Culture has allowed me to expand and multiply the venues and voices. Like most of us, I am a microblogging, social-networking, apps-loving, tweeting USAmerican. I'm never happier than when I'm virtually present in multiple places at one time.

More important than all that, I am a Christian whose life is defined by the witness and words of Jesus. God is revealed to us in the words of sacred Scripture and in the Word, Jesus the Christ. Words are important. They reveal God, inspire faith, form lives, impart wisdom, give direction, and much more.

Christians of the first century did not have access to the full canon of Scripture. They had the same Bible Jesus had, the Hebrew Scriptures. And followers of The Way in various churches had a letter (or letters) from Paul, James, Peter, John, and the writer to the Hebrews. They were people of the Word, but they also were people of The Word Made Flesh and knew that they formed the body of Christ on earth. The members were interdependent, of "one accord in prayer"—not in politics, propositions, or programs, but prayer.[1] Gatherings of Christians were communities of prayer, practice, participation, knowing, and being known.

> We were missionaries, disciples, Jesuits.
> —KEITH RICHARDS, DESCRIBING WHAT IT WAS LIKE
> TO START THE ROLLING STONES WITH MICK JAGGER[2]

This is a fairly accurate description of the Googler world as well, both the believing and unbelieving segments. Googlers tend to live by values that early Christians would recognize. They believe there is more truth in relationships than in propositions. They yearn to do more than interact and stay in touch with others. They want to *share life* with others. They do not seek a spirituality that escapes flesh and blood. They understand that to be "incorporated" in a body is to be enfleshed, but an enfleshment that is not corporate but corporal. While Gutenberger Christians keep busy parsing a Greek root to uncover the exact meaning of "submit" in Ephesians 5, the Googlers of the world are friending another two hundred people, reading the twenty text messages that came in during the last ten minutes, and meeting someone for coffee. The Gutenberger church might think of Googlers as superficial and bent on wasting time, but what is superficial about devotion to relationships?

CLIFFSNOTES TO TGIF CULTURE

As with any culture, there are natives and immigrants. Natives were born into the culture and, as a result, the culture's identifying characteristics are largely invisible. You don't think about oxygen; you just breathe it. If you're a native English speaker, you don't lie awake at night parsing *pare, pear, pair,* and *père.* But immigrants do. To them, the culture is exotic and often confusing. It's interesting but unsettling. To Gutenbergers (but not Googlers), TGIF Culture is an odd thing that has happened in the world.

Meanwhile, TGIF Culture is invisible to Googlers. They operate within it without thinking about it. Googlers couldn't imagine living any other way.

So what is this new culture? As we use it here, TGIF does not stand for Thank Goodness It's Friday, nor is it the acronym for a chain of family restaurants. TGIF is the Googler Culture that is built on Twitter, Google, iPhone, and Facebook—the most visible and relied-upon tools of relationship and life.

Every Gutenberger is right now undergoing a brain transplant. Cognitive scientists credit the rise of TGIF Culture not only with changing the way we access information and communicate with one another but also with reformatting our brains. Researchers have found that surfing the Internet and having an overabundance of data at our fingertips recalibrates brain synapses.[3] It is called brain "plasticity." An onslaught of tweet-length messages plus thirty-five hundred "sermons" (advertisements) a day selling us everything from hamburgers to Hampton Inns, plus texting while we're Facebooking and IMing and checking e-mail and looking up movie times and doing a little online banking—all of this is taking its toll.

Your brain is being short-circuited and maybe even shorted by sound storms and data avalanches. Everybody is only too eager to share, and now they have multiple venues for instant self-expression. The prospect of sitting alone in a quiet room, pondering or ruminating or praying, is most people's idea of torture. The prevailing ethos is to be connected 24/7, even if you hardly ever see one another in a physical sense.

Long gone are the days when a friend would send you a postcard from some faraway location and then return home before the postcard landed in your mailbox. Now we expect a moment-by-moment account of the friend's travel adventure. (As with most things, being connected 24/7 is a two-edged sword. This could be considered an invasion when your parents want to get involved. Who wants to Skype with Mom and Dad when it involves sitting at your computer just so your parents can see you when you're half-asleep and wearing a wrinkled T-shirt and pajama bottoms? Plus, they want you to keep sending them photos and clever videos, and even the GPS coordinates of your new apartment. You know if you give in, they'll be at their desktop taking a street-level look at your building and calling to see if they can stop by for a visit.)

How did they miss the point that communication in TGIF Culture is largely virtual?

> Distance is no obstacle to getting in touch—but
> getting in touch is no obstacle to staying apart.
> —ZYGMUNT BAUMAN
> ON THE CELL-PHONE GENERATION[4]

And again, there is another side to this. I have found no empirical evidence that thumbing your way through life has advanced the scientific enterprise, or furthered art and culture, or done even one thing to enrich the use of language. Much of human contact has been reduced to acronyms, misspelled words, emoticons, missing punctuation, and mindless replies to meaningless revelations. (I don't care what is on your grocery list and whether you took a nap this afternoon.) These things pass for conversation, a thing that used to thread the fabric of society. For many in TGIF Culture, it's more like stitches to close a wound, and we're wondering if it will leave a scar.

Educators wonder if children will soon stop learning the mechanics of printing the alphabet by hand. That skill is called upon so rarely, it's almost vestigial. (Already, cursive writing is in danger. How long is hand printing likely to survive?)

FOR GOD SO LOVED A GOOGLER WORLD

If we had any doubts that God wants a relationship with us, Jesus's life on earth supplies the final proof. God didn't send us a treatise; God sent a Person. And in our culture, either Googler or Gutenberger, it's often hard to find Jesus amid the clutter of words. While it might seem that Googlers (the thumb-texting acronym crowd) treat words too lightly, they are driven to find and maintain connection with one another.

In their dogged tweeting, blogging, Facebooking, and IMing, Googlers have stumbled onto the heart of Christian faith and meaning. Oddly, they have arrived at a place that echoes the earliest Christians and their faith communities. I'm not saying that TGIF Culture is more consciously in tune with God than are the Gutenbergers. But I am saying that Googlers (of any age) recognize a need in their lives and they act on it. Repeatedly. Some would even say constantly.

While Googlers cannot be thrown off the relational scent, it can be argued that Gutenberger Christians never picked up the trail to begin with. Sure, if you go to church on Sunday you might hear talk about a personal relationship with Christ. And you might notice announcements of the meetings of small groups with the purpose of encouraging deeper relationships. But too often these are programmed and ultimately ineffective.

Gutenbergers might be more adept at describing in words what a relationship is and why it is needed. But Googlers are light-years ahead when it comes to the practicum. They pursue connection with a tenacity not seen since Elizabeth Taylor's sixth wedding. Googlers are driven to find meaning and touchpoints with others. I don't endorse the narcissistic sharing of personal minutiae, but I support sharing for the purpose of connecting. And so does God. There is nothing more boring than reading the memoirs and minutia of someone you don't care about. But there is nothing more exciting than reading the memoirs and minutia of someone you honestly care about.

I believe it is more natural to incarnate the gospel in TGIF Culture than in the world of the Gutenbergers. In other words, Googlers (be they disciples or not) are better positioned to encounter and engage with the Jesus of Scripture than Gutenbergers have been, since Gutenbergers were inclined to refashion the Jesus of Palestine into a Western-size-fits-all Savior. The church may wake up to find that Jesus's time has come in TGIF Culture because it is more organic than linear, more kinesis than stasis, more circle than square. For this reason, Googlers may be the best hope for the future of the church in the West.

Gutenbergers suited their times well. But in the Googler world—the age of experience, participation, image, and connection—Gutenbergers have proven to be unwilling to let go of their fixed position. Meanwhile Googlers, for a variety of reasons, are more adaptive to the future while being anchored in the past. To add to the sadness, many Gutenbergers are putting more and more distance between themselves and what God is doing in the world.

While Googlers expend enormous amounts of energy seeking to satisfy their urge to connect, Gutenberger Christians continue to pursue their fascination with terminologies, definitions, formulas, and what Sigmund Freud called "the narcissism of small differences." While Googlers are getting by with acronyms and finding friends everywhere, Gutenbergers are delving into words about words that have been written about God's words. It's an overstatement, but in place of vulnerable, transparent, biblical relationships, Gutenbergers often choose a spiritual path that leads away from the practical outworking of life and faith and people.

Let's Ask a Bigger Question

Is Jesus a person or an assertion? Is he personal connection or heated argument? Several years ago I wrote a book that posed one central question: "How did Christians get the point and miss the Person?"[5] Now more than ever, the question needs to be answered because it captures the divide that exists between Christian cultures. At the same time, it reveals the elemental search for meaning and connection that drives Googlers in just about every area of life.

Neither Gutenberger nor Googler Culture is defined by demographics (age, income level, educational attainment, career or profession, ethnicity). Rather, we are looking at two cultures of very different psychographics. Gutenbergers are oriented toward clarity and certainty, which require finding answers to questions and solutions to mysteries.

They gain confidence from rectitude and exactitude. As a result, they value the texts of Scripture for the authoritative words and their apps.

The other culture, the one we're calling TGIF, uses the word *text* as a verb more than a noun. They text to keep in touch with other people. Texting is connection, belonging, self-expression, friendship, and community. It is a way to get to know others and to help them get to know you. Life and faith are best lived out when they invite others to join in. Life is at its best when it involves other people. Beliefs that are isolating or distancing from everyday experience might be interesting to think about, but as a way of life they are useless. Why would anyone think Christian faith should or could be divorced from relationships?

In later chapters we will look more closely at the contrasts between Gutenbergers and Googlers, and we will attempt to identify what each culture brings to the life of faith. Here are a few of the contrasts in summary.

WORDS AND THE WORD

Gutenbergers value precision and rationality. In many ways their faith is the pursuit of details that explain the ways of God and the reasonableness of belief. They value the meaning of words and are confident that words serve to clarify truth and make God knowable.

It's not surprising that Gutenbergers are so attached to words. The printing revolution that was launched by Johannes Gutenberg rewrote the book on communication, information dispersal, education, rhetoric, and the propagation of religion. With the invention of movable type, the printed word became as central to the training of Christians as hand-lettered Torah scrolls had been to the ancient Jews.

I'll quote Marshall McLuhan here, since to not do so would make everyone wonder why. He is famous for saying that "the medium is the message."[6] He wrote a celebrated book using that phrase as the title, pointing out that the meaning of a message (what is communicated by words) is unavoidably shaped, altered, biased, and "massaged" by the delivery system—the medium. This is akin to the phenomenon of a laboratory researcher muddying the results of his research simply by being present as an observer. The researcher's body temperature affects the ambient room temperature. His breathing adds carbon dioxide to the atmosphere. His physical presence causes lab rats to behave in ways that vary from their activities when they are isolated from humans. Amazingly, science moved forward for generations without realizing that a neutral observer was in truth an active participant in any experiment. The research data and resulting conclusions were automatically massaged by a researcher who thought he was doing nothing more than standing idly by.

Likewise, Gutenberg's movable type and the bound volumes it produced had the unplanned effect of intensifying the tendency among Christians to place their confidence in words. More than ever before, Christian ministries focused on the propagation and distribution of words. Proclaimed words had always held sway, as the Scriptures were read aloud whenever Christians gathered. But with the ability to mass-produce Bibles and books and to obtain them at affordable prices, Christians could study God's Word as well as words written about the Word. Depending on the stature and reputation of the commentator, words used to convey ideas about the words that God spoke could take on an authority of their own. If you don't believe me, talk to a Methodist about John Wesley, a Presbyterian about John Calvin, an Anabaptist about Menno Simons, an Episcopalian about Thomas Cranmer. Or read five current, popular-level Christian books and notice how many of the authors quote C. S. Lewis, Oswald Chambers, Augustine, or Billy Graham.

It is not wrong for monotheists to hold words in high regard, and especially the words of God. I will never argue against the power of words. I am, after all, a writer, speaker, and educator. But something—or, I should say, Someone—can get lost amid a multitude of words. God's most perfect, most glorious, most human, and yet most divine communication to us is Jesus, the Word made flesh. It is possible for the Word to be obscured by words. Emmanuel, God in human flesh, God with us! How can sheets of paper covered with type do justice to God's Son, the God-Human, Lord of the universe, and the living Expression of Three-in-One?

Printed text can never hope to capture the full meaning or the inexpressible glory of "the Word [who] became flesh and dwelt among us."[7] Is it possible that the Gutenberger fixation on precision and exactitude delivered by words might be preventing people from connecting with Christ and following his example in loving people?

GOOGLERS AND DEPENDENCE ON TEXT

Googlers love words because words are expressive. They lie at the heart of communication and lead to connection. But Googlers also are sensitive to the abuse of words, knowing how words are manipulated to advance agendas and causes that contradict the plain teaching of Christ. Words are written and spoken and preached in ways that twist God's truth to support a fund-raising campaign or promote a cause or defend a theological system. There is no question that words are powerful, influential, emotive, and danger-ous. Words are useful tools, but words are not truth.

Jesus told us, using words, that he is the Truth. He is also the Word become flesh. You might have seen the bumper sticker that says, "I was looking for Jesus but got mugged by one of his followers." Googlers, while not poster children for "God, save me from your people," can document how the Gutenberger church has been getting it wrong for a long time.

In being able to read and write, Jesus traveled the information superhighway of his day. But he never departed from the way of connection and community. Even when he unleashed his harshest criticisms of temple leaders and teachers of the law, he met them on common ground, quoting Moses and Isaiah. He said, in essence, we spring from the same Source, the history of God and the prophets, the story of God's people, but you guys have been getting the story all wrong.

So as we take a fresh look at the church in the Age of Google, we realize that too many Christians for far too long have been propping up the culture of Gutenberg. Rather than rooting the practice of Christian faith in the timeless, timely, and time-full ways of the Founder, the church in the West clings desperately to the canons of the Age of Reason. As we look at Googlers and their practice of Christianity, we see clear con-trasts from the ways things have been done since Gutenberg's famous invention.

Googlers are drawn to relationships as much as they are to ideas, which gives them a head start in the heart-first (not head-first) practice of Christianity. It is easier to talk to Googlers about Jesus than about five points of Calvinism or whether Israel still enjoys most-favored-nation status with God. The person of Jesus is more attractive than thoughts and teachings about Jesus.

If you are a Gutenberger, you might argue that what I'm saying can't stand up to a strongly analytical approach to Christian belief and practice. I would agree. Hard analy-sis can cast doubt on just about anything. But I'm not advancing a new proof. I'm advo-cating a new view of Jesus that takes his personhood more seriously than the theological positions that read a lot like a job description for the Son of God. Let me suggest a series of contrasts:

Jesus is message more than manuscript.

He is story more than instruction manual.

He is a personal letter, not the envelope it comes in.

He is a launching pad, not a storage locker.

He is self-defining, not an entry in a Bible dictionary.

He is mystery, not equation.

He is the Transcendent made immanent, not systematic made simulation.

He is miracle more than logic and reason.

He is personal experience and direct reality, not a syllabus or lesson plan.

Jesus did not come to earth so that later generations of his followers could prove a point. He *is* the Point. He is time spent together, not a list of seven rules for success. He is intimacy, not statistical analysis. He brings unimaginable riches and spiritual wealth but never adds up on a balance sheet. Following him is messy yet holy.

Googlers intuitively are drawn to the real Jesus, the One who is not mediated by Gutenberger attempts to impose formulas and propositions and structure. The mess we call church has the greatest message in the world. But when the message is modified to emphasize the church and not to introduce Christ, the world can't hear our message for our mess.

TALKING WITH YOUR THUMBS

Typesetting went digital not long before the wired culture went wireless. Wireless went to Cloud, and it won't be long before Skype will give way to avatars and holograms and teleporters. My concern is not the effect that evolving technology has on faith, but how culture (of which technology is a part) shapes Christian beliefs and forms biases, and the way Christianity is practiced in the context of culture.

Much is made of orthodox belief, and rightly so. Orthodoxy is crucial. But where in open-source culture is there a similar emphasis on the practice of our faith being open to the Source? The Gutenberger world has shaped the beliefs and practice of Western Christianity within the influence of the Enlightenment. In fact, "modern Christianity" is arguably more modern, more Gutenberger, than it is Christian. The life of the Spirit largely got lost amid facts and functionalities. Words became weapons and a means to score points against an opponent, leaving behind a bombed-out, barren, infertile Christian landscape.

> Something unknown is doing we don't know what.
> —WERNER HEISENBERG'S UNCERTAINTY PRINCIPLE
> AS EXPLAINED BY SIR ARTHUR EDDINGTON[8]

Whereas Jesus was fond of asking questions to draw out his listeners, words in the hands of Enlightenment Christians became a way to level accusations, to solidify positions, and to clarify who was and was not a member in good standing. These things went largely unchallenged in the Gutenberger church. Sadly, Gutenbergers failed to grasp the practical, relational, lived-out meaning behind all the right words. There are a lot of pastors out there with the right words and with the right theology but with no people. If you have the right theology but aren't reaching people and aren't in relationship with your culture, what does it profit a pastor or a church?

Meanwhile, Googlers recognize the reality of something inside them that has for too long gone unanswered, and the private pain of living under mushroom clouds of fear and despair that contaminate their daily life. What is the truth about truth? Googlers ask. Is there such a thing as "absolute truth"? If so, is absolute truth the same as abstract truth? Is truth primarily something known to the intellect, or is truth something known to the soul? Is truth an intellectual assertion or a soul moment, or both? Why was one of Jesus's signature phrases "I tell you the truth"? Are there different kinds of truth? And what does it mean to live "untruthful" lives?

The heartbreak of broadened brokenness makes Googlers yearn for a living relationship with Christ. But, Gutenbergers counter, Googler Culture is so narcissistic. And it takes a cavalier attitude toward absolute truth, the authority of Scripture, and the creeds of Christianity. Perhaps. Perhaps not. But in my experience Googlers are not cavalier about the things that matter most. They are interested in the core, the heart, the elemental matters of life and faith. That is how so many of them end up finding the Word, the Person who is relationship and meaning.

Only Jesus can satisfy the persistent longing at the heart of us all. There will be time later on for formulations and words that are creedal and descriptive, enlightening and reformational. Even Arminian and Reformed, Anabaptist and Anglican, Pentecostal and dispensational.

I have no axe to grind against Gutenbergers. I was born one, was bred as one, and spent much of my adult life eating bread from its table. In fact, I was a Gutenberger among Gutenbergers. In the early days of my coming up through the ranks, I held the jackets and clerical collars of particularly zealous Gutenbergers as they threw brickbats at the digitized, globalized culture on the horizon.

That was then. I have repented publicly and privately. Now we live in a TGIF world. Gutenberger Culture is the fringe culture, and the Gutenberger church has moved far from the heart of life, closer to edges of the ledge. Googlers are culture makers, and I am convinced they hold the secret to ministry and mission. So if you're ready to throw a brickbat, don't hand me your jacket. I'll be standing over there, alongside the ones you'll hit, learning how Googlers create community and live their love for Jesus.

Interactives

1. What is your text-to-voice call ratio? Describe the differences and why you prefer the one you do.
2. Why do you think 87 percent of African Americans and Hispanics own a cell phone, compared to 80 percent of whites? Why are Hispanic and African American adults more likely than whites to be wireless-only?
3. T. S. Eliot's poem "The Waste Land" is available from Touch Press in an interactive iPad edition.[9] What poems or stories would you like to see in this interactive form? How might the church use this form of interactivity to tell its story?
4. Is the digital book taking us back to scrolling? Google books scroll, but Kindle, iPad, and Nook seem uncertain. Are you a page turner or a scroller?
5. Marianne Sawicki defined doctrinal theology in this way: "the selection and abstraction of certain elements from Christian Scripture, the refinement of those elements by philosophical means into declarative statements, and the arrangement of those statements into a systematic presentation that is asserted to be true in itself and also representative of its scriptural source."[10] How interested in doctrinal theology should your church be? How do you respond to Sawicki's definition?

A Tale of Two Cultures

Why Googlers Will Save the World, and Why They Might Not

A charge to keep I have, a God to glorify;
A never-dying soul to save, and fit it for the sky.

—Charles Wesley

No one gets to pick their birth date. Unfortunately. If I could have chosen any time in history in which to live, I would not have picked this one. My academic training is as a historian. History is my home. This gives me the advantage of time travel of a sort. In my mind I can live anywhere. And when I'm considering a favorable era, I don't pick the teenage years of the twenty-first century. I much prefer high Victorian culture and the late nineteenth century.

This fascination goes way beyond the occasional mental excursion. Visit my home at Orcas Island, Washington, and you'll enter a time warp. My small house is stuffed with heavily carved furniture that the arts and crafts movement of the early twentieth century rebelled against. Wherever you go in our two-thousand-square-foot home, you find yourself transported at least one hundred years into the past. Even more, you will be greeted with high Victorian rituals of courtesy and hospitality—one of the most important being two desserts (or "two puddings," as the Brits liked to say). A good Victorian meal begins with multiple appetizers and always ends with two desserts.

You and I get to choose how we will furnish our homes, but we can't choose our moment for ministry—for one simple reason. You can't pick your birthday.

In the Marx Brothers' movie *Animal Crackers,* Groucho asks, "Where are we?" Chico replies, "You can't fool me, we're right here." God put us "right here." And like it or not, "right here" is our unchosen responsibility. As an old Stephen Stills song had it, "If you can't be with the one you love, honey, love the one you're with."[1] Likewise when you can't get the world you'd prefer, love the world you've got. I might prefer to live in a world of gracious manners and elegant accoutrement, but I'm more than one hundred years too young. You and I can have two desserts if we choose, but the world we minister to has been chosen for us. And it doesn't look or sound or respond like any world that preceded it.

If you are native to the TGIF world, the unprecedented contrasts with what went before will be largely invisible. If you are an immigrant from another era, as I am, you'll need to plug in your GPS.

No More Secrets

We live in a kiss-and-tell world in which celebrities are famous for being famous, and it's not unusual for even ordinary citizens to have thousands of fans and followers. The rapid proliferation of social media—including Twitter, blogging, Facebook, texting, and live chats—seems to prevent people from keeping anything private. Who knew that the ever-present opportunity to share things about oneself would be so effective in convincing people they should share everything? Forget privacy and good taste—follow the tweets of certain people and you'll be better versed on their sleeping, eating, and bathroom habits than you are on your own.

> To serve the present age, my calling to fulfill,
> O may it all my powers engage, to do my master's will.
> —CHARLES WESLEY[2]

With all this public sharing of personal stories, where does that leave Christians and the proclamation of the gospel? The mass media have never been more democratic. We all have equal access, and anyone with an opinion, a story, a rant, or an urge to show photos of their grandchildren (or their pug) to the world can do so. You can reveal what you're preparing for dinner tonight and make it available to a potential audience of millions. The opportunity to gain exposure for a message has never been greater, and that should hold an irresistible attraction for Christians, Christian ministries, and the church at large. Micro media is now mass media, but how is it being used for God's kingdom?

In the world of media, every journalist wants an "IWT" tag: I Was There. Each of us is here, but too many signs point to Christians who wish they could be somewhere else—or at least occupying space in a different time. Each one of us gets a thousand months on earth, and God chose you to live yours here and now. When you stand before your Maker, will you get your IWT tag, or will you receive an MIA or AWOL tag instead?

NOAH, ESTHER, AND YOU

"A Charge to Keep I Have, a God to Glorify" is how Charles Wesley put it in the first hymn listed in every index of every Methodist hymnal. The song goes on: "to serve the present age, my calling to fulfill."[3] In order to fulfill and be faithful to our calling, we need to be in a state of "here-ness" and faithful to the time and place and people to whom we have been divinely assigned. We are to love the ones we're with, knowing that these are the ones God chose for us to love. Like the biblical Esther, we have been raised up "for just such a time as this."[4] We have been entrusted with preserving the past, "the faith that was once for all delivered to the saints."[5] But we also have been entrusted with shaping the future, which comes only from feeling the texture of the times we're in.

This "such a time" world has a right to expect a kiss-and-tell default setting from disciples of Jesus. The TGIF world demands that, as Christians of the early twenty-first century, we make sure the old, old story is new and hot...and that we bring the promise home again, in a way our current world can understand.

The Bible says Noah was "a righteous man...in his generation."[6] If he showed up today he would frighten more people than he would intrigue. A seafaring desert dweller, smelling of multiple species of cooped-up animal dung, and work hardened after decades of building a ship far from a significant body of water. Uncivilized and premodern and physically embodying the epithet "tool user." Who would know what to do with a man like Noah? He would be given a 1950s-era gospel tract that he couldn't read and sent to the homeless shelter for a shower, a change of clothes, and a hot meal.

Noah answered the call and preserved humanity. He is a hero for all time, but his mission was for his generation. What is our call today, and how eager are we to answer? It is easy to be faithful or pious in a generation that has passed. But who will be a Noah or an Esther in the TGIF world? Will we be devout, not in another time, but in our generation?

Augustine liked to say that God is younger than us all. If Jesus is always the youngest person around, can we be as young as Jesus, who never finishes saying what there is to say because his words are truly apocalyptic—a continuous unveiling?

POP CHRISTIANITY OR BAD BUDDHISM?

Here is the problem with much of the "spirituality" that is making the rounds. Too much of today's pop Christianity sounds like bad Buddhism or pseudo Islam. Christianity is not a vague, amorphous, ethereal religion; nor is it a prescribed set of ritual practices, whether they be liturgical or litigious, religious or political. You can try to get rid of flesh and blood and make Christianity into a religion of excarnation, but you will fail. Christianity is and always has been a religion of incarnation. It puts on flesh and blood. As a living and breathing faith, it is inescapably material, physical, and cultural. Christianity speaks in the locative case.

Jesus was an immigrant on earth. Abraham became one as soon as he walked out of Ur. Jacob took his family to Egypt to survive a famine. We all are from somewhere else, it seems. Some of the most successful websites are those promising to help you trace your ancestry and claim your ethnic pedigree. It seems that everybody loves to probe and parade their immigrant story. But when it comes to living as immigrants, there is far less ardor. We're glad our ancestors did the immigrant thing so we can live off their sacrifice. We are far less eager to make similar sacrifices.

> I don't own a computer,
> have no idea how to work one.
> —WOODY ALLEN[7]

But life on earth is an immigrant experience. If you were born before 1973, you are an immigrant in the current culture whether you want to be or not. Perhaps you've heard the joke about watching reruns of *Seinfeld* on your iPhone, wondering why Jerry uses a telephone the size of a gym shoe. Ten years ago no one would have believed that a cell phone would be the clearinghouse for everything in a person's life short of cooking dinner. And now that we have centralized the daily duties of life in one handheld device, no one wants to go back to a landline life. Except, it seems, the church.

Immigrants settle in. They start speaking the language and enjoying the fruit of the land. And why not? Familiarity is comfortable, undemanding. Finally, you feel as though you can relax. But you can't, because the world does not stop or even slow down. In fact, today's world evolves faster than Google spins out a new upgrade. No longer is staying put an option. If you're not willing to move with it, the world will move without you.

I know this because my life has been a three-act play: Analog Childhood, Digital Youth, Google Adulthood. I am convinced that the potential of Googlers (those born since 1973, although Googler status is more a psychographic than a demographic thing) to stay in tune with Jesus while in touch with their culture is greater than anything the Gutenbergers were able to accomplish.

Christians may be fascinated with the future, but too many of us don't want to live in it. The problem is that Gutenbergers act in the same way that every group of immigrants has acted: when finding oneself in a new world, immigrants circle the wagons and protect their familiar ways. Immigrants huddle in ghettos to preserve the old language and rituals. No wonder more and more of us suffer from border syndromes: as people living with identities in both worlds, we are confused, uncertain, afraid, disoriented, on edge.

> Arm me with jealous care, as in thy sight to live;
> And oh, thy servant, Lord, prepare a strict account to give.
> —CHARLES WESLEY[8]

Any culture will demand this of us: that we not hide or be hidebound. Most of us hide out of fear of change or anger at the range of change required of us. To be sure, fear is a normal protective response to changes that threaten our comfort, convenience, and security. But fear also can be an adaptive response. Healthy doses of fear can serve to propel us out of binding circumstances and into positive action. Riven with fear, we can be driven to resist life-sustaining change or we can be dynamically driven to embrace a new and exciting future. Christians need to find ways to transform disabling fear into an impetus for innovative and life-giving change.

Get to Know
Your Neighborhood
Gutenberger and Googler

The nature of the church is cross-cultural. At Christmas, we celebrate baby Jesus's birthday in Bethlehem. At Pentecost, we celebrate the body of Christ's birthday in Jerusalem. A missionary church requires fresh adaptations of the faith as it spreads across space and spans through time. There is no such thing as an untranslated version of Christianity. God crossed cultures when God became human and lived on earth.

Here is a playful glossary of cross-cultural perspectives that can be found in every church:

Gutenbergers: It's necessary to be right.
Googlers: It's necessary to be in relationship.

Gutenbergers: God is in charge.
Googlers: God chose to be among us.

Gutenbergers: Need a good light for reading.
Googlers: Need to recharge their reader.

Gutenbergers: Theology explains God.
Googlers: Jesus explains life.

Gutenbergers: Capital campaign.
Googlers: Homeless campaign.

Gutenbergers: Statement of faith.
Googlers: Life of faith.

Gutenbergers: Build something.
Googlers: Meet someone.

Gutenbergers: Water-tight arguments.
Googlers: Fluid apps.

Gutenbergers: Fit in.
Googlers: Fit together.

Gutenbergers: Church history informs belief.
Googlers: Everyday life requires faith.

Gutenbergers' top temptation: Make Individual our god.
Googlers' top temptation: Make Community our god.

Gutenbergers' top challenge: A culture of words and
      individualism that has lost its ability to propagate.
Googlers' top opportunity: A culture of images and relationships
      that breed virality, the petri dish of revival.

Interactives

1. In Alan Hirsch's *The Forgotten Ways,* he distinguishes between Hellenistic and Hebraic approaches to life. In the Hellenistic approach you give people the right ideas and expect they will change their behavior. Hirsch refers to it as thinking "our way into a new way of acting." In the Hebraic model of knowledge, you educate whole people in the context "of life and for life," or what Hirsch calls acting "our way into a new way of thinking."[9] Was Jesus more Hellenistic or Hebraic? In light of Hirsch's examples, which way do you think Jesus formed his disciples? Give examples.

2. Discuss this affirmation by Albert Einstein: "The most beautiful emotion we can experience is the mysterious. It is the fundamental emotion that stands at the cradle of all true art and science.... To sense that behind anything that can be experienced there is something that our minds cannot grasp, whose beauty and sublimity reaches us only indirectly: this is religiousness. In this sense, and in this sense only, I am a devoutly religious man."[10] Does Einstein sound more Gutenberger or Googler?

3. In one of the final interviews of novelist Graham Greene, John Cornwell concluded with the question of what Greene's Catholicism meant to him.

The author replied: "It's a mystery…which can't be destroyed…even by the Church."[11] What are some of the mysteries that "can't be destroyed… even by the Church"?

4. Stockholm Syndrome takes effect when a kidnap victim becomes emotionally attached to his kidnapper. The name is taken from a 1973 bank robbery in Stockholm, Sweden, when the robbers held bank employees hostage for six days. When the employees finally were freed, they defended their captors. When people have Stockholm Syndrome, the abuse warps them so that being held captive seems preferable to being free. They forget the benefits and the promise of freedom and cling to captivity.

5. Is it possible to contract Spiritual Stockholm Syndrome? For instance, is it possible to forget who we are and fall in love with the things that capture us? What are some of the things we fall in love with? How do we fall out of love with the things that hold us hostage?

6. Have you ever been a slave to something? What freed you from the influence, person, habit, or force that held you?

THE GOD OF CREATIVE CHANGE

Following God into the Guaranteed Unknown

> We would rather be ruined than changed. We would rather
> die in our dread than climb the cross of the moment and let
> our illusions die.
>
> —W. H. AUDEN

Change is God's signature on life. The Creator creates, and humans are made in the Creator's image. That means we also are made to create. *Creation* is another word for change, and to be creative is to be adept at change—to be an artist of transformation, harnessing the energy of fear and engaging the desire for the new and unknown.

Fear awakens us to danger, but creativity inspires us to climb out of ruts to embrace life. Those who don't face the future with fear and trembling have something missing from their faith. Or said another way: their faith is so listless that even appropriate fear can't arouse it. But the future is not a Thomas Kinkade painting. Far better to look ahead and be ready, to anticipate the future, even if it puts the fear of God the Creator into us.

In my lifetime I will need to learn six or more different preaching styles to keep the bread of life hot from the oven. A quick example: I was taught never to speak of "me," only of "one" to avoid talking about myself in the pulpit. The old rules prohibited telling personal stories. How can it be that everything has flipped?

The elders used to boast the wisdom of experience, while youth was granted qualified praise for supplying the energy and faith to generate idealism and optimism. Now the birthright of youth is the wisdom of present experience, knowing what works in the world. Meanwhile, the crown of old age echoes the virtues previously ascribed to youth: hope, optimism, and idealism. Elder wisdom is the wisdom of hope informed by history.

We can be so hidebound in our routines that we either deny that change is needed or pay it lip service while refusing to muster the energy necessary to change. There is a struggle between being right and being righteous. Some Christians are so fixated on being theologically sound they are sound asleep to what God is doing. Wendy Wasserstein has a word for lazy contentment with the world that was or the way things are: "lethargiosis."[1]

One of the reasons so many churches function in digital and discipleship dead zones is that we have failed to make the distinction our ancestors did between the *res significata* (thing signified) and the way of signifying (*modus significandi*). The deposit of faith stays the same, but the deposition changes. The way the truth is presented can change (and needs to change) without the substance of truth varying.

Each new generation needs to start fresh, but not from scratch. This is one reason Googlers need Gutenbergers, and vice versa. When we separate ourselves from the inherited memories of our ancestors, when the texts and traditions of the past do not join the present, the future is in jeopardy. There is no future without the past. Updating is fixing the bugs, removing the toxins, and improving the connection to the original Operating System. The passion of turning dead zones into live wires is one of the reasons I'm passionate about John Wesley and the early Methodists. They had a profound sense of Christianity's locative case, its "here-ness."[2]

Is the church too allied with fear (or paralyzed by it) to move past the necessary discomfort and into the world that has been thrust upon us? The key to whether this will be the best or the worst of times will be the church's ability to enter the new world with passion. Even John Calvin said that faith is false until it is *in corde* (in the heart) as well as *in cerebro* (in the head). The world is not moved by mildly interested, middle-of-the-road, play-it-safe people. And the TGIF world, especially, is not looking for a new, improved, better-reasoned argument. Gutenbergers love that stuff; Googlers have already moved on. In the words of Ray Palmer, which I grew up singing:

May thy rich grace impart
Strength to my fainting heart,
  My zeal inspire;
As thou hast died for me,
O may my love to thee
Pure, warm, and changeless be,
  A living fire.[3]

FEAR OR PASSION?

Beatle Bob (a.k.a. Robert Matonis) is a Methodist at heart. This St. Louis man has gone to see music performed every night, starting in 1996. That's more than four thousand shows. "I was a full-time concert goer" may not be what I'd like on my headstone. But I do want Beatle Bob's passion, for he understands intuitively what the Hebrews understood: to "know" is based on participation. You don't know something by being detached and distant, but only by being in relationship with it, by having personal knowledge of it and being taken in by it. You have to enter into "intercourse" with the subject.

The greater the participation, the greater the passion. Little wonder Søren Kierkegaard insisted: "If passion is eliminated, faith no longer exists."[4] Passion is one of the principle signs of our participation in the life of the divine. I want the passion of a live-music lunatic like Beatle Bob. I want the passion of Eugene Ormandy, who dislocated his shoulder while conducting the Philadelphia orchestra. But rather than pursuing music at that level, I want this type of passion for Jesus and a Jesus passion for the world. Too many Christians haven't had a passion great enough to dislocate their coffee lid, let alone a shoulder.

I want the passion of Jesus and the compassion of God. I want the passion of Paul, Augustine, Catherine of Siena, Calvin, Luther, Wesley, Pascal, Sojourner Truth, Karl Barth, Howard Thurman. Up the intensity. Start the cheering and clapping. Whenever I hear Ginny Owens singing the refrain "I don't wanna be a flame, I wanna be a raging fire,"[5] I start singing like I'm in the shower.

There is no excellence without passion, without intensity of intentionality. St. Bernard made the case that there is no true understanding without passion. "If anyone desires to grasp these writings, let him love. It is vain for anyone who does not love to listen to this song of love, or to read it. For a cold heart cannot catch fire from its eloquence."[6]

When you live out of your passion, you don't drag yourself out of bed and head to work. In fact, you don't work a day in your life. You serve, you play, you help, you love, you suffer. You were born to play in these ways, not to work at getting through life. In fact, when the Christian tradition uses the word *passion* to refer to Jesus's suffering and death, it means two things: love and willingness to suffer.

Social historian and broadcaster Studs Terkel called himself an agnostic. But just before he died he wrote a memoir titled *Touch and Go.* On the last page of his book he included a quote from William Sloane Coffin's benediction at a Yale commencement. These are the last words of a self-proclaimed agnostic, or "cowardly atheist." When you read them I dare you not to see the gestures for an authentic Christian:

> O Lord, take our minds and think through them,...
> take our hearts and set them on fire. Amen.[7]

Passion for Christ is infectious. Passion for love is viral. Passion to bear the cross is one of the primary ingredients of revival.

PETER, PAUL, AND MARY

Exactly what can the future expect of you and me, assuming we are driven by faith and God's Spirit? Pressed for an answer, I say, "Peter, Paul, and Mary." Or I scrunch a serious face and say, "The tonsures of Peter, Paul, and John." Let me explain.

The future demands our hands. As the body of Christ, the church exists to be the hands and feet of Jesus in the world. St. Peter the apostle was the disciple entrusted with the church, and the future desperately needs a thriving, vital, hands-on church.

The future demands our head. The head of the body is Christ, and the mind of Christ is imperative for right now, the teenage years of the twenty-first century. Paul the apostle is the one most helpful for our understanding of what is the mind of Christ.[8]

The future demands our heart. Mary and John symbolize the heart of the gospel. We need the example and inspiration of Mary, whose let-it-be heart trusted the impossibility of a virgin birth and who, as the mother of Jesus, pondered the mystery.[9] And John, whose writings best portray the beating heart of the gospel and the pulsating mystery of faith.

You say, "Okay, Peter, Paul, and Mary are immediately recognizable. But what about 'the tonsures of Peter, Paul, and John'?" By the seventh and eighth centuries, monks would cut their hair in a pattern to symbolize devotion and obedience to Christ.

Each pattern was said to convey an apostolic aura, one originating with St. Paul, another with St. Peter, and another with St. John.

The Pauline or Eastern tonsure consisted of shaving the entire head. In iconography, Paul is most often depicted as a bald man. The Petrine or Roman tonsure (the one we're most familiar with) is a bald spot on the top of the head. The size of the spot varied from a button to a bowl. In iconography, Peter is most often portrayed with a thick head of hair. The Johannine or Celtic tonsure consisted either of a triangle pointing toward the face or a semicircular forward arc. This was the rarest, most controversial, and most mysterious of the tonsures.

> If you don't like change,
> you're going to like irrelevance even less.
> —GENERAL ERIC SHINSEKI[10]

Aside from hands, head, heart, and tonsure, there is another Peter-Paul-John way to think of what the future requires of us: the simplicity of Peter, the complexity of Paul, and the simplexity of John.

THE SIMPLICITY OF PETER

The early church father St. Irenaeus (d. 202) liked to call the Son and the Spirit together "God's two hands." Jesus came to the world as God's hands and feet; Jesus comes now as bread and wine so that we might come to others as Jesus's hands and feet.

It's as simple as that.

Or in the even simpler words often attributed to St. Teresa of Avila: "Christ has no body now on earth but yours, no hands but yours, no feet but yours; yours are the eyes through which Christ's compassion looks out on the world, yours are the feet with which He is to go about doing good and yours are the hands with which He is to bless us now."[11]

Simplicity means to strip things of their irrelevancies and see them in simple, communicable terms. Ernst Gombrich, the Austrian art historian, was so devoted to the mastery of simplicity that he ran the text of his best-selling *The Story of Art* past a sixteen-year-old for fear his writing had been infected with academe's love of gnarly phrases. Christianity cannot be reduced to one or two phrases, but the essence of Christianity can be expressed on just one page. How long is the Apostles' Creed? How long is the Nicene Creed?

After Sir Isaac Newton finished writing his *Principia* (1686), the text that unlocked the secrets of the physical universe, he worked on a parallel volume to unlock the secrets of the spiritual universe. In this unpublished, 550-page manuscript (now housed in Jerusalem), Newton outlined eleven "Rules for Methodizing the Apocalypse." Rule nine was basically this: God, like Nature, acts in the simplest way possible.[12]

> The less alive two entities are, the more obvious
> the need for a well-designed interface becomes.
> —APPLE COMPUTER

The more complex the machine, organism, or culture, the more simple the interface needs to be. That's one reason why I love the metaphor of the Simple Church. But too often when you hear it elaborated, the Simple Church seems to be a synonym for the accretions of the modern church or for flamboyant strategic planning processes. One of the best examples of the Simple Church was lived out by Count Nicholas Zinzendorf's Herrnhut community. It centered its life on one word, a word that became key to all of Moravian theology. In German it is *Einfach;* in English it is "simplicity." The more complex the world gets, the more we need simplicity.

Living Without Complications
My family's home is furnished with heavily carved, high-Victorian couches and chairs that showcase the woodcarver's skill. I'll never forget the day I stood in an antique store, staring at a Shaker chair. I admired its simplicity and then looked at the price. I almost passed out. Six figures for a simple chair?

When the store's owner came over, I asked why the chair was so expensive. It was so plain it almost made you want to apologize. The antique dealer said: "In fancy, florid, Gothic furniture like yours, the flaws of the material and the flaws of the artist don't show. The defects and mistakes are covered up by the ornamentation. But when you look at the simple lines of this Shaker chair, you can see very quickly whether there are any mistakes or defects. There is no margin of error. Only a master artist can make a Shaker chair."

It's that simple.

We need to strip away the fancies and embellishments. We need to call upon the skill it takes to carve the simple. Discipleship is the process through which we strip away all that impedes the love and mercy and grace of Christ through us to the world. My friend Vern Hyndman likes to say, "Disciples start out as barrels and become pipelines." We start out conserving and move to dispersing.

My favorite metaphor for the type of Simple Church we need is the *Trümmerfrauen,* or "rubble women." Germany was reduced to rubble at the end of the Second World War. There was the rubble of cities leveled from bombing, and another kind of rubble from the concentration camps. Germany's cities contained an estimated 400 million cubic meters of rubble, with almost nothing available to clear the debris but the simplest tool of all, the human hand.

Enter the rubble women. The Russians were the first to use the term *Trümmerfrauen.* When the Red Army entered bombed-out Berlin on May 29, 1945, they conscripted all women between fifteen and sixty-five (sixty thousand of them) and gave them the toilsome task of clearing away rubble. While the rubble women rebuilt war-torn Germany by hand, they cared for the wounded, buried the dead, and salvaged belongings. You can hear the testimony of the rubble women:

On our knees we sifted through the burnt ruins, the debris and ashes. Like search dogs we sniffed among rotting limbs, flowers torn from roots, charred photos of people who did not survive. Our sharp eyes picked out bones and teeth, keys, shoes, a bit of lace, used tin of rouge, pages ripped from books. With tender and careful hands we gathered the pieces of metal, flesh, paper. Voices howled or whispered through the ditches and mountains of dirt, but they were too loud or too soft, or the language one we'd never heard before. We tried to grab the voices by the throat and make them explain what had happened here—in clear, solid language: nouns and verbs, words that cannot be misunderstood. No adjectives or adverbs, no qualifiers, no conditionals.

An army of women, we stood at the barbed wire and admitted what we really searched for. We spoke distinctly, in simple language that could be understood by a child. Here is what we said: We are not looking for poetry, not yet, not while our nostrils still choke on the smell of burnt flesh, and yellow-gray particles drift from the sky into our eyes, and everything we reach for turns into human bone. Is it too much to ask (we cried) for a sentence that can be clearly diagrammed, with a subject that leads to a predicate, in which every word is identified and has its function? We need a language that will make sense of the devastation, the horror that was rained on us—not by a God of the Wilderness, but instead by men with eye-slits so narrow they

cannot let in the light, minds cramped and cobwebbed as black mouse-
holes.... With a sigh, we return to our task. Kneeling, sifting through the
debris, searching the rubble for meanings ripped from words.[13]

The world as we know it has been demolished and deconstructed by the annihila-
tive forces of postmodernity. What the church owes this deconstructed world is the
grueling, backbreaking task of rebuilding and reconstruction. The Simple Church is the
church of the rubble women, a church that speaks with its hands in the midst of dust
and ruins.

The Complexity of Paul

The more complex life becomes, the more simple we need to make it. This is the fundamental principle of complexity science: that complexity in the world derives from simple
generative rules and regularities. The universe is a marvelously complex system arising
from splendid simplicities. Hence the key to navigating complexity is simplicity.

Still, we must navigate complexity because life is just not that simple. If simplicity
underpins complexity, complexity overlays and overcasts simplicity. In fact, the human
species survives to the extent that it complexifies to adapt to a changing environment. It
diversifies, rather than specializes. Healthy organisms are diverse and differentiated, not
uniform and franchised.

Life operates on complex levels. There is an irreducible complexity to life that makes
the idea of accidental creation inconceivable. A living cell, for instance, contains some
100 million proteins of 20,000 different types. The genome of a simple bacterium has a
genetic code some 4 million letters long. The mechanism needed to translate this into a
living organism is "so complex, so universal and so essential, that it is hard to see how it
could have come into existence."[14]

The complexity that drives human life is multiplied by the complexification of our
social and personal lives. No wonder we live with terrible pressure. We may be tired of
terrible, but we process information four hundred times faster than the rate of our Renaissance ancestors and without the four hundred extra hours. So we're terribly tired as
well as tired of terrible.

That's why it is not enough simply to talk about Simple Church. As movie mogul
Samuel Goldwyn once replied to an idea he didn't like, "You are partly 100 percent
right." Every side has a flip. To be fully 100 percent right, we must also talk about Complex Church. And then flip it once more.

Far too many people are stuck in the Gutenberg world, intoxicated by the familiarity and held in the sway of its simplicity. But they are blind to the reality of the new world's challenges and endless complexness. What appears to us today as obvious and clear-cut choices were, at the time they were being made, maddeningly difficult. When life is a colorful mix of clashing contradictions, it can be best to serve up a salad. As Kurt Vonnegut is said to have observed: too many people are trying to construct a philosophy (or, one could add, a theology) out of bumper stickers.

The best example of complexity theory, of a nonlinear, self-organizing, complex adaptive system, is the doctrine of the incarnation. Christians take this mind-boggling doctrine for granted. Why, of course the God of the universe would assume human flesh and enter everyday human life in first-century Palestine. It's far too easy to make it sound simple. If you grew up hearing this teaching, it does seem simple. But put yourself in Mary's place. She was a teenage girl. Without her knowing it, the Spirit of God "came upon" her and she, having never engaged in the procreative act, was pregnant. That part was evident, but what about the rest of it?

God decided to father a Son in partnership with this unmarried girl? Who among us, hearing the words of the angel to Mary for the first time, would respond with, "Oh, of course. God does things like this"? No, there would be no casual acceptance. Incarnation? The suggestion that God the Creator would be enwrapped in human flesh? That can't be right.

But once a doctrine becomes familiar, it quickly becomes overly familiar. We set aside the parallel truth, which is just as revolutionary. It is this: incarnation asserts that the religion of Jesus must take physical, material, organizational form that is culturally indigenous. God did not come to earth as Albert Einstein or Seth Godin or Mickey Mantle. He came as a baby who grew up to be a craftsman and then an itinerant healer and teacher. He lived fully in his culture, which helps explain why so many of those who met him and heard him had such trouble accepting him as the Anointed One. How could he be this One? After all, he was born to an anonymous teenager in a backwater village. This guy is the Messiah? Can't be.

Faith Incarnated in You

Again, the way of life that Jesus introduced is one that is incarnated in one's culture. And as one era arrives and disappears to be replaced by a new era, lived-out faith will collect and reflect the culture in which it appears. The notes on a page of music never change. But every time the notes are played or sung, the sound is different: what changes are the lips, the bow, the baton, the interpretation by the players.

Incarnation means embracing the complexities of the zeitgeist on terms defined by God. We know the Spirit by the Spirit's fruit, which means we know the Spirit only by embodiment. But that embodiment is self-organizing and adaptive within the limits set in motion by God. Like a virus that mutates, the practice of faith learns and changes its behavior, depending on its context. Nothing illustrates this quicker than translation, the need for faith to learn the language of another culture. For example, the Japanese word for "mother's sister" is the same as that for "father's concubine." In Brazilian Portuguese, the word for eating and having sex is the same. To be precise, *comer* (to eat) and *dar* (to give) are the terms in common use for the taking and giving roles in sex.

The doctrine of the incarnation says God makes the infinite finite; that God makes the very being of God small for us; that God's humanation in Jesus means God works little large; that the whole of faith is encapsulated in a very small package: one act of love with cosmic significance.[15] But even more complex: the act of incarnation is replicated in every one of us. Here is how Paul presented the complexity of incarnation: To the Jew, become a Jew. To the Gentile, a Gentile. To the TGIF world, a Googler.

To the Greek Christians in Thessalonica, Paul talked about the resurrection this way: "For since we believe that Jesus died and rose again."[16] He used the intransitive verb "to rise" with Jesus as the subject, as Greeks would think of the Phoenix who rose spontaneously. To the Jewish Christians in Rome, Paul talked about the resurrection this way: "It will be reckoned to us who believe in him who raised Jesus our Lord from the dead."[17] He used the transitive verb "to raise" with God as the subject and Jesus as the direct object, as Jews would think of God who is the subject of history.[18] Same truth, different context, different way of expressing it to two different audiences and cultures.

God "humbles" the Godhead by bringing God to earth to reach every one of us. That is 107 billion of us, the total number of humans who have walked on planet Earth. Consider the astonishing complexity of 107 billion little incarnations. Consider the mind-boggling difference between an Emmanuel God-with-first-century Palestine and Emmanuel God-with-twenty-first-century Paris or London. Consider an Emmanuel God-with-Bach and an Emmanuel God-with-Bono. Jesus is the same yesterday, today, and forever. But for Jesus to be the same yesterday, today, and forever, he needs to become "fresh every morning."[19] Jesus is fresh-baked bread and fresh living water.

Incarnation—Simple and Complex

One of the gospel's favorite symbols of the incarnation is Living Water. Water is an apt image to help us think about simplicity and complexity. Complexity is seen as a third way that mediates inactive order at one end of the continuum and disorder or chaos at the other. Think of static order as ice. Think of chaos as steam. Complexity is liquid water, perhaps the second most favorite image among scientists to illustrate complexity theory.

Forget "the earth is flat." This world is fluid. To flatten the complexity of a situation is to endanger the future. The world today is a dangerous place. Some cheer that it is "dangerously flat." Others sneer that it is "dangerously curved."[20] I claim it is dangerously fluid. But whether curved or flat or fluid, the world is dangerous. In the complex Pauline theology:

1. Small is big if God is in it, so Paul encourages the church to do little large, to look at life through both ends of the telescope.
2. The details of how you live have direct implications for your future and your place at the Parousia.
3. We are justified by grace alone, which means the whole is greater than the sum of its parts.
4. The more the gospel is embodied in the diverse cultures of the world, the more complete and the more powerful is the full stature of the body of Christ.

Here are indirect parallels in complexity science and in complex, nonlinear systems:

1. Small, simple inputs can have massive consequences.
2. Small, simple changes in initial conditions produce radically different outcomes (for example, a difference of one part in 1016th in the ratio between two fundamental forces could have meant that no stars were formed).
3. The whole is greater than the sum of its parts.
4. The more rich the interactions, the more diverse the relationships, the greater the creativity and adaptability of the system.

"Complexipacity" is a key skill for the church in the TGIF world. The word was coined in 2008 by designer Tom Snyder to name a paramount survival skill: the capacity to "assimilate complex ideas, systems, problems, situations, interactions, or relationships."[21]

Complexipacity is the recognition that sometimes complex thought calls for the use of complex words. The result of simplicity is often a splendid lucidity, but sometimes lucidity is achieved at the expense of the truth. Consider how we talk about the Persons of the Trinity. In recitations of the Nicene Creed, the affirmation of Jesus being God is rendered in more contemporary language as "begotten, not made, *of one Being with* the Father."[22] This rendering is not the same thing as the early Nicene (CE 325) language of "consubstantial with." As Clifford Longley has argued, Tertullian's phrase "consubstantial with" (the Greek *homoousios*) is more honest since it "sounds mysterious and profound" while "'being' sounds familiar and is therefore misleading." Longley's last point is as profound as it is nuanced: "Whatever 'being' means when applied to God, it is not the same as when applied to a carrot, or indeed to you and me."[23]

The triune identification of the disciple of Jesus as spirit and soul and body may be theologically complex, yet this is Paul's Greek/Christian attempt to identify the totality of each person.[24]

THE SIMPLEXITY OF JOHN

There are two words I wish I had invented but didn't: *glocal* and *simplexity*. Like the word *glocal*, which brings together the global and the local, *simplexity* yokes the simple and the complex. The mystery of simplexity is the complex embracing the simple and the rational embracing the incomprehensible. Three of the best biblical examples of simplexity are the mixed mysteries found in the doctrine of the Trinity, the Lord's Prayer, and John's gospel.

> Certainly it is heaven upon earth,
> to have a…mind move in charity, rest in providence,
> and turn upon the poles of truth.
> —FRANCIS BACON[25]

The Lord's Prayer, which is in truth the Disciples' Prayer, has both a simple elegance and a bowing to the complexities of human existence. The doctrine of the Trinity braids together the three-in-one Godhead in a unity comprised of uniqueness.

John's gospel has been called "a stream in which a child can wade and an elephant can swim."[26] In John's gospel, we find the polarities of truth most loudly proclaimed. One minute, the Son is equal to the Father ("I and the Father are one."); the next minute, the son is subordinate to the father: "The Father is greater than I."[27] In John, Jesus is both most divine and most human.

On one hand, Jesus came not to judge the world.[28] On the other hand, Jesus came for judgment.[29] The kingdom is here, and the kingdom is coming.[30] Truth is both Hellenistic and Jewish, "wisdom" and "mystery," culminating in Jesus's declaration that he is "the way and the truth and the life."[31] Yet don't forget that Jesus has many sheep "not of this fold"[32] and Jesus is the true light that enlightens everyone entering this world.

In these three—the Lord's Prayer, the doctrine of the Trinity, and the gospel of John—there is an artful combining of two or more melodic themes to form a contrapuntal conversation. Each theme acknowledges the presence and participation of the other and is altered by the exchange.

Simplexity is like an elegant Flemish needlework. The complexity looks like the loose threads and stray knots on the reverse side of a tapestry. But the beginnings and endings are eventually matched up with the finesse of an artist whose simple scenes blare forth on the front side. To experience the presence of God is to live in simplexity, an unfathomable mystery of absolute sobriety and almost giddy intoxication. To know God is not to banish mystery, but deepen it.

The language of mystery is not the language of mathematics, science, or philosophy, but the language of symbol, metaphor, liturgy, and story. In fact, before the third century, what we now call "sacraments" were called "mysterion," which comes from the Greek word *mustes* meaning "close-mouth." *Mystery, mystic,* and *mute* share the same root, which testifies to the incomprehensible, unfathomable, paradoxical nature of truth. The Latin author Tertullian is responsible for taking the terminology of military induction, *sacrament,* to discuss Christian practices connected with baptism. But Tertullian's use of sacrament was intended to deepen the mystery, not banish it. In his words, "All things go out into mystery."

It makes perfect sense, then, that the mystery of sacraments lies at the heart of Christian faith. Sacraments reconnect humanity and more importantly, individuals, with God in ways that are simple, real, local, and mysterious. The hunger of the TGIF world is for reconnections with the things that are simple, real, local, and mysterious.

One of my students, the Nobel laureate Ted Moeller, coined the phrase "Give me mystery, or give me death." Another of my students hides behind Shakespeare in condemning the Enlightenment. "You would pluck out the heart of my mystery," Hamlet exclaims.[33]

As in most things of life, the choice between simplicity and complexity is not an either/or proposition. It is both/and, and/also, one and the other. We mentioned earlier that the fear of God is a necessary component of entering into the future. The future has arrived, so let us fearfully and fearlessly embody Christ on earth as our faith is stirred to meet the challenges of the TGIF world. But there is another future coming that needs our enthusiastic embrace: "thy kingdom come on earth, as it is in heaven." In the "Our

Father, who art in heaven," can we hear "heaven" as not just a location above and beyond us, but a living presence and lifestyle *among* us?

Interactives

1. How can we, as the body of Christ, become an incarnation of hope and community to the world without mimicking the latest marketable trend?
2. Do we listen to the generations that came before us or after us? I mean, really listen? Malachi spoke of the hearts of parents turning to their children and children to their parents. Then there is the Joel/Acts passage that promises an outpouring of God's Spirit to young and old, women and men, enslaved and free. Whose wisdom do you build upon?
3. What sounds of TGIF Culture can you hear in the following quote: "My favorite book is one nobody owns, yet everyone reads at least passages from it; a compilation which earlier ages called the Book of Nature, where a starry night's almost my favorite page"[34]?
4. How is the Bible both simple and complex? Give an example for each.
5. Parker Palmer contends that "We can know reality only by being in community with it."[35] What do you think he means? If you lived by this vision, how might it change your life?
6. Do you see evidence that TGIF Culture is increasingly post-Christian, if not anti-Christian? If so, give examples. A senior member of the USAmerican Catholic hierarchy confided to George Weigel that he was fearful of this scenario coming true: "I will die in my bed; my successor will die in prison; and his successor will die a martyr."[36] Do you think this is overstated? Understated? Why?

Singing Strange Songs in the Lord's Land

Life Wouldn't Be Interesting
If You Didn't Feel Out of Place

Say not, "Why were the former days better than these?"
For it is not from wisdom that you ask this.

—Ecclesiastes 7:10, esv

Martin Luther King Jr. taught only one college course in his life. President Benjamin E. Mays asked him to teach a course in social philosophy at Morehouse College (1961–1962). Eight students signed up for it—six males, two females.

Throughout that semester the students took few notes. Forget any taping of King's lectures and seminars. Those who did take notes didn't save them. There were no photographs taken of Professor King at the lectern. No saved syllabi. No saved papers, marked up and graded by King himself.

These are the only people in the world who can legitimately call themselves "students of Martin Luther King Jr." And yet they missed their moment. None have any evidence of having taken the course, other than the class registration records of More-house College, and the fact that their professor gave them a grade.

One of the saddest things you can say about anyone? They stood in the presence of greatness and missed it.

Let's not miss our moment.

> Help me to watch and pray, and on thyself rely,
> Assured if I my trust betray, I shall forever die.
> —CHARLES WESLEY[1]

I admit it. This is not the moment I would have picked.[2] I am a product of Gutenberg Culture, but now find myself in the TGIF world.[3] I prefer the world of paper and ink to bits and bytes. No wonder so many of us are feeling like novelist James Ellroy, who summed up his life in a few words: "I was frayed, fraught, french-fried, and frazzled."[4]

I want to be careful not to treat any generation or cultural group as if it had a single personality, mind, and will. But for the sake of psychographic as opposed to demographic

Can Googlers and Gutenbergers Get Together?

If the shifts in culture that I've been describing are largely invisible to you, you're probably a Googler. You can be a Googler by birth (they tend to be younger than Gutenbergers), or by worldview (a Gutenberger can be influenced and even won over by Googler Culture). No matter what culture you identify with, you have likely run into conflicting assumptions, values, and expectations between the two tribes. Here is a short questionnaire that points to some of the issues that differentiate the two groups. Respond to these statements with "agree" or "disagree." Then find out if you're more Googler or Gutenberger.

1. Gutenbergers need to loosen their grip on all the rules and start listening to God.
2. If Gutenbergers were serious about "winning the world for Christ," they would make more of an effort to get in touch with what's going on in the world.

clarity, I like to say that I was born B.C. (before cells). My kids were born A.C. (after cells). I was born just after the bee's knees were the cat's pajamas and when phones were a useful and rapidly spreading technology. Today, mobile devices are no longer phones; they are a person's link to the world. They are a relationship.

I use Martin Cooper's invention of the cell phone in 1973 as the dividing line between the B.C. and A.C. cultures for good reason. "Mobile is at the center of everything," Jeffrey Cole insists. "It's truly the transformational device."[5] Mobile devices are overtaking personal computers—the days of the workstation desktop are over.[6] In the relatively brief span of time since 1973, a whole host of media decided to cohabit and compete for our attention during our every waking moment.

These technologies are radically reshaping our relational dynamics in both the real and virtual worlds. I don't make this statement lightly. What started out as a system limited to making and receiving calls began, in 1973, to evolve into the arbiter of life's relationships and an inseparable companion on the journey.

Try this experiment: While sitting in your car at a traffic light, do a quick survey of the motorists around you and those passing through the intersection in front of you.

3. It looks like Gutenbergers didn't read the tweet about Jesus saying it's impossible to serve both God and mammon.

4. God hasn't resided in a building since the temple was destroyed in CE 70. Why don't Gutenbergers know that?

5. Jesus wasn't a Christian, so why are Gutenbergers convinced that he died so humanity could convert to evangelicalism?

Scoring: Count your "agree" answers and give yourself one point for each. A score of 5 is *bona fide* Googler. Scores of 3 and 4 indicate a strong Googler leaning. Scores of 1 or 2 show that you are either a born Gutenberger or a Googler who has very mixed feelings.

To think about: What might happen if Googler Christians and Gutenberger Christians started talking to each other and started really listening to each other? If you are a Googler, what can you bring to the church that more accurately reflects Jesus's model for the life of a follower?

What percentage is driving while they make a phone call, send a text, or play Angry Birds? A single piece of technology has become so indispensible that many of us can't tolerate driving to work or the grocery store without at the same time being in touch with someone who's not in the car with us.

Sadly, the mobile device has intensified our inability to be alone. Even for a few minutes.

And the ever-present mobile device is just one characteristic of the TGIF world. The technologies of the Google era require new protocols for living, loving, dying, and dis-uniting. Look at what lies behind that statement. Marissa Mayer, a Google vice president, boasts that credit card companies can predict with 98 percent accuracy two years in advance when a couple is going to divorce, based on the couple's spending patterns.[7] And we are supposed to feel reassured at hearing this? Not only do people who are driving to the health club feel compelled to use the phone, couples can't even keep their deepest secrets from the eyes of Visa and MasterCard.

In the Agricultural Age, there was the extended family.

In the Industrial Age, there was the nuclear family.

In the Virtual Age, there is something new: the polysemous family.[8]

This is only the tip of the iceberg. Internet dating is now not a last resort but a first

Are You More Gutenberger or More Googler?

If Gutenbergers and Googlers didn't look at things differently, life would be much less interesting. Here is a short questionnaire that points to a few of the ways the two groups differ. Respond to these statements with "agree" or "disagree." Find out if you're more Googler or Gutenberger.

1. Googlers take life seriously enough.
2. Googlers who claim to be Christians are *really* sold out to following Christ.
3. Googlers should follow the same rules as the rest of us.
4. It's time for Googlers to get on board with what God has been doing through the church for centuries.
5. The noticeable absence of Googlers at 11 a.m. on Sunday mornings shows they're not truly committed to Christ.

resort, plus a form of entertainment. There is long-distance love, Second Life dates, and virtual marriages.[9] In India, for example, millennium-old traditions of arranged marriages are giving way to online dating services such as BharatMatrimony.com. Throughout Asia and Africa, millions of people without personal computers are able to hook up through myGamma, a Singapore-based mobile phone social networking site. In China, *wang hun* (online role-play marriages) are straining definitions of marriage even though the partners never meet face to face.[10]

ARE YOU AN IMMIGRANT?

When I was born, contacts were lenses, not connections.

I was bred to be afraid of defeat, of getting licked. Our children, when they're licked by something, aren't bred to think they're defeated; they're just being slobbered on by life. When I was born, teenagers went into a drug store, asked for some cigarettes, and then, in a whisper, asked for some condoms. Today teenagers go into the drug store, ask for some condoms, and then, in a whisper, ask for cigarettes.

When I was born, children accessed information through authority figures. We are now raising the first generations of children that do not need authority figures to access

Scoring: Count your "disagree" answers to questions 1 and 2, and give yourself one point for each. Then count your "agree" answers to questions 3, 4, and 5, and give yourself one point for each. A score of 5 is full-on Gutenberger. Scores of 3 and 4 indicate a middling Gutenberger. Scores of 1 or 2 show that you are either a born Googler or a Gutenberger who has been learning from Googler Culture.

To think about: We all are most comfortable when we're around people who agree with us and uphold our viewpoint. But does a lack of conformity to Gutenberg values really indicate that Googlers are not committed to following Christ? St. Paul said a toe in the body of Christ can't tell a finger that it's not needed because it isn't a toe. What might happen if Gutenberger Christians decided to listen to Googlers and learn from them?

information. It is the total reversal of historical learning modes. Looked at objectively, children need adults to help them assess, understand, and process information. The reversal is that, now, adults need their children to help them access information. In immigrant communities, the children teach their parents the new culture, the language, and the ideas. Today, adults need to listen to their children, because they are the natives and adults are the cultural immigrants.

Children can speak to virtually anyone, anywhere, whether they "know" one another or not. John Zogby calls them history's "First Globals,"[11] Members of the TGIF generation are natives of a global empire with the shared experiences of movies, music, and material culture, a common language of hieroglyphics and abbreviations, and the instant awareness of what's in and out, trusted and fraudulent. These "shared universals"[12] are evangelizing cultural particulars, as global homogenization transmits tribal identities. Paradoxically, local traditions burn more brightly under the pressure of the new and the tyranny of being current. The more global and generic our brands, the more a local oddity is the mark of authenticity.

I understand what it's like to be an immigrant, because I am one. I am not intuitively TGIF. And while the word shifts to this new culture, Gutenbergers still hold the positions of power. It is no mystery why Googlers marvel that the leadership of the church is so out of sync. Likewise, we don't need to guess at reasons why Gutenbergers are more and more confused in a world that doesn't seem to work like it should. Unless something is done, matters will only get worse. We have not begun to imagine the backlash against baby boomers for stealing all the jobs, all the pensions, all the Social Security benefits, and all the professorships, and then pulling up the ladder behind them. The boomer church is not admired by Googlers. Far from it.

Theologian Bernard Lonergan said that part of the human condition is for each of us to have a personal "scotoma," a blind spot that blocks our openness to wisdom.[13] We develop scotomas to blunt truth that might upset the status quo and require change. A looming example is to recognize the spiritual implications of this cultural shift, and to understand what it will take for educational and religious institutions to come to terms with the change.

The blind spots may change, but every age has them. A member of the theology faculty at a school where I don't teach criticized me for teaching students in the virtual platform of Second Life, because "it can get kind of creepy in there." Was this person pretending that there are no creepy places or people in real life? No matter how new the moment, we have been here before, so many times. Social networking may be creating new kinds of community, but wasn't the church the original social network?

Everything is older than you think.
—English local community historian
W. G. Hoskins[14]

I like to define nostalgia as recalling the fun without remembering the pain. Every age is equidistant from eternity. Every age can say "these are the best of times, these are the worst of times." No problem is ever solved; it is only resolved for the moment, shortly to raise its head again in new guise. We waged war on poverty, and there's still poverty. We went to war against drugs, and there's still drug abuse. We made war on homelessness, and there still are people without a place to live. The core problem isn't the poverty, the drugs, the homelessness. The problem isn't the augmentation. The problem is the human heart.

And sometimes the gains and losses of augmentations are identical. The upside of TGIF Culture? Everyone has a voice. The downside of TGIF Culture? Everyone has a voice. TGIF empowers the one just as it empowers the many. Everyone is discovering their voice, because in a TGIF world every voice matters and every voice can be heard.

If Jesus were here today (which he is), he would run to embrace people in these new social spaces. Jesus taught us to be "in" the world, whatever that world is, but not "of" the world, or "out of it" either.[15] Christians are always standing at an angle to their age.

Of course, cultures also have scotomas, the places where a culture is blind to wisdom. Or as Marshall McLuhan warned us, "every new technological innovation is a literal amputation."[16] New media creates new problems along with new opportunities. Shane Hipps riffed on McLuhan like this: "No technology is neutral. Every technology has an innate bias, and it will use you. Once you become aware of its bias, you can use it."[17]

Sometimes the amputations were long and painful. For example, even after the appearance of gummed envelopes and postage stamps in 1840, the tradition of sealing letters and other missives was continued for decades.

Sometimes the amputations were close to immediate. The Reformation was not good for the beeswax business, since the Reformers turned people away from candle-lighting rituals and toward the candlepower of the Word. Once the electric light genie was let out of Edison's brain, it could not be put back again or even turned off. Herbert Hoover wanted to commemorate Edison's death in 1931 by turning off the lights across the country. He was advised that such a blackout would cause great harm.[18]

How many of you reading this book were taught how to use a slide rule? How many know what a slide rule is? The augmentation of the calculator led inexorably to the amputation of the slide rule. Would any of you like to lament that amputation (though my calculus teacher in high school fought it)? The artificial intelligence of GPS navigation systems has solved the problem of getting from point A to point B and soon will threaten the survival of map publishers. The augmentation of text messaging is leading willy-nilly to the amputation of cursive writing. It is hard for me to lament that amputation when no one can read my handwriting anyway.

> An eight-year-old today sees the internet with about
> as much fascination as you see the toilet.
> —INVENTOR AND ENTREPRENEUR
> DEAN ("MR. SEGWAY") KAMEN[19]

Sometimes the amputations are frighteningly unpredictable. I know this because I had a personal role in one boomer-generation amputation. The augmentation known as television brought with it a hit series that became a cultural institution (and my favorite show), *Bonanza*. Can you guess when the network scheduled *Bonanza*? Sunday night at 8 p.m. That meant it presented head-to-head competition with another long-standing cultural institution, the Sunday-night church service. My generation was forced to choose either church or the Cartwrights. We know who won.

There are other augmentations whose amputations prove the law of unintended consequences, or as Edward Tenner put it, "Why Things Bite Back."[20] The overuse of antibiotics has produced super bacteria that trump the power of the drug. The development of "safer" football helmets tripled neck and spine injuries; computer keyboards cause wrist injuries; chairs deform our bodies and weaken our spines. (We forget that comfort is a very recent concept: only a very small percentage of the world's population used chairs until a few centuries ago.)

We amputate some things at our peril. One of the two humans competing against Watson the IBM supercomputer, in the first ever "Man vs. Machine" *Jeopardy* competition, conceded defeat by scribbling a cheeky line from *The Simpsons:* "I, for one, welcome our new computer overlords."[21] Allow me to differ: I, for one, do not welcome any "overlord"...other than Christ.

There is also the potential in every augmentation for apocalypse. J. R. R. Tolkien was the most successful author of the twentieth century. A constant theme in Tolkien's

The Lord of the Rings is the barbaric uses of technology. Studies have shown that when East Germans were allowed to watch USAmerican soap operas, it reduced their interest in politics and pacified the populace. As one East German dissident lamented: "the whole people could leave the country and move to the West as a man at 8 p.m.—via television." The more time spent watching Western television, the less interested East Germans were in political change.[22] Television viewing habits in East Germany proved that Karl Marx was only half right: it was media, not religion, that was the "opiate of the people."

New media enable people to be generous and kind. But they also enable bullies, heresy hunters (a.k.a. ODMs or Online Discernment Ministries), jihadis, and spammers to stir up cauldrons of hatred that boil over and scald everyone within spraying distance. TGIF may be viral, but many viruses you don't want to spread. Hate can be spread as easily as love.

TGIF does not just democratize; it also can be used for authoritarian and propagandistic purposes. That's why Hugo Chavez is on Twitter, and it explains why the Chinese government is so Internet sophisticated. Clay Shirky calls this "the dictator's dilemma."[23] TGIF aided popular uprisings in Tunisia, Egypt, Libya, and other nations. But repressive regimes love the Internet for its help in keeping an eye on what their citizens are up to. Dictators have used USAmerican technology and tools to censor their nations' citizens and pocket Facebook passwords.[24] Even if authorities lose their monopoly on the flow of information, they gain access to a new kind of social control: the ability to manipulate and monitor the flow.[25] "In the past, the KGB resorted to torture to learn of connections between activists," Evgeny Morozov says. "Today, they simply need to get on Facebook."[26]

More than two thousand years ago, a mathematician named Archimedes is claimed to have said, "Give me a lever long enough and a fulcrum on which to place it, and I will move the world."[27]

Here is the lever: the simplicity of Peter.

Here is the fulcrum: the complexity of Paul.

Here is the will to use the lever and the fulcrum together: the simplexity of John.

It is time for all of us to move into the TGIF world, and to move the TGIF world toward the gospel. Social networking has created a culture that breeds virality. And this virality could easily become the virtual petri dishes of Christian revival. Googlers are poised to carry out this mission, but they face heavy winds and foreboding challenges. Some of the major promises, and perils, are outlined in the chapters that follow.

Interactives

1. If you were to open the door to the future, to change, to transformation, what doors in your life would you need to open?
2. In one of T. S. Eliot's most celebrated poems, "Murder in the Cathedral," four knights are sent by the king to kill Thomas Beckett. They start to enter the cathedral, and the initial reaction of the priests is to bar the door. But the archbishop intervenes by demanding that the doors to Jesus's house, if truly a "house of prayer," should always be left open. The sanctuary should be free, not a fort:

   > The church shall be open, even to our enemies.
   > Open the door![28]

3. Charlie Peacock reflected: "When I used to hang out with drunks and addicts, they would say, 'More will be revealed.' When I started hanging out with Christians, no one talked like that, or lived like that. They were largely a people of dry, almost mathematical certainty. The only time mystery entered in was when someone quoted 1 Corinthians 2:9, 'No eye has seen, no ear has heard, no mind has conceived what God has prepared for those who love him.'"[29] Discuss when and why you have felt the same. Or have you never felt this way?
4. The bottom has fallen out of classical music. Why? Because it has failed to engage its time and place.[30] How appropriate is it that the Los Angeles Philharmonic Orchestra's new concert hall is called the Walt Disney Concert Hall?
5. "I've never had any ambitions, only enthusiasms."[31] So testified James Hodgson (former US secretary of labor and ambassador to Japan). Do you like this distinction between "ambitions" and "enthusiasms"? What are your "enthusiasms"?
6. Arguably the number one magazine for youth ministers, *YouthWorker Journal,* devoted its first 2011 issue to technology and youth culture, under the heading of "Tuned In, Turned Off," here is a sample of what the "experts" told youth ministers:
   - With today's technology "spiritual life wanes. You can't fit prayer into a multitasking habit."

- "Every time we put a piece of technology between us and the person communicating with us, we're living one step removed from reality."
- Technology devalues the interpersonal relationship and harms his or her ability to socialize in person.

You get the picture.[32] If you continue reading in the magazine, you also learn that things such as Twitter, Google, iPods/iPhones, Facebook, and video games are causing kids to stay up late and lose sleep. In fact, "heavy media users between the ages of 8 and 18 were more likely to have poor grades, experience more trouble with their parents and ironically become more bored than their less media-saturated peers."[33]

Reflect on the images of TGIF Culture being portrayed by these "youth ministry experts." Which ones do you think are accurate, and which aren't? What does it say about the church when the top youth ministry journal peddles such negative perspectives?

PART II

—

Twitter

In the Beginning Was the Tweet

How Twitter Produces a Better Follower of Christ

> Quickly, tell me everything in two words!
>
> —F. T. Marinetti
> in "Futurist Sensibility" (1912)

If anyone tells you that when Twitter was launched (2006), the social-networking world was turning cartwheels, don't believe them. Some of the world's biggies were so unimpressed they didn't bother to grab their own Twitter handles. This includes Burger King, Bank of America, Berkshire Hathaway, Eli Lilly, GE, GM, Macy's, Sears, VW, Wendy's, KFC, Nike, Walmart, Hyundai, Walt Disney, Coty, and Comcast, to name several.

One person, however, can claim prescience. He recognized Twitter's potential far ahead of the pack and used it to help change his address to 1600 Pennsylvania Avenue. How else do you explain what got a dark-skinned guy with a Kenyan father and the middle name Hussein elected president? Barack Obama tweets. (You know it's the president's personal tweets when posts are accompanied by his initials, "BO.")

Twitter has reached epidemic proportions. This social-networking medium has grown so fast that the site still can't easily handle the traffic. The Fail Whale icon shows up all too frequently (a sign that the volume of tweets has exceeded capacity). When you're using Twitter you get the same feeling our ancestors must have had when they picked up a telephone receiver and heard a neighbor droning on and on, tying up the party line.

Fail Whale or not, I can't imagine life without Twitter. I've been microblogging since 2009, and it is an almost hourly connection to the wider world. A case can be made that if not for Twitter, the social fabric of daily life for millions would suffer a mortal blow. (Should I defend tweets during worship?)[1] Twitter is not just a handy way to tell the world you're headed to Kroger to pick up bread and milk. It is a catalyst for popular uprisings, political movements, the unseating of tyrants, mass demonstrations calling for civil liberties and democracy. In political revolutions taking place around the world (the "Jasmine Revolution"[2] or "Arab Spring" of 2011), or in helping relief efforts in the midst of natural disasters (the earthquake and tsunami that hit Japan in 2011), Twitter gets all hands on deck long before governments, large relief organizations, and even the news media know what's going on. The greatest archive in the world, the Library of Congress, has decided to dedicate its resources to stockpiling every post ever entered into the Twitter stream, assuring that you and I and every other Twitterer past, present, and future will enjoy online immortality.

Jesus, Twitter, and You

From the start, Twitter changed things. And every hour it changes something else. And if you cooperate, it can change you. I don't mean by giving you a wireless megaphone to announce the color of your nails or the acquisition of a new pickup truck. I mean Twitter can make you a better Jesus-follower.

I shared this view with a group of Christians, and an audience member told me afterward, "It takes a lot of *chutzpah* to argue that Twitter makes you a better Christian." Well, not as much chutzpah as was displayed in 1983, when President Ronald Reagan hosted at the White House a kosher-catered birthday celebration for The Rebbe (Menachem Mendel Schneerson).[3] The guest of honor attended the party via video link.

Now that's chutzpah.

But maybe it's true that getting the highest benefit from Twitter takes chutzpah. This kind of cultural chutzpah may explain why a study found that of all the social media (Facebook, LinkedIn, GooglePlus, and so forth), tweeters are the most religious.[4] For me, social media stretches far beyond a cultural icon of religiosity. The vehicle of Twitter is, in many ways, the ultimate medium for discipleship. Let me explain the five leading ways that Twitter has changed my life and made me a better follower of Jesus. You might realize a few of these changes have taken place in your life as well.

1. The Art of Following

Twitter only knows two categories: whom you follow, and who is following you. Twitter's categorical imperative is one of followership, not the fast track to leadership, which is so inherent in our culture. In Twitterdom, you are who you follow.

> I woke, the dungeon flamed with light;
> my chains fell off, my heart was free,
> I rose, went forth, and followed thee.
> —Charles Wesley, "And Can It Be"[5]

Picture Bob Dylan for a moment. Few people have had greater impact on popular culture than this offbeat singer-songwriter. For five decades he has provided some of the most dominant soundtracks to the human imagination, not just in North America but around the world. His dramatic conversion to Christianity in the 1980s is still not understood, and the church has never embraced him as a brother. But this is Dylan's own description of his journey from drugs to discipleship under the tutelage of the Vineyard movement:

> Jesus tapped me on the shoulder and said, Bob, why are you resisting me? I said, I'm not resisting you! He said, You gonna follow me? I said, I've never thought about that before! He said, When you're not following me, you're resisting me.[6]

As Dylan understood then, and hopefully still does, Jesus's category is "leader." Our fundamental category is "follower." Even when Jesus calls us to the front of the line, we still lead from behind. For the last fifty years the church has made a fetish of a word that is hard to find even once in the New Testament ("leader") and has ignored a word that is found hundreds of times (*mathetes* or "follower," "disciple"). Leadership is, at best, a function. Followership is an identity.

Christianity is all about following, but that is hard for us to accept. We want to be the leader who takes people to success and greatness. Jesus says, "I'm your leader who takes you to the cross." Leaders wear crosses. Followers bear crosses. No wonder some find Jesus too demanding and break off their relationship with him. No wonder Jesus turns to his disciples and says, "Will you also go away?"[7]

The rallying cry of the first-century church was "Jesus is Lord." What is a faithful translation of that statement in today's language? It bears no relation to "Jesus has called me to leadership." It does not translate as "Jesus is my Inner Virtue" or "Jesus is my Core Value." It does mean "Jesus has called me to follow him." And with a bit more elaboration: "Jesus is the Messiah, the Son of the Living God. And I will follow him."[8]

The first words Jesus's disciples heard? "Follow me."[9] Jesus's words were not interpreted in a directional sense ("Let's go north!"). They knew he was calling them to be caught up in what he was doing. Jesus never once used the word *leader* or anything like it to refer to his disciples. He himself "led" with towel and trowel as he portrayed God's dream for the world.

Dreaming of a Kingdom

We translate "God's dream" as "kingdom of God." Instead of being a "lead" church or a "lead" pastor or a church "leader," we should think instead of being a "dream" church, a "dream pastor," or a "dreamer." Who will be the dreamers of the future? Who will build a dream church? Who is going to build a dream world? And if you could dream in this way and build on such dreams, what would it look like? Wael Ghonim (the former Google executive who TGIF'd Egypt's uprising) proclaimed to the world, "Now our nightmare is over. Now it is time to dream."[10] Do followers of Jesus still know about dreams?

Twitter is a daily reminder that events big and small don't rise and fall on leadership, but on followership. Who am I following, and who is following me? The name "Christian" (meaning "little Christ") was given to believers in Antioch[11] because people saw in each other the Christ they followed.

Paul said, "Follow me as I follow Christ."[12] In Twitter's ethic of followership, I am constantly reframing reality in ways that are more Jesus—more grace-full, more forgiving, more loving, more humorous—and helping my "followers" to better follow Christ. I am constantly on the prowl for things that could encourage, enrich, inspire. I want my tweeps (people who follow me and whom I follow) either to smile after reading one of my tweets or to shake their heads and sing, "What a Tweep We Have in

Jesus." In my ongoing battle with self-transcendence over self-absorption, Twitter has helped me become more others focused.

For the One who taught us to be "in" the world but not "of" the world, the question is not, would Jesus tweet? The Pulitzer Prize–winning historian Dan Fehrenbacher was asked in a talk-back session: "What would Abraham Lincoln have said about busing children to achieve school desegregation?" Fehrenbacher paused, then drily replied, "I guess he'd have said, 'What's a bus?'"[13]

The real question is not, would Jesus tweet? but, what would Jesus tweet? The Twitter question of "What are you doing?" has been replaced in my mind with "What is God doing?" and "Where do I see Jesus?" and "What am I paying attention to?"

With a new list of followers every day, and an unlimited number of potential followers, I am reminded daily that the most important people in my life are ones I haven't yet met. I also am constantly surprised and consistently blessed by the revealing directions in which followers take my tweets.[14]

2. SOUND BYTES CAN BITE

Diogenes is often called "the first philosopher." If so, the first philosopher was also a graffiti artist who posted history's first tweets. Diogenes wrote on the walls of a large portico where he engraved his words for passersby to read. He became famous for these pithy, compressed sayings.

Some writers (like Diogenes, Confucius, Rumi, Emily Dickinson) come by concision naturally, so that their one volume compares to the entire corpus of another writer. Others need help in being compressed. But in a TGIF Culture, we all need to learn the ability to craft sound bytes that bite. We need more bits of condensed images that sear into one's soul with sharp and saucy impact. If you doubt the legitimate provenance of such an approach, consider the greatest master of sound bytes that bite: Jesus.

The Gutenberg world loved to biggerize and supersize. We grew adept at biggerizing food, biggerizing life, biggerizing church, biggerizing homes. The problem is that being the biggest and best is *not* a missional strategy. Identity is more important than bigness. McDonald's has roughly eighty food items, while In-N-Out Burger has four. In 2010 the average In-N-Out Burger location did $2.25 million in sales, about the same as McDonald's. Kmart went bankrupt. Why? Not because it didn't understand TGIF. But because it had nothing special that set it apart from high-end Target and low-end Walmart. Linens 'n Things didn't go bankrupt because it didn't understand

TGIF Culture. It went bankrupt because it cloned Bed, Bath & Beyond, offering nothing unique.[15]

The "get big or get out" (or at least "get out of the way") mentality is killing us, not to mention killing our family farms, our family businesses, our mom-and-pop shops, the very family itself.

In a world that has been shrunk by speed and with almost every facet of life accelerating, we want the whole shebang in two sentences. The truth is it takes more work to distill thought into two sentences than two pages. In the best of Twitter, the language is distilled, restrained, made to be sipped rather than quaffed. There is a lot of distilled theology on Twitter, but if the liquor of distillation doesn't taste very Jesus, I don't keep sipping.

A Gutenberg world was the master of the long sentence and short thought. A TGIF world is the master of the short sentence and the long thought. There are some 100-page books that feel long and some 1,000-page books that feel short.

If you can't say it in everyday words, you probably don't understand it yourself.[16] Lord Macaulay contended that the "two great creative minds" of the late seventeenth-century England were both Puritan: John Milton and John Bunyan.[17] In his *Lectures on European Literature* (1818), Samuel Taylor Coleridge remarked that John Bunyan's *Pilgrims' Progress* is a book that "delights every one."[18] It has been called the "most read book in English history apart from the Bible."[19] Dr. Samuel Johnson said it was one of only two or three books that he finished reading, wishing it were longer.[20]

Twitter teaches conciseness, but we have to supply the substance. This is Googler Culture in its simplest, most direct manifestation. If you can't say it in less than 140 characters, you can't say it in a way that can connect with a Google world. The first task of a missionary is to learn the language. No missionary has a future in missions who is clueless of the culture they're in.

In 1986, with $286 million dollars to insure a successful hostile takeover, corporate raider Asher Edelman took control of Ponderosa Steakhouse. After signing the papers that made him the chief owner, Edelman celebrated the takeover by inviting the CEO of Ponderosa, Gerald Office, to join him for lunch. When Office and other Ponderosa executives walked into the Ponderosa Restaurant, Edelman sat down and waited for a waiter to bring the menus. Here was a buyer who had spent $286 million to sit down at a restaurant that built its reputation, identity, and clientele as a buffet.

In a Google world, downsizing is upscaling. TGIF people are looking for Old-MacDonald-Had-a-Farm kind of farms and "a village life," the title of a new collection of poems by Louise Glück:

You ask the sea, what can you promise me
and it speaks the truth; it says erasure[21]

The future favors the small, the start-ups, the bonsai versions over the big-box verticals.

Small actions can have huge consequences. Small pads (even as small as iPads) can launch big ideas. You can tip the world from the tiniest tweet. In spite of all the cautions against trading in caricature and cliché, most of history's greatest books and thinkers have distilled their thoughts into the equivalent of a 140-character tweet. In fact, history has shown again and again that the single killer sentence is what changes the world.

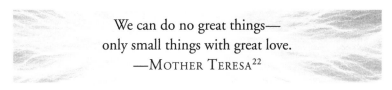

We can do no great things—
only small things with great love.
—MOTHER TERESA[22]

No one was better at tweets than Jesus. He was a master at sound bytes that bite with terseness and immediacy. Bursts of illumination have always flashed at the most unexpected moments and condensed places in history:

Pythagoras's theorem: 24 words

The Lord's Prayer (English): 70 words

Archimedes's Principle: 67 words

The Ten Commandments: 179 words[23]

Of course, some things are simply not blurbable or tweetable. Hence the sermon on the mount, the nippy anecdotes called parables, Paul on Mars Hill. There also are ways of stating truth that are not hospitable to compression. One of the big debates in the sixteenth century was whether the King James Bible or its Catholic counterpart, the Douay-Rheims Bible, was the better translation. In some ways, the Douay-Rheims Bible was more compressed, but the King James Bible was more elegant. Here is Philippians 2:10 first in King James and then in Douay-Rheims:

At the name of Jesus every knee should bow, of things in heaven, and things in earth, and things under the earth.

In the name of Jesus every knee bow of the celestials, terrestrials, and infernals.[24]

But Jesus was always tweeting the gospel in pithy, memorable phrases, and even expressed his gospel in The Great Tweet: "Love one another as I have loved you."[25] His followers would be well advised to RT (retweet) everything he said. Twitter's retweet is viral and will prove to be more powerful than Facebook's "like." What's more, Jesus desires not only to be "liked" but to be retweeted. Jesus dealt in clarifying truth and was the Master at truth simplified, de-codified, de-legalized, commonized, intensified. Retweeting is the twenty-first-century equivalent of the parables of yeast and the mustard seed. Retweeting Jesus is spreading the virus of the gospel.

3. Explore the Surface

To say that someone is bubbling in or around the surface of a subject is not a compliment. In fact, Robert Runcie, former archbishop of Canterbury, said despairingly that "the Church is like a swimming pool; the splashing goes on at the shallow end."[26] He went on to call the church to leave the shallows, get to the deep end of the pool.

Splashing in the shallows is perhaps the greatest critique of Twitter: its numbing, crushing banality. Do I really need to know what time you finished brushing your teeth or what brand of toothpaste you used? Do I really need to see a picture of your kid in the hospital with a fork through his nose with the tweet "What happens when you run with a fork?"

But life is not just about the depths. Life is also about the surfaces. Every depth has a surface, and careful-enough attention to what's on or near the surface can reveal depth. There has been powerful art of the shallows with an emphasis on the surface: in Andy Warhol's Brillo boxes and Campbell's soup cans, surfaces are searched and depths are skimmed, unfathomed but not unearthed.

I spend much of my life with academics who spend their careers exploring the depths. Many of the deepest thinkers seldom reach the surface. You come up for the air of communication and relationship, and when you spend all your time in the depths you find yourself cut off from those who could benefit from your knowledge. You end up talking to yourself. People with highly sensitive seismographs for souls, like writers and artists, often rail against the shallowness of living and refuse to compromise and play in the spray. That's my theory for the high incidence of suicidal behavior, if not suicide, among artists and poets.

We need a theology of the surface in tandem with our theology of the depths. As Alice in Wonderland might have reminded us: "All this digging deep I dislike because if you dig deep all you dig is a pit into which you may fall yourself, or a well at the bottom of which there is nothing but treacle."[27] We need both surface and depth, not the surface replacing the depths. When I look for something to tweet about, I find myself paying attention to life in heightened ways. With Twitter every day is an awakening to things that never would have registered before. Twitter gives me openings through which I can dive into newly discovered depths.

Life is a bunch of little things. These little things add up, and Twitter reminds me to be grateful for the little things and to celebrate the little and the simple. In my list of "50 Reasons Why I Love Twitter," Reason #33 is "A place where serious people can think serious thoughts about trivial things." Terry Tempest Williams, in her book *Finding Beauty in a Broken World,* wrote: "I used to believe that truth was found only below the surface of things. Underground. I was a disciple of depth.... But something changed.... I am interested now in what my eyes can see, what my fingers can touch."[28]

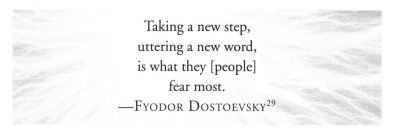

Taking a new step,
uttering a new word,
is what they [people]
fear most.
—FYODOR DOSTOEVSKY[29]

The best beer is a subtle symmetry between froth and substance. The best life is a dance of depth and surface.

The waters around Greenland are filled with giant icebergs. Closer to the shore are small ice floes. If you watch carefully you will see that the icebergs and the ice floes move in different directions. The reason is simple: small ice floes are responsive to the waves and winds. But icebergs, with 90 percent of their mass below water, aren't affected by the surfaces, only by deep ocean currents.

There are surface currents and there are deeper currents of God. Both are valid and important. But even in my surface tweets, I try to bring readers to the edge of the depths, and then to tempt and torment them not to leave until they have at least wet their feet in the profound and the deep.

Life is a conscious interplay of surfaces and depths—part of my weirdness is that I am sociable on the surface but monastic in the depths. One of the highest compliments you can pay me? "Sweet, you do shallow well."

4. There's a New Global Commons

Four months after joining the Twitterverse, I submitted this tweet: "Approaching my four-month anniversary on Twitter. Can't imagine life without it now...love hanging out at the new global village commons."

Immediately I got back this tweet: "send a link 2 the global village commons, plz."

Some people never get it.

This new global commons was the reason I entered the Twitterverse. My social-media mentor Aaron Linne challenged me to think of Twitter like a medieval village green. If we were living a millennium ago, our lives would revolve around a village commons. In the course of a day, we would physically pass each other many times and exchange greetings: "How was your lunch?" "Who you working for now?" "What are you carrying?" Wireless technology enables the same multiplicity of personal exchanges to take place today, except now it's with people from around the world. Twitter is the new global commons.

Like soothsayers reading entrails, I conduct "twee-leaf" readings. Twitter connects me both to others and to what's hot, what's current, what're the reigning gossip and styles of this new global village. With Twitter I can keep one ear perpetually pinned to the ground.

There is nothing sadder than Young Turks turned into Old Geezers. It can happen overnight. In fact, I like to think of myself as the "pastor" of this Twitter parish. In the course of a day's passings ("postings") on the village commons, I try to find ways to encourage my "parishioners" (Barnabas blasts, I call them), and be a positive, healing energy in their lives.

When my congregation seems bent on carpet-bombing Twitter with greeting-card aphorisms, I yearn to know what they had for lunch and what they're feeling. Don't give me quashed quotations. Give me the inside scoop, your personal equivalent of what John Franklin (1786–1847) recorded in his log during the infamous 1820 voyage through the Coppermine River and the Northwest Passage: "We drank tea and ate some of our shoes for supper."[30]

The question social media pose is one easily answered: Are the residents of your global commons reflective of our global community? Or are they only mirrors of yourself? Are the tweets streaming your way ones of plurality and diversity, or uniformity and homogeneity? How many people of different races, classes, continents, and religions

Follow Me, or Not

My friend Tom Cottar gives five reasons why you should follow him on Twitter. So I came up with "Five Reasons You Shouldn't Follow Me on Twitter":

1. I promise to make you mad. I will prick and prod you as I probe the boundaries. I'm as good at squirm making as I am lip smacking.
2. I like puns…so you'll groan a lot. Aside from Jesus, who founded his church on a pun (Peter, the rock), one of my heroes is E. V. Knox, who disarmed everyone in 1916 by declaring in *Punch:* "I take thee, dearest margarine, for butter or for worse."[31] Do not follow me on Twitter if you don't have a sense of humor.
3. I change my mind, a lot of times because of your replies and pushbacks. So if you're looking for consistency, constancy, and stone stability—if you're looking for someone who doesn't sometimes change his mind—don't follow me.
4. I like surprises and randomness. I am captivated by the connections caught from seemingly random collisions. Links lurk everywhere on Twitter, and I lurch when they delurk.
5. I paddle on the surface sometimes, don't always dive deep. Sometimes all you get is a premise and a punchline. So if you're too sophisticated to play in the shallows, I'm guaranteed to disappoint.

are part of your social universe? Are you following people who don't follow you? Do you have any disabled or special-needs people following you, those you're watching out for and taking special care of? Have you moved from the stereo of dialogue to the surround sound of pluralogue?

When I was growing up, we were taught that the human body has "vestigial organs," by which were meant organs that once were important but today are not needed and thus can be ignored. One hundred eighty body parts were seen as vestigial, including the appendix, coccyx, pituitary gland, thymus gland, pineal gland, and tonsils.

Now we know that the appendix produces antibodies that protect the intestines. Tonsils protect against infection by filtering germs we inhale. The coccyx has muscles that help hold our pelvic organs in place. The thyroid gland controls metabolism and growth. In other words, there are no vestigial structures in the human body, and none in the body of Christ either.

But there are limits to diversity. You can't embrace pluralism without being exclusivist.[32] Sometimes you will connect with people with whom you really don't want to connect. That's what the Block tab is for—when sweetness and light will only work against you. In one of my tweets I mentioned a book I had read where the author estimated there were a quarter of a million "sacred sex workers" in India. Someone named Margie immediately retweeted another retweet of my tweet. Something bothered me about the tone of her retweet, so I looked further into who this retweeter was.

The location of Topeka, Kansas, gave it away, and my shuddering went into seizures as I saw the website: www.godhatesfags.com. Margie Phelps is the wife of Westboro Baptist Church pastor Fred Phelps and mother of their thirteen children. But as soon as I could block this new follower, I found others in their network retweeting me and trying to follow me. Such is the power of the new global commons. People such as Fred Phelps and Koran-burner Terry Jones, insignificant voices from invisible churches, can use TGIF to gain global attention for evil. In fact, "He's a Terry Jones" is my new moniker for a penny-ante pastor whose significance is grotesquely magnified by the lens of the Internet. Sadly, social networking makes celebrities of people whose leading credential is attacking others.

But the potential for good is even greater. Iranian Mir-Hossein Mousavi was chosen by *Time* magazine in 2010 as one of the most influential people in the world. In 2009 Mir-Hossein Mousavi ran for president of Iran. Prime minister of Iran from 1981 to 1989, Mousavi campaigned for Iran's highest office as the leader of the Green Movement, promoting a "Green Path of Hope" and bathing Iran in the color green. After repeated attempts were made on his life, and at a time when no one knew whether Mousavi would survive the election, the world read this June 21, 2009, tweet to Iranians from Professor Zahra Rahnavard, Mousavi's wife: "Let the wolves know that in our tribe / If the father dies, his gun will remain. / Even if all the men of the tribe are killed / A baby son will remain in the wooden cradle.[33]

Thanks to Twitter, I can pray the real "Lord's Prayer" like never before: "*Ut omnes unum sint.*"[34]

5. Social Solitude

Cloister means closed. Everyone needs some closed doors, especially amidst the gregariousness of a web world.

I'm a hermit at heart. Twitter is made for hermits. It enables me to shut myself off without shutting anything or anybody out. It enables me to simultaneously give myself away and never stop hiding. You might call the Twitterscape one of social solitude. And yet, like any "global cityscape," all of us are inescapably connected.

My life is like a barbell: lots of weight on the social end, and lots of weight on the solitude end, with not much in between. The thin middle in my life is primarily standing in lines at airports, which connects the socialness with the solitude. Twitter now lets me do my solitude in society; it lets me be anonymous in groups.

But the currency of a Twitter world is relationship, and Twitter helps me keep my friendships in good repair. Gutenberger Culture developed a personal and private relationship with the text. The content was the commodity or the information. In a TGIF world, the content is the connection or the relationship. Seventy percent of all jobs today are found through networking. TGIF Culture is a link economy where the one who dies with the most links wins. To add links is to add value: the more links you have, the more value. Finally, we have a culture that celebrates the value of relationships.

Sometimes when I am speaking, I stop and ask, "Who is the most important person you will hear from or meet tonight?" After a pause, I say, "Not me. Forget me. It's that person in front of you, or to your right, or behind you, or to your left. Those people are more important than any speaker. I hope you'll connect with me in some form, but they're the ones who make your network."

You might think of Twitter as the TGIF replacement for a phone booth. (Do native Googlers even know what a phone booth is?) Our kids have missed the experience of hunting down a cold, damp, phlegm aquarium that smells of urine and smacks of a pimp's rolodex, hoping they have a quarter in their pocket and then hoping the receiver hasn't been yanked from the phone. You go inside and try not to touch anything while making a call. Soon, phone booths will be no different from outhouses: kept alive in memory because they no longer exist in the world.

But the motivation behind inventing the phone booth has much in common with Twitter: How do we do private in public? Twitter is smashing the boundary between private and public; it provides new ways of being private in public.

> Private faces in public places
> Are wiser and nicer
> Than public faces in private places.
> —W. H. Auden[35]

Can we truly be private in public? The danger is that our privacy will be policed by strangers or the government. We can be surveilled like never before, and our communications can be censored, limited, and confined by legal constraints. The tension between tweeting in a world without boundaries and within the invisible boundaries of a glass fishbowl will remain a struggle to protect, retain, or regain freedom of authenticity from the glare of voyeurism. This applies at both ends of the political spectrum: dictatorial heavy-handedness in limiting citizens' allowable range of communication, as well as democracy's Big Brother policy of spying on Internet searches, as well as e-mails and text messages.

Every now and then you tweet something that is less a comment than a comet. Not too long ago I tweeted a question: "Can you side with hurt people and not get hurt? Can you love in a world that hates, & not get hated? Can you sacrifice in a world that takes & not get taken?"

The conversation went on for days. There were those who said "You can" and those who said "You can't." I came to see that both were right. Of course you can. Or more precisely, you can't. But Christ can.

Canadian author Margaret Terry posted her response to my tweet on Facebook: "The world has always hated and will continue to hate. But LOVE is bigger than the most hateful heart. I choose love. With it I can side with hurt people and not own their hurt, I can give freely without worry about being taken and at the end of the day I can fall into love's arms no matter who hates me."

My personal answer to my own tweet came in the form of another tweet. It was my way of moving on but with greater insight than before: "Even when you're taken for a ride, if you know the road you're on, nothing can deter you from the divinely appointed destination."

Interactives

1. I have a soft spot for the person who invented that eerie glow you can place under your car. His name is Andrew Wilson, and he lives in Branson, Missouri. At least his name was Andrew Wilson, until September 15, 2004. That's when he legally changed it to They. When asked why, he says, "People are always saying 'They said this,' and 'They said that.' Hey, somebody had to step up and take responsibility."[36] What would it mean for the church if Googlers woke up to a new name and took full responsibility for the gift they are? Do you think the church would receive their gift or reject it? Why?

2. One of the greatest dangers of merging your online and offline life, says business thinker Tony Schwartz, is that we come to treat ourselves, in subtle ways, like computers. We drive ourselves to cope with ever-increasing workloads by working longer hours, sucking down coffee, and spurning downtime. But "we were not meant to operate as computers do," Schwartz says. "We are meant to pulse." When it comes to managing our own energy, he insists, we must replace a linear perspective with a cyclical one. It is a myth, he says, that "the best way to get more work done is to work longer hours."[37] Schwartz cites research suggesting that we should work in periods of no greater than ninety minutes before seeking rest. What do you think about his theories and advice? What do you do to keep reminding yourself "I am not a computer"? How are you at Sabbathing?

3. The King James Version of the Bible was written in such a way that it attracted writers as diverse as Melville, Faulkner, and Bellow. It was the earliest and deepest source of high literature in the English language. Do you think one reason the value of literature and the sense of literary style are vanishing from Googler Culture is because the Bible is vanishing from this culture?

4. When is the last time you read the Bible in the King James Version? Has it in any way shaped your life? If so, how?

FIVE WAYS TWITTER CAN CHANGE THE WORLD

Your Life as a Follower, in 140 Characters or Less

> Nothing is more important than to know where Jesus abides and where he may be found.
>
> —C. K. BARRETT

By now you know that I'm not just a fan of Twitter, and not just a follower, and not just committed to tweeting. I am all of those things, but my relationship with Twitter goes way beyond that of the basic, straightforward user of a social-networking tool. Twitter has the potential to change me, you, and anyone who follows you or me—if we're devoted to following Jesus. Think I'm overstating this? Take a look at five ways Twitter can bring about big changes, starting with us.

1. TWITTER HELPS YOU BECOME TRANSPARENT

The new global commons of Twitter makes social networking the twenty-first-century equivalent of a small town. If you grew up in a small town, you know one thing:

busybodies reign. There are no secrets. Everyone in town not only knows what skeletons are hidden in what closets, but also holds the keys to one another's closets.

In TGIF Culture, everyone's life and secrets are exposed to the world. Little Brothers are watching. They are watching our streets and buildings, and they watch us online. Don't believe me? Research the word *Tiannamen* (hypersensitive China still calls June 1989 "the incident"), and see if before long there isn't a strange knock on your door. A colleague sent me her new book, which includes a chapter titled "Invite a Terrorist to Church." When I tried to tweet the title, Twitter refused to post it. I tried repeatedly, and Twitter shut me down.

You claim a First Amendment right to free speech? Try to tweet that chapter title. You are no longer completely free to choose your own vocabulary, because you might choose a word that runs afoul of Little Brother's thought police.

More than seven million public and private surveillance cameras keep watch over the citizens of England,[1] and if you are near one when you happen to do something bizarre, untoward, or odd, you could become a star on YouTube. Everything that is done by anyone can and will be shown to everyone…for free. Combine video surveillance with secret listening technology that monitors cell-phone traffic, e-mail communication, and your location, which is announced by your cell-phone signal. Your every move and utterance are captured as they happen. You and I are the target of maximum security lockdown treatment, and we haven't done anything to warrant it.

An argument can be made, and has been made, that the free flow of information on the Internet can make us less free.[2] What is unfettered is the overstepping of bounds by government, the intelligence community, hackers, and bored cyber geeks. They invite themselves to listen in, watch, and store details of your life, relationships, thoughts, and communiqués that used to be considered private and even sacred. The TGIF world is an open book that keeps your life on file.

During the Cold War, the United States and the Soviet Union stockpiled nuclear warheads at a rate that far exceeded the need. Both nations possessed enough long-range weaponry to obliterate each other's homeland. And not just the capacity to kill off the citizenry; I mean the ability to annihilate both nations. This was a national defense doctrine, and it was known as Mutual Assured Destruction (MAD). The idea behind it was that if the USSR knew in advance that launching a first strike would guarantee an out-of-proportion counterstrike that would incinerate Mother Russia, the Soviets would think long and hard before pushing the button. And likewise for Washington.

The Age of Google and the networking of every phone, computer, and GPS on the planet means the global village (another Marshall McLuhan coinage)[3] knows my business and yours. It's a Digital Age version of MAD. And if MAD reigns globally, will it inspire us (or threaten us) sufficiently to be gentle and forgiving with one another? Will the knowledge that our secrets can be exposed motivate us to protect the secrets of others? Or will the platform we have assumed, with the democratization of mass media, bring out the worst in us?

Have you ever watched *The Real Housewives of New Jersey, MTV Cribs, Cops,* or the bleeped-out freakfest on *Jerry Springer*? A camera and the promise of mass exposure do odd things to people. Knowing they can be seen and heard by a mass audience tends to bring out their basest instincts.

In the future, the ultimate status will not be those who are famous, but those mysterious types who manage to maintain some anonymity and mystery. They come on the scene and disappear, leaving the masses wanting more. It is assumed that the public has a "right to know," and keeping oneself unknown will feed the frenzy.

Your Life on Screen

In 1999, Matthew McConaughey starred as Ed Pekurny in a movie about a hit reality television show. As the star of the show, Ed was asked to do nothing more than go through his daily routine, with a camera crew following him 24/7. Ed thought it would be exciting—until he tired of the continual exposure and lack of privacy. Welcome to *EDtv*.

TGIF Culture is moving us to a world where everything we do or say will be available for viewing. Status updates and tweets soon will be replaced by continuous "lifecasting" or "lifelogging." Everything you say or do will shape your personal brand, either making it more positive or negative. Your identity will either be created in advance to win followers, or will be re-created by those who view your life and cast judgment on its value.

Regular tweeting is a discipline of transparency. The knowledge that my tweets will be read by thousands of people keeps me more focused on my mission, makes me less whiny and complaining, and keeps me more sensitive to what others may need to hear. It's a discipline to serve others and to simply express what I'm feeling myself.

My faith dominates every arena of my private life. But when I insist that my faith dominate every arena of everyone's public life, especially when I share that public space with people of no faith and different faith, then I become not a herald of Jesus's mission but a cuckold of Satan's mischief. Jesus shared a drink with the woman at the well in order to offer the gift of life; he didn't need to drown her in the water in order to make a point. Before I attempt to bend the arc of history, Twitter reminds me daily that I must first try bending and arching myself.

If sensitivity is a necessary ingredient of transparent space, authenticity is the life-giving element of transparent space. To make myself transparent is to be an authentic disciple of Jesus, which means avoiding the temptation to become a duplicitous disciple or even attempting to duplicate Jesus. When the transparency of Twitter meets the transparent authenticity of Jesus, tweeting is at its best. In the world of social media, we don't want to impersonate Jesus, but to "personate" Jesus. A Twitter disciple of Jesus makes authentic transparently visible.

2. A Semiotics Lab of the Spirit

During a television interview, the late humorist Sam Levenson recalled an incident when his two-year-old son accidentally swallowed an aspirin tablet. Mrs. Levenson became extremely worried. What impact would an adult aspirin have on a child?

In a panic, she called her mother and asked, "What should I do?"

The child's grandmother, conditioned by years of experience, replied, "Give him a headache!"

Twitter gives me headaches.

Some of these headaches come from tweets of clotted reasoning, along the lines of that used in a small town in Texas that had only one fire truck. One day the taxpayers passed a levy to finance the purchase of a new fire truck, and the question became: "What will we do with the old fire truck?"

Someone came up with this answer: "Let us use the old fire truck for false alarms."

Twitter gives me brain headaches, and also faith headaches. Plus, I get futuring headaches as I monitor tweets that hit the panic button about the future and then run.

Part of the shift is that we now talk to many more people in one day than we did previously in an entire month. In the Gutenberg world, think about how face-to-face contact limited conversations. In one day you would talk to members of your immediate family, a number of colleagues at work, perhaps a neighbor or a few friends after work. If you stopped at the store, you'd say hello to someone in the dairy section and you'd thank the bagger. And if one of your kids had a ball game in the evening, you might run into other parents in the bleachers. So on a good day, you might talk to twenty or thirty people.

When you tweet, with one short comment you can talk to thousands. And as a follower of others on Twitter, you can hear from thousands. This is interaction among real people, and you are just as much a part of the conversation as anyone else. Never before has it been so easy to keep in touch with so many. Never before has it been possible to speak to and hear from so many people on such a variety of subjects, opinions, insights, questions, and perceptions.

Twitter is my semiotics petri dish, my laboratory for ministry, the place where I sink probes into the culture to find out what God is up to. God is, as always, up to a lot. However, the rapid decline of a doctrine of providence has done great damage to the human imagination.[4] It is difficult to muster much optimism, or even to think in terms of steps toward a workable solution, when trust in divine attention to and investment in human well-being is in decline. The absence of attention to divine providence gives us a dual legacy of singular responsibility and a pervasive sense of world-weariness. If I no longer had a sense of shaping a life in accordance with design, I would not need Twitter. But who can turn the pages of history with serene indifference when you believe in the meaningfulness of time and in the moving hand that turns the page?

God's finger is still stirring the waters, and when I use Twitter I know God is involved. Twitter is the social-media equivalent of an overstuffed sandwich that, bitten into at any point, squirts out an unmanageable sluice of ideas and leads. Thanks to Twitter I can be an information omnivore—someone who gobbles up information and shares references and ideas of others. I can also be an incarnation omnivore—someone who gobbles up evidences of God's activities and broadcasts this awareness as widely as I can.

The dualisms of today are not between body and spirit, but between feeling and thought, emotions and reason, head and heart. Twitter is my way of bringing the two together, a daily proof that there are other modes of cognition besides rational ones.

> One thing I ask of you, Lord, that I never use
> my reason against the truth.
> —OLD HASIDIC REFLECTION ON THE KINSHIP
> OF *RATIONAL* AND *RATIONALE*

Twitter is my subjective counterpoint to Sherlock Holmes's objective, cold-logic reasoning. Much like the television show *Criminal Minds*, it enables me to use psychology and anthropology, not just reason, to solve problems (that is, crimes). Through Twitter I get a feel for the context, and a feel for the subject, and work through problems that way.

What Twitter virgins don't understand is that Twitter is unsurpassed as a meteorological tool. In real time it brings forth an atmospheric wealth of narrative information and signals the location of rich veins of reflection and research waiting to be opened. In fact, it has been claimed that "At the beginning of this century more individuals have attained possibilities for self-expression and choice than at any other time in modern history."[5]

The Test of Resonance

Twitter has a Resonance Test that it uses to decide which ads—or what it calls "promoted tweets"—to allow. Those that aren't retweeted or forwarded or talked about are dropped. If something doesn't capture the imagination, it doesn't survive. This is the new scorecard for a TGIF world: not the power of your statistics, but the resonance of your story. Resonance is voice authenticated by lifestyle.

For followers of Jesus, the power of influence should never have been based on rank but on resonance. The numbers were never with Jesus. Even on the cross, he could convince only 50 percent of his audience. But the resonance of his story, and the power of his voice authenticated by his vocation and lifestyle, made Jesus the most influential person who has ever lived.

There can be no resonance without connection and union. When something resonates, we find a piece of ourselves in it. When something resonates, we hear words of the same substance that is found in our souls. When something resonates, we find that others are like us when we were convinced we were alone in feeling this. When something resonates, we feel the vibrations in our soul.

Urban monk Shane Claiborne is the most sought-after speaker on Christian college campuses today, both in USAmerica and around the world. He is founder of a community in Philadelphia called The Simple Way, a community of less than one hundred people. But Shane's voice has been so authenticated by his vocation and lifestyle that the resonance of his witness is global. They aren't asking him to "show me the money!" or "show me the numbers," but to "show me the story."

The true test of success is not found in the *Book of Numbers,* but in those *Books of Stories* we call Matthew, Mark, Luke, John, and especially the book of Acts. It is resonance that will rock the boat, break the glass, ring the bell, and bring the walls down, just as it did for Joshua.

3. Wabi-Sabi creativity

In the Gutenberger world, it was trial and error. In the Googler world, it is trial and success. I have talked to more than a few people who tried Twitter but quit for the same simple reason: they could not be satisfied with less than the perfect tweet. Twitter is a daily reminder that I am chronically human.

Wabi-sabi is the Japanese tradition of celebrating the beauty in what's flawed or worn, decrepit or commonplace. I call it the art of imperfect beauty. Wabi-sabi offers an inspiring new way to look at your home, your life, your ministry, your church, and your tweets.[6]

An ancient Japanese legend tells about a young man named Sen no Rikyu who studied hard to master the rituals and customs associated with the Way of Tea. When he deemed himself ready, he presented himself to tea-master Takeeno Joo, who tested the younger man by asking him to tend the garden. Rikyu swept, raked, and cleaned up the ground until it was perfect. But before submitting his immaculate garden to the master, he shook a cherry tree, causing a few flowers to spill onto the ground.

To this day, the Japanese revere Rikyu as one who understood to his core a deep cultural thread known as wabi-sabi. Emerging in the fifteenth century as a reaction to the prevailing aesthetic of lavishness, ornamentation, and rich materials, wabi-sabi finds beauty in imperfection and profundity in earthiness. It is the art of revering authenticity above all.[7]

Here is a very simple example of how hard it is for Western cultures to understand wabi-sabi. In the West, when porcelain is cracked or when fissures start to form, the blemishes are repaired in such a way that you would never know it was flawed. In the East, cracks in porcelain are traditionally repaired with a lacquer into which gold dust has been mixed, emphasizing the fissure rather than effacing it. The gold dust features the qualities of *sabi,* signs of aging through use over time, and *shibui,* modesty or understatement. Gaps in a cup's glaze are intended to express the same qualities, as well as disclosing *tsuchi-aji,* the "taste" of the clay.[8]

To discover wabi-sabi is to understand God's hallowing of hollowed-out, broken people to bless a harried world. Wabi-sabi understands the singular beauty of wetlands, the raw richness of repentance, the tender acceptance of another day lived with all its marvels and mistakes. Wabi-sabi celebrates things as they are, without leaving them the way they came. Wabi-sabi knows when to push and perfect something, and when to accept and appreciate something as it is. Wabi-sabi dreams the magnum opus, but obliges the *parvum opus,* or what in TGIF language is called the beta version, the trial model getting a field test. A wabi-sabi home does not confuse godliness with cleanliness and is at peace with the dirt of its surroundings. If wabi means an aesthetic of less is more, sabi combines ideas of never being afraid to try. The only fear is an unwillingness to try.

In a wabi-sabi Twitterverse, you're only as good as your last tweet, but every tweet is sacred. Christianity is a wabi-sabi religion that makes the unthinkable ultimate, the horrible beautiful. The Father let the Son die on a cross that was plunged into a garbage heap—an old, ugly, rugged cross. The worst imaginable circumstance, death on a cross, brought the most glorious outcome, God saving people from sin and death. The saving act is perfect, yet "flawed" by beatings, blood, mockery, injustice, spikes driven through flesh, suffering, and death.

4. GET FULL VALUE FROM THE SIMPLE

Two radio personalities were talking about texting and how much they engage in it. A caller came on and told why she liked to text or tweet messages. It went something like this:

"There are some things that are just better to text or tweet. Like if you call someone [on the phone] and ask them if they want to go to dinner. They start out with 'Hi, how are you?' This takes at least five minutes." Then,

"Want to go out and eat?"

"Sure, where do you want to go?"

"I don't know, where do you want to go?"

"Why don't you pick? I am not really hungry."

It can go on forever. But the same conversation texted goes like this:

"Want to go eat?"

"Sure."

"Applebee's?"

"See you in 15."

You can be succinct without being shallow. Simple is too often equated with simpleminded, when in practice simplicity should be linked to tough-minded and clearsighted. Only second-rate minds are afraid of the simple.

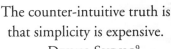

The counter-intuitive truth is
that simplicity is expensive.
—DEYAN SUDJIC[9]

Simple is hard. A writer will tell you that writing short is much more difficult than writing long. Capturing an idea in a few words, and conveying it with impact and clarity, is much harder than writing an extended book chapter about the same idea.

An ancient Chinese philosophical text (*Han Feizi*) narrates an exchange between an emperor and a painter. The question arises: Which subjects are the hardest and easiest to depict? "Dogs are difficult," the artist replies, "demons are easy."[10] Poet Samuel Butler (1612–1680) touted the ability to name a cat the true test of the human imagination.[11]

The simple, familiar things are the hardest to get right. It's much easier to portray mysterious entities and monstrosities than the commonplace and everyday. A "simputer" has been in the R&D stage for decades without being introduced to the computer-using public. But in another culture, a "simple computer," selling for less than two hundred dollars, is close to being introduced, after being developed by a nonprofit trust in India for the rural population.

Don't undervalue simplicity:

- A simple flashing phrase like "moral dementia" can imprint something in the mind like nothing else.
- A simple life (hence the "Live Simplers") can inspire more supreme satisfaction than a hedonistic life of opulence.
- A simple test of what the military calls "mission clarity" is this: Can you tweet it?

5. Tweets Are Stories: Cherish the Story

Every face is a life story. Every wrinkle and crack chronicles an episode, every sag of skin tells of adventures, some good, some bad.

> Not knowing what happened before you were born means being a child for ever. For what is human life unless it is interwoven with the life of our ancestors, by the memory of ancient history? Moreover, recollecting antiquity, and providing examples from it, provides authority and credibility to one's discourse as well as enormous pleasure.
> —Cicero[12]

Every person you meet is a living book, but a book that needs to be opened. Twitter helps open those books to the stories that lie within people you care about, and who care about you. With each tweet you receive only a shard of a story, but the whole is present in every part, and the whole story can be felt in every shard.

Twitter also opens my life to a dialogue of souls carried on across boundaries of space and time. Thanks to Twitter I can pay heed to ancestral voices on a daily basis and learn to think out of a communal consciousness.

One of the most memorable characters I have met is an artist/drama teacher/arts consultant to churches and member of the Anglican Church of Canada. I first met Peter Mansell at Huron College as part of a "53rd Weekend" experience. He was sitting under a very old white pine, praying while he soaked up the sun. We struck up a conversation, and he confessed that wherever he goes, his first act is to scan the landscape for its oldest members—the oldest tree, the oldest person, the oldest building, the oldest street. Then he personally engages these elders and pays his respects as he learns their stories.

I do the same with tweets. The older the quote or the more ancient the wisdom, the more time I spend with it. In many ways, the more up-to-date the text or tweet, the sooner it will be dated. The Christian tradition is a palimpsest, where each culture inherits a pattern laid down by tradition. But each culture then adds layers of colors, cross-hatchings of designs, and filigreed images that bring untold dimension and depth to the landscape. When you lose your past, you lose your future. When you lose your future, you lose your life.

One of Sir Isaac Newton's favorite quotes was from Bernard of Chartres, who used to say that we, "like dwarfs on the shoulders of giants, can see more and farther not because we are keener and taller, but because of the greatness by which we are carried and exalted."[13] Every generation has great expectations of the succeeding generations: our failures finally redeemed; our mistakes not to be repeated; our disappointments reversed. These are but a few of the expectations we project on the shoulders of our youth.

But before we throw all these great expectations on them, we need to look over our own shoulders to our ancestors, stop giving our predecessors the cold shoulder, and let them lift us up on their shoulders. Life ought to be a robust collaboration between the living and the dead. If we are not careful, TGIF Culture will lose the knack for dealing with the past.

> One does not...ignore the great voices of the past.
> One does not awaken each morning with the
> compulsion to reinvent the wheel. But if one is
> servant...one is always searching, listening, expecting
> that a better wheel for these times is in the making.
> —ROBERT GREENLEAF[14]

The Germans have a great expression: *schulterblick* ("shoulder look"; *schulter* means "shoulder" and *blick* means "to look.") Twitter is one way I bring the past, present, and future into conversation, and when all three are talking to one another, there is that telltale tingle between the shoulder blades, the shivers-up-my-spine proof that the timeless, the timely, and the timeful have become one.

Brad Meltzer is a novelist known for his thrillers. His murder mystery that brings together the world's greatest villain, Cain, and the world's greatest superhero, Superman, has an ending that I hesitate to give you because I don't want to spoil such a great novel. But without giving too much away, here is how Meltzer leads up to the end of his book. (There are two more pages following this excerpt. I have issued the spoiler alert.)

The Book of Truth is written in the one language the whole world speaks.

It's a picture.

And it's glorious.

At first it looks like an etching, but the way it's framed at the corners—like a stamp…or a seal. The horn…this is the carving that was on the horn. Someone pressed it in ink and rolled it like a rubber stamp. Right onto the skin.

I study the lines, which are rough, almost primitive. The pale brown color…it's dried blood. Ancient blood. But what makes my eyes well with tears is the picture itself: It's rudimentary, with poor, crude dimensions—but there's no mistaking the image of a young child sitting on his parent's lap—his father's lap—as the man whispers something in his ear.

A story.

A father telling his child a story.

My brain turns into the skid, searching for traction. At first I assume it's Adam, whispering to Abel…to Cain…it's gotta be one of his sons. My eyes scan it again, inspecting each ragged line for clues. The way the father leans in close…the way the boy dips his head downward, like he's relishing every detail. I think of Bible stories from when I was young—of Noah and his quest to save God's creatures. I think of Jerry Siegel, alone in his bedroom, staring at his ceiling. And of course, I think of my father and all of the secrets and stories I missed. So much harm comes into this world when the wrong thing is said. But that's nothing compared to the pain of what goes unsaid.

The image blurs from my tears, but with an eye-blink, they're gone. And I see father and son and story. Clear as can be.

Roosevelt…Roosevelt was right. It is a birthright—a mark—a

sign—the ultimate remembrance—a "book" that Adam created to pass all earthly knowledge. The instructions are right there:

Tell your story.[15]

Social media such as Twitter can be retooled as a discipleship tool. It can be a transformative vehicle to faith, a powerful spiritual discipline, and a relational connector to God, fellow Christians, and the world. Whatever tools we use in service to Christ (whether words, images, music, audiovisuals, social media), they can be used for our own satisfaction or used to the glory of the Savior.

Be a Twitter-disciple. Use social media to strengthen your faith, and Twitter can be a truly transformative and evangelistic tool for recognizing God within the world—a virality of meaning. Tweet for Christ? Why not!

Interactives

1. Three ways you probably shouldn't use Twitter are to refer to birth, death, or therapy.[16] Can you think of any other topics that should not be tweeted? Do you have any nightmare examples related to birth, death, or therapy? Discuss.

2. I have argued that Twitter can make us better disciples and can change the world. But what about the downside? Do you feel we are feeding our hunger for celebrity culture and gossip by "snacking" on updates during the day? Why or why not?

3. Sing the old gospel song "Where He Leads Me, I Will Follow."[17] Now discuss the theology of followership presented in that song.

4. Check out the "Twitter Bible," which puts the more than 31,000 verses of the Bible into nearly 4,000 short-form tweets. Actually titled *And God Decided to Chill,* the German-language book is a compilation of tweets by more than 3,000 German Christians who participated in a church project that summarized 3,906 Bible sections into 140-character messages. Some of the hypothetical tweets from Jesus include:

> "40 days without food. Satan doing a full court temptation press. Does he really think he can win?"

"Just healed ten lepers, only one came back to thank me. Nothing worse than ungrateful ex-lepers."

"Watching my disciples as I ascend to heaven. They look helpless. Will send Holy Spirit soon."[18]

What if your church were to do a *Tweet Book of the Bible*?[19]

5. In a TGIF world, is this how the resurrection would go down? Watch this YouTube video, "Sunday's Comin'," by Igniter Media: www.youtube .com/watch?v=ZRiIpsbJW8o.

6. Check out http://wiffiti.com, which makes it possible to read and view feeds from various places, including Twitter, on a screen. How might you use this in worship?

7. Twitter users agree to comply with terms of use, which includes some small print. When you use Twitter, this is what you agree to: "This license is you authorizing us to make your Tweets available to the rest of the world and to let others do the same. But what's yours is yours—you own your content."[20] In other words, you may own your content, but don't forget that WE CAN DO ANYTHING WE WANT WITH YOUR CONTENT FOREVER. Discuss the implications of this "small print" codicil.

PART III

—

Google

Jesus, Master Storyteller

Jurisprudence Kills, but Narrative Brings Hope

> We lived in the country, we lived in the city,
> now we shall live on the Internet!
>
> —Sean Parker (played by Justin Timberlake)
> in *The Social Network*

Nobody likes a know-it-all. Except for one. Know-it-alls were *en vogue* in the days before the Gutenberg era turned everything into an individual discipline. In fact, you could debate about which individual in history truly knew the most about everything. My candidate for the last world-class know-it-all is Gottfried Wilhelm Leibniz, a Renaissance thinker from the seventeenth century. He commanded expertise in fields as diverse as ornithology, metallurgy, blood-borne diseases, metaphysics, literature, and philosophy.

In the postmodern era, there is no debate about the name of the world's unrivaled know-it-all: it's Google.

Everybody loves Google, not just the Googlers. You see even hidebound Gutenbergers relying on it for everything from NFL scores to reruns of TV shows to recipes to home remedies for gout. But Gutenbergers' use of the Internet has its limits. Suggesting that a church website is the twenty-first-century equivalent of a church steeple is asking them to enter a foreign land.

The Gutenberger default setting is print: Ask for a phone number, address, or movie time, and Gutenbergers will reach for a catalog-thick yellow-page directory. Discuss a family vacation, and a Gutenberger will feel most comfortable mapping it out using a road atlas.

Not so the Googlers. Ask a Googler who starred opposite Gene Kelly in *Singin' in the Rain* and she will whip out an iPhone and give you the entire cast in a matter of seconds. Googlers are native to the Google world. The idea of picking up a book to obtain data (be it an encyclopedia, home medical reference, or *Oxford English Dictionary*) is as foreign to them as a Gutenberger loading an app that enables his cell phone to talk to him in *Jersey Shore* dialect.

These differences—and others that are far more significant—are what positions Googlers as the world's best hope. And not just the world at large, but more specifically the world of faith.

Anyone older than forty will freely admit that the world changes at a dizzying, disorienting pace. But for Googlers, change is life. It's not daunting; it's hopeful. It presents the possibility that advances might be introduced that will improve the lives of humanity. Imagination, vision, and the desire to make change a positive force are traits Googlers have in abundance, and these are reasons the Christian community needs to take Googlers seriously.

They are not idle dreamers; they act on visions and turn ideas and possibilities into reality. They see where things can be improved (communication, access to information and technology, better ways of connecting, just to cite a few). Meanwhile, Gutenbergers—the untiring, unretiring boomers—talk a good game, but it has been talk more than action. They were the master QED generation (*Quod Erat Demonstrandum*—"which was to be demonstrated") when what the world needed was a QEF generation (*Quod Erat Faciendum*—"which was to be done").

If boomers had only learned to pray, "Help me, Lord, to do all I know."[1] Boomers developed an acute ability to stare at frightening and insoluble problems. They give things careful thought. They honed the skill of making dog-ate-my-homework, devil-made-me-do-it excuses about why they failed to address the elephant in the room. To those who grew up in the shadow of the QED generation, it must have seemed that never before had there been so much talk of love and so little love.

Googlers are the QEF generation. For them there is nothing worse than talk that doesn't walk. Yet Googlers are not in denial about the challenges of the future or the burdens of the past that they've inherited. The threats humans face are real. The way forward is less one of daisy-strewn paths of scientific progress than tempting paths of pathologies masquerading as "way forward" and road-bombs of ruin lurking around every turn.

But Googlers bring to the table an abiding conviction that our difficulties are God's opportunities if we don't run from them. TGIF Culture is much more oriented toward picking up a difficulty and presenting it to God in faith and trust. The human spirit rises to the occasion, and the divine Spirit does the best of things in the worst of times.

During the dark days of the Nazi Blitz of London, the trustees of the Bodleian Library at Oxford, perhaps the closest the Western world came to the Library of Alexandria, wanted to expand facilities in order to prepare for the next century. So they drafted plans and began construction during the firebombing, when more than a million homes in London alone were damaged or destroyed by the Luftwaffe. That was QEF initiative long before the Googlers arrived on the scene.

THE OLD RULES NO LONGER APPLY

The Internet has altered the rules of almost everything. As a benchmark of cultural evolution, it may rival the invention of the wheel, the script, or brewing beer as the biggest augmentation in history. It is undermining old assumptions and unleashing new learning that previously was bottled up in ivory towers and leather tomes. It is changing what we know, how we know it, and how we live according to what we know.

But with any augmentation there come related endangerments. The good news of a Google world is that information about everything is available free (but not ad-free) to everyone. The bad news of a Google world is that it takes only one suicide bomber with the wrong use of the right information to blow us all up. Globalization and Googlization democratize innovation, making the power of one person immense. In the new world, each person can be an inventor and innovator who can change the world.

And bear in mind that right now we're ogling the Model-T stage of the Googlescape. The former high priest of Google, Eric Schmidt, boasts that more content is being created in forty-eight hours than was produced from humanity's beginning until 2003. But the real issue has little to do with the power of digital technology. The closest comparison to Google's power to turn your life around is the person who went from being depressed and miserable to being miserable and depressed.

It's easy to be web-wise and life-stupid. You can't build a better future on technology. You build a better future on human dignity and the common good. It requires the addition of what you bring to it, and the eagerness to see what God is doing. Google

Search doesn't just bring facts faster; it brings friends closer. Google Maps doesn't just show you how to get there; is shows you how to enjoy getting there. Google Earth lures me away from a planet of iPads and iPhones on a spinning ball that rotates, and onto a shimmering blue viburnum that reveals a burning bush of God's presence. Google nudges me to see the flame when I'd otherwise be blind even to the glow.

Google wants to "save the world." It is telling that the company chose not to use the language of "change the world," but "save" the world. I suspect the inspiration for its corporate slogan came from an incident that took place in 1978 and is now legendary. On his first day as president of Yale University, the late Bartlett Giamatti issued a memo stating, "I wish to announce that henceforth, as a matter of University policy, evil is abolished and paradise is restored. I trust all of us will do whatever possible to achieve this policy objective."[2] The informal corporate slogan of Google is "Don't be evil," and the sixth point of the ten-commandment Google philosophy proclaims: "You can make money without doing evil."[3]

If you doubt Google's effectiveness as an evangelist, consider its biggest convert to date. A few clues: He heads up the largest single supplier of health care and education on the planet. His organization has as many members as there are citizens of China, 1.3 billion members and 17 percent of the world's population.

The title of this person? The pope.

Popes are not prone to admit mistakes. They will, however, at times apologize on behalf of the church for its missteps and mistakes. Pope John Paul II, for example, apologized on more than one hundred occasions for the "sins" of the church. His first e-mail was a 120-page missive addressed to Catholics in Oceania, apologizing to victims of sexual abuse committed by priests.[4]

On rare occasions popes will even confess to scientific and technological errors. For example, Pope John Paul II wanted to place a statue of Galileo, the father of modern science, in the Vatican as a tacit acknowledgment that scientific inquiry is not a threat to faith. One can only wonder how Galileo, crushed by the Inquisition and confined by Pope Urban VIII, would feel about this belated papal embrace.

Who would have thought the current pope, Benedict XVI, would dare to confess a mistake? But he has. Benedict confessed to the world that he should have Googled before making certain decisions, especially regarding the ideological bent and/or the history of abuse attributed to certain priests. Pope Benedict XVI admitted he should have used the Internet to search out more detailed data. The pope is an immigrant Gutenberger in a Googler world. Here are his exact words:

I have been told that consulting the information available on the internet would have made it possible to perceive the problem early on. I have learned the lesson that in the future in the Holy See we will have to pay greater attention to that source of news.[5]

The pope is now a Googlephile.

The great god Google is not God. But Google may very well be consulted as much as the gods were in premodern times. How many users turn to Google not to learn but to live? In a Gutenberg world, people who felt their life was unraveling tried to glue it together using drugs and alcohol. In a TGIF world, people use Google as the glue.

The editor at Cambridge University Press, the world's oldest publisher, admits in an astonishing aside that "95 percent of all scholarly enquiries start at Google."[6] We've come a long way from the days of Duke Humfrey, who donated more than five hundred books to Oxford University between 1439 and 1444. Oxford fixed each book in place by chains, so valuable was each volume.[7]

This does not mean that *The Little Engine That Could* has been rendered obsolete by The Search Engine That Would. Even Robert Darnton's *The Case for Books: Past, Present, and Future* is published in print, audio, and digital editions.[8] I can love the idea of a library without walls at the same time that I love my lair with books piled so high on all eight sides that they threaten to bury me in an avalanche of ink. After all, one of the top websites sells—guess what?—books. Thanks partly to Amazon's franchise system of bookselling, wherever you go online, everyone is selling books. Churches, charities, corporations. Sometimes it seems the web is one giant bookstore.[9]

Besides, books and original documents are artifacts that tell stories in and of themselves. Anthony Grafton tells of one researcher who sniffed 250-year-old letters in an archive. When he smelled vinegar on the documents, he knew he could use the letters to trace the history of disease outbreaks in the village. In the eighteenth century, towns plagued by cholera sprinkled vinegar on items to disinfect them and hold back the plague.[10]

If the web is not a giant bookstore, then it surely is a global library. You might even call it the twenty-first-century equivalent of the Library of Alexandria. Yet it's a library that rests in the palm of your hand. We now have all of human knowledge, in a literal sense, at our fingertips, searchable in an instant. Almost.

In thirty-five years, Andrew Carnegie managed to build 1,700 "free" public libraries across North America (plus 660 in Great Britain and Ireland). In thirty-five years,

Martin Cooper's invention of the cell phone managed to lure more than half the human population into paying for active mobile-phone subscriptions.[11] The adoption of the cell phone has been more than rapid; it has been rabid and revolutionary.

> Maslow's needs hierarchy ought to be changed
> to breathing, food, water and phones.
> —KEN DULANEY[12]

Universal online access to all knowledge is on the horizon. Maybe not in my lifetime, but surely in my kids' lifetime. Brewster Kahle wants to build the world's largest digital library. Openlibrary.org is creating a catalog of every book ever published. Internet Archive alone is scanning more than a thousand books a day, in direct competition with Google's book digitization project. The Google project has this aim: "to organize the world's information and make it universally accessible and useful."[13] As I write these words, Google has digitized 15 million of the estimated 130 million titles printed since Johannes Gutenberg perfected the press in the fifteenth century. Two trillion words have been scanned so far, representing 11 percent of the books published between 1500 and 2008.[14]

Googlers don't judge a book by its cover or by whether it possesses a cover. But there is a lot of silliness written about a culture where coverlessness is the norm. Nicholas Negroponte, founder of the MIT Media Lab and father of the One Laptop per Child project, has predicted that the physical book will be dead in five years.[15]

Talk about "irrational exuberance."[16] There is no doubt publishing is coming to an "inflection point"[17] that will shuffle the ratio of unit sales of e-books and e-readers to print books. And Borders did declare bankruptcy in 2011. But in some ways book sales and reading are stronger than ever. It's a matter of whether you'd rather feel cornered by the market or feel you have a corner on the market.

Far from the TGIF world being hostile to books, almost every link you click takes you to a bookstore. Every Googler is a book dealer, and every blogger is a hawker of books. Even if old models of bookselling are on the way out, millions of people still want to be part of the old model. And every author for the past two decades dreamed of being a "chosen one" for Oprah's Book Club.[18] Princeton historian Anthony Grafton got it just right: "these streams of data, rich as they are, will illuminate rather than eliminate the unique books and prints and manuscripts that only the library can put in front of you."[19]

TEXT AND IMAGE

In the Google world we are controlled by the virality of images and icons, pictures and pixels. It's a world not unlike the premodern period, long before the name Gutenberg held any meaning. A world not unlike that inhabited in the thirteenth century by the major contender to Mama T (Mother Teresa) as the most venerated Christian in history.

St. Francis is known for many things—being from Assisi, engaging birds in conversation, espousing poverty, embracing the leper, establishing the Franciscan Order of Friars Minor (OFM), wearing hair shirts. Of all his alleged sayings, the one most repeated is "Preach the gospel at all times, and if necessary use words." Beside the fact that it is highly unlikely St. Francis ever said those words, the quote is supposed to minimize the importance of sermons. The truth is that St. Francis was a master communicator and preacher of sermons. It's just that he chose image and story over words as the media for sermonizing.

> Storytellers are not priests who commune with an
> ethereal realm, but artisans, like dumpling-makers.
> —TIM GAUTREAUX[20]

This is why St. Francis came up with the idea for the first nativity scene in 1223. How does one convey the Christmas story to an illiterate congregation, especially when the village was becoming obsessed with the consumerist components of the holidays? Why not a sermon with live images and a living reenactment of the story? St. Francis positioned real animals outside a cave on the outskirts of Grecco, dressed people in biblical-era robes, and placed in the manger a life-sized wax figure of the infant Jesus. So popular was the *presepio,* as it was called, that other towns in Italy began featuring nativity scenes. Then wealthy families commissioned sculptors to make life-size wooden figurines, and finally individual families placed small creches in front of their homes. Whenever you look at a creche, you are looking at a medieval sermon that used image and story rather than words.

If someone asks, "What is Christianity about?" do you give them words or images in a story? You tell them about Jesus, his birth, the events surrounding his arrival on earth. Jesus Christ is the gospel, and the gospel begins with a story. You don't explain Christmas by telling about laws or commandments. You don't tell about doctrines and creeds. You don't even relate just one story, as if that covers it all.

Like St. Francis did for his audience, you tell word-proof Googlers stories about Jesus. You tell about a person who lived, died, and rose again that we might live and die to rise again. You tell them the old, old story of divine love imaged in human form, a love that wants to be made new in every human image. You don't hand them a book; you give them an image and a story.

Jesus is all about narrative and metaphor, what I call narraphor, not a list or a formula. Think about his teaching method. He used metaphors, paradox, parables, and stories, and—at times—even seeming nonsense to convey the deepest and most precious truths ever communicated. And not just a couple of times, as if by accident, but time and again. This was Jesus bringing his A game.

> To tell new stories will require skill,
> as well as enthusiasm and imagination.
> —MISIA LANDAU[21]

Narraphor is the essence of Christianity. If truth be told, narraphors are the essence of human life. To be human is to have a story. Unlike white sharks, black widow spiders, red fox, blue whales, gray parrots, brown snakes, and every other colored creature, human beings construct narratives, whether they write them down or not. And all humans edit narratives with the pen of complex, sense-making minds. Our

Learning from the Storyteller

Gutenberger Christians learned to read the Bible as a textbook, searching for the most important lesson to be learned. King David's poetry and Jesus's parables were not valued for their form and beauty, but were mined for the ore of ordinances and touchstones. It would be similar to asking Emily Dickinson to write an instruction manual for assembling a bicycle. The directions would be beautifully stated, but all you're looking for is which nut fits which bolt.

Christians are part of the greatest story ever told and the greatest story that ever will be told. We live the true storybook life. Our lives are storytelling brains make each one of us a unique matryoshka doll of stories within stories that explain why we are the way we are.

The Gutenberg world put us on weak narraphoric diets. Explanations and arguments gained favor, and they make weak stories. The truth is we need rich narrative feasts, especially as children. Growing up we need stories as much as we need spinach. What lasts longest in memory are the things that seem most ephemeral: images, stories, songs, gestures, jokes, metaphors, phrases. With every human relationship, you are being blessed to step into a sacred story because each person's story is a sacred mystery between that person and God. When you are graced with that gift of story, it is something to be handled very carefully, even reverently.

> I vote for no more leaders, please, but storytellers, poets, teachers, painters, dancers, dulcimer pluckers, crooners…we could take hints from Garrison Keillor.
> —JOHN BLASE IN A FACEBOOK POST

If you're a follower of Jesus, your vocation is story. That's your business and calling. Jesus-followers are in the story business. And in that story, image is everything. For Jesus is the image of God. It is one thing to say "God is love." It is another thing to say "God so loved" and image that story in a person who acted as God does.

to be a continuation of that story, and we are to continue to tell that story in all its glory. How do you talk about your faith? Do you try to explain it, or do you talk about it in narrative form?

Consider the elements of the best stories: They have a beginning, a middle, and an end. They involve actors and the acted-upon, givers and receivers. They feature tension, conflict, obstacles, drama, emotion, and release. They point to a meaning that is higher and deeper than face value.

David told his stories in verse; Jesus used narrative. Study these two master storytellers and see what you can learn about the spirituality of storytelling and storycatching.

Gutenbergers don't want to hear this, but we have reached the end of the Gutenberg story, where the coinage of the realm was words used to make a point. The narraphor coin, or more precisely the narrative-metaphor-story-image coin, is the unit of currency in the new TGIF social world.

THE WINTER COUNT

The USAmerican poet Thomas McGrath penned a suggestive poem called "Letter to an Imaginary Friend," in which he immortalizes the ritual of the "winter count." It is built around this one narraphor:

> But all time is redeemed by
> the single man—
>   Who remembers and resurrects
>   And I remember
>   I keep
> The winter count.[22]

The winter count is what American Indians of the northern Great Plains used to keep track of their history.[23] Their calendar went not from January to December but from winter to winter. They called an entire year a "winter," an annual cycle that covered the first snowfall to the following year's first snowfall.

Near the end of a winter, tribal elders met and assigned meaning to the most important events in the life of the community. They talked until they agreed on one narraphor—one story and one image—that would summarize the entire winter and trigger memories of all that happened. The winter was then named after this event and image.

One person in the community was trusted with the task of designing and painting onto a buffalo hide a pictograph, an image that told the summarizing story and triggered memories of the entire winter. That person was called the Keeper, and the hide on which all the symbols of the passing years were painted was called the winter count. The first winter image would appear in the center, and in counterclockwise fashion the years or winters would spin out in a spiral.

The Keeper of the winter count was one of the most respected members of the community. The role of Keeper often was passed down from father to son. If the images on a winter count faded or if the hide became worn, the Keeper would make a new copy to preserve the information and conserve memories of the past. Some winter counts also were drawn on paper or cloth. The winter count was the American Indian version of the annual report. Our annual reports are written by accountants; theirs were pictured by storytellers. The children of the community were introduced to their past by the Keeper of the winter count, the storyteller whose task it was to remember and resurrect.

What serves as today's memory keeper? This is different from a record keeper or note taker. The task of characterizing a year is not a matter of profit and loss, or statistics, or bare facts. It is an image or metaphor that captures life during a certain span. Where do we have this in the human community? Who is the Keeper of the winter count in your community? And what of the faith community? Why aren't charities and churches keeping pictographs of the winter count?

We're fighting a new kind of cultural war on the news channels just like we're fighting a new kind of culinary war on the Food Network. Up until now, every war proved to be in some way a war of words. It is sometimes said that Churchill's refusal to pronounce the word *Nazi* with a "t" sound won the war for the Allies. Up until age thirty-nine, Adolf Hitler's father Alois carried the surname of Schicklgruber. Can you imagine history being the same if Adolph Hitler's father Alois Schicklgruber hadn't changed his name to Alois Hitler?

But in the era of Google, warring narraphors have replaced wars of words. Ever watch Food Network and its story wars, as symbolized by *Iron Chef Amercia*? In the battle of the cultural kitchens, who ultimately wins? The one who out-narrates the opposition, the one who tells the better story. Show me a successful business, and I'll show you a triumph of storytelling.

Not long ago, Apple produced a series of television commercials in which the competing PC was characterized as a hapless, clumsy, unattractive dweeb. The commercials weren't selling superior technical specifications but Mac's cooler image.

The one who weaves and leaves the best story wins.

> A story is a way to say something that can't be
> said any other way, and it takes every word
> in the story to say what the meaning is.
> —NOVELIST FLANNERY O'CONNOR[24]

A young, aspiring playwright went to see George Bernard Shaw for some coaching. "What's the secret of your success as a storyteller?" Shaw said, "Well, it's really quite simple. Every play boils down to the same thing. My plots are all the same. Act I, curtain rises, girl meets boy, curtain falls. Act II, curtain rises, girl falls in love with boy, curtain falls. Act III, curtain rises, girl marries boy, curtain falls."

"But Mr. Shaw," the young playwright protested, "what's so exciting about that?" Shaw smiled and said, "Same girl, different boy."[25]

Storytelling links the premodern world with TGIF Culture, and vice versa. Image, metaphor, and paradox carried the day before the arrival of written language, and long before there was movable type. In the image-obsessed Google world, narrative is the verbal image that holds its own against the visual onslaught.

Googlers are the hope of the present and the future, in the world at large and in the world of faith. Googlers are, in large measure, the storytellers. This is not to say they have cornered the market or perfected the art, because in certain ways they are tone deaf to the essentials.

But there is reason for great hope.

Interactives

1. What happens when technology breaks free of religious and moral moorings? Give a few examples. Is it just a matter of time before this break takes place in USAmerica? How will human history be altered if and when that happens?

2. Biologist E. O. Wilson in *The Creation* argues that humans today display "a mix of Stone Age emotion, medieval self-image and godlike technology" which together "makes the species unresponsive to the forces that count most for its own long-term survival."[26] How would you critique his assessment? Or do you agree with it?

3. Leonardo da Vinci is quoted as saying that image and sound were the two perfect media, one for responding to the visible world, the other for responding to an invisible world.[27] What do you think he meant by that? How might that perspective help us understand worship in Googler Culture?

4. In what ways does the church speak the loudest? How does it express itself as a body? Through its resolutions and political declarations, or through its liturgies and hymns, its confessions and creeds? Discuss.

The Infallible Story

Giving Good News the Placement It Deserves

Never mind the facts. Just give me the truth.

—Groucho Marx

We tend to think of storytellers in mythical, epic terms: crazed creatures wandering lonely roads, or aged gurus in hooded robes who live in caves and commune with the dead. But storytellers are really artists who craft art with tools. Artists like those Iron Chefs as well as the straightforward short-order chefs who cook up simple food. Storytellers, like good chefs, create art so that the body can live and bathe in beauty, truth, and goodness. The great storytellers bake beauty biscuits. They construct truth tiramisu and mix up goodness goulash.

Jesus was the greatest storyteller of all time. Hence this warning: society kills the storytellers first. Plato was right. If you want to change the world, don't bring in the politicians who make the laws; bring in the poets who tell the stories.

Jesus was crucified not for being a bad theologian, but for being a compelling communicator of God's kingdom and extremely good at telling stories that subverted establishment law and order. In fact, Jesus had a secret recipe for expert storytelling. In utilizing the recipe, Jesus worked by paradox, by defamiliarization, by reframing ("You have heard it said, but I say"), and by participation (what we call "crowdsourcing" or "brainteasing").[1] This is what C. H. Dodd's classic book on the parables calls "interaction metaphors." Jesus's stories are irreducible interaction metaphors that "tease it [the mind] into active thought."[2]

It is essential that we closely follow the Master Storyteller. To do that, we need to practice his recipe for compelling narraphors. Googlers live in the perfect era to excel as storytellers and to use the power of stories to change the world. But will they? Here are five of the six blind spots that could prevent TGIFers from being great storytellers in the bloodline of the greatest storyteller of all time. (For the sixth blind spot, continue reading to chapter 9).

1. The Urge to Cut the Umbilical Cord

I have participated in too many conferences where the Scriptures were ancillary to the topics at hand, and where the proceedings seemed more tethered to leadership literature and business gurus than biblical literature and God. If Googlers are to save the world, they must never cut the umbiblical cord to our Source and source material.

On the other hand, I have attended (and spoken at) too many conferences where the Scriptures were approached as a rule book or an answer book, an encyclopedia supplying specific answers to specific questions. If Googlers are to save the world, they must let the blood flow through the umbiblical cord.

One response to living in a world that is coming apart at the semicolons is to hunger for more grammar and rules, not less. The bible of authors and publishers is the *Chicago Manual of Style*. It first appeared in 1906 with a letter- versus spirit-of-the-law dictum that encouraged authors to read the book as legislation for the grammatical norm, but allowing freedom for the exception. "Rules and regulations such as these, in the nature of the case, cannot be endowed with the fixity of rock-ribbed law. They are meant for the average case, and must be applied with a certain degree of elasticity."[3]

But in the most recent edition, the authors conclude that today people need "firmer rules and clearer recommendations,"[4] given the complexity of the times and the need for someone to make decisions for simplicity's sake. The new *Chicago Manual of Style* stands ready to be that book of rules. But why, in one of the most creative ages since the Renaissance, do we need a manual that lays down the law on creative people? Apparently, it is necessary due to the fact that we populate a world of constant destabilization and creative destruction. Every day we are made aware of new apps for our mobile device and offered constant software upgrades.

And what of creative people of faith, which would include storytellers? There are lots of *Chicago Manual of Style* churches ready to do your thinking for you. And what of the Bible? Is it a legal textbook bent on making the boundaries clear to keep the imaginative people in line? I would argue it is like a battery of love-energy. To read the Bible for knowledge is tiresome. To read the Bible as docudrama is boring. To read the Bible as a book of rules is deadening. But to read the Bible as a love letter from a Friend, and to meet that Friend in the text of Scripture, is to pack your bags for a lifelong journey.

The Bible can be a tomb or a manger. For Irish theologian John Scotus Eriugena (c. 817–c. 877), "Christ's tomb is Holy Scripture, in which the mysteries of his humanity and divinity are secured by the weight of the letter, just as the tomb is secured by the stone."[5] But for other theologians, such as Martin Luther, the Bible is the manger in which Christ is laid. "The Bible is alive, it speaks to me; it has feet, it runs after me; it has hands, it lays hold of me."[6]

If you approach the Bible as a tomb, then you go there to pay your respects to an authority on how to live and die. But the instructions are found in a dead letter, and dead letters are in debt to death. Flemish philologist Justus Lipsius was such a literalist about Roman historian Tacitus's writings that he "offered to recite the text of Tacitus with a knife held to his throat, to be plunged in if he made a mistake."[7]

But if you approach the Bible as a manger, then you go there to find a living Christ. You find a Christ who wants to be born in your life so that you become, by letting the images and stories of this book become your images and stories, a living letter, a fifth gospel, a "Jesus Manifesto."[8]

Approaching Scripture as a Manger

The Scriptures are the Living Word. You can be a strict constructionist and still believe the Bible is a living organism, a Word-made-flesh. This does not mean that the Word changes, but it does mean that truth is both a given and a giving. Truth is always participatory, the crossbeam of transcendence and immanence. There is a divine revelation and a human response. Taking the Bible as the literal word of God is different from taking the Bible literally. Jesus was killed by the Scripture-toting and Scripture-quoting people of his day. A literalist reading of the Torah is what got Jesus killed.

Like Jesus, the Bible is both divine and human, and its authority resides in the divine-human partnership. That is the key to understanding the authority of the Scriptures. Jesus is interactive. If he is just talking to himself, what's the point? He wants you to jump in, because if you're not engaged there isn't much reason for any of this.

The Bible is the words of men that also are the words of God. The Bible is the greatest witness to the God of love, and the love of God, that ever has been written. Yet at the same time, there is no other book that reports in such detail and honesty the cries of "Where is this God of love?" If you don't pick up the Scriptures and let them live in you, no matter how much you venerate the Word or defend its honor, it still is a dead letter in your life. It takes a daily exercise of reading, interpreting, and applying the images and stories. That is what activates the Scriptures' life and power.

If the Scriptures are a dead letter in your life, the problem is not with the Scriptures. The problem is with you and your blockages. The problem with some of the people who most strenuously defend the Bible's honor is that they never really *read* it. Instead, they reference it. The more people brandish the Word, it seems, the less people breathe the Word until they and it become one.

> He not busy being born is busy dying.
> —Bob Dylan[9]

I believe the Bible from Genesis to Genuine Leather. When I die, you'll find my heart pressed between the pages of this book. Why? Because in it I have found the images and stories that keep working their magic, working as healing powers in my life. The Bible will do this for all of us, now and to the end of time.

2. The Distrust of Metaphors

I have said already that Googlers represent the greatest hope for rescuing the world. They were born into a culture and in a time that is ready to be rescued, and Googlers are native to the habitat. They instinctively seek out paths that are consistent with the way of the Master Storyteller. They don't hide their neediness. Far from it. They energetically pursue answers to the longings that draw people to God.

But Googlers, like anyone else, are apt to overlook the ingredients that are most essential to a successful recipe. And as we look at the recipe Jesus developed, we have to make a case for metaphor, the back end of narraphor.

William Shakespeare is considered by many to be the greatest writer ever. *King Lear* is well-known to be his greatest achievement. The play is based on a twelfth-century written folk tale that was circulated orally much earlier. A monarch had three daughters he loved dearly, but banished the youngest when she refused to tell him how much she loved him. She would say only, "I love you as meat loves salt."

Later, the king was expelled from his kingdom and cut off from his wealth by the abusive elder daughters. Homeless and looking nothing like a king, he stumbled onto a wedding feast. The bride recognized him, but he didn't her. She ordered the cooks to serve the wedding guests meat without salt. The guests pushed the meat away because it was so tasteless. Even the old and hungry king couldn't swallow the savorless, unsalted meat. And at that moment he recognized the bride. He also realized the true meaning of his outcast daughter's words when she said she loved him "as meat loves salt."[10]

The medieval tale ends happily, but Shakespeare's *King Lear* is a tragedy. In both versions, however, there is the spurned love of a devoted daughter who believes that only something greater than words can convey the depth of her love. And there is a father who can't think in metaphors. King Lears are found in every generation, but this TGIF world platforms the loud voices of word-obsessed literalism and those who can speak only the flatland language of data, facts, blueprints, and formulas.

> A shilling life will give you all the facts.
> —W. H. AUDEN[11]

Still, Googlers know that *text* is a verb. The Bible is not a text but a telling, a series of divine stories enriched by one another and reborn when they are retold. If a poem is a machine made out of words, as William Carlos Williams has argued,[12] then a church is a body made out of metaphors. Indeed, the biblical language of "the body of Christ" and "the bride of Christ" is rich metaphor.

Words as Images

Most often I use the words *metaphor, imagery,* and *picture* interchangeably. I do insist that *allegory* and *analogy* not be included in this definitional imprecision. Metaphor, imagery, and picture all share in common a bringing of words to life in visual form. They all speak the natural language of the brain.

Images and metaphors create in us new receptacles and capacities for understanding and action. Words delimit and divide a subject into points and principles. Points are sharp and piercing: they are hard to pick up. In contrast, images are uniting, inviting touch and embrace. Metaphors link things. They create common identity and expand our horizons of what is known and can be known. That is one reason that *text* is a verb, especially when we refer to biblical text.

What prevents real change from happening? Of the Four Horsemen of the Apocalypse—inertia (static is satanic), fear, impatience, self-deception—inertia kicks the hardest. For some people, change is life. For some people, change is death. For all people, change is difficult. And for all people, change is mandatory.

Our real problem has less to do with learning new behaviors than letting go of old ones. The truly brave are not those who don't feel fear, but those who conquer fear enough to let go of old habits. Cognitive scientists such as George Lakoff have proven that to overcome the inertia of old patterns we need new "frames,"[13] new "mental pictures"[14] or metaphors that can redefine and reinvent how we perceive reality. To change how we live we have to "reframe."[15] Just like you need to format a disc, you need to format your brain.[16] That's what metaphors do: reformat.

> A world ends when its metaphor has died.
> —ARCHIBALD MACLEISH, LIBRARIAN OF CONGRESS / POET[17]

Sigmund Freud is vilified, debunked, and demonized. But he is constantly quoted and, when not quoted, is used as a modifier. How often do you hear a habit, utterance, or behavior referred to as "Freudian"? His lingering influence is the power of his metaphors, not his perspective on the mind. We link his name still with his leading metaphors: the id, the ego, the superego, the Freudian slip.

But the Master Storyteller reigns as the master of the metaphor. Jesus is without peer for reframing. One example: Jesus reframed the Hebrew conception of *Shema* (morality and justice) with perceptions of "Love your enemies," "Go the second mile," "Return good for evil," "Forgive seventy times seven."

Jesus's rich images and metaphors are communicated in words, of course, and Gutenbergers learned how to parse and exegete his words. But such a tight focus on the mechanics of language can blind you to the bigger picture. In the Googler world, the primary cultural currency is image and metaphor. Biologically as well as socially, metaphors are primary and primal. When you dream, you aren't reading a script; you are watching the movie. (Some of the Gutenberg-influenced Reformers, such as Martin Luther, didn't like dreams for precisely this reason: they were all images, no words, and thus sired by Satan). The natural language of the brain is metaphor, which explains why creative children register more dream activity than noncreative ones.

When you rearrange images in people's minds, you are doing brain surgery and, by extension, life surgery. Jesus's ministry can be seen as metaphor surgery—which is soul surgery. He replaced one way of looking at God and the world with new mental models. "You have heard it said, but I say" was one of Jesus's favorite segues. What came next? A new frame, which often was an unsettling image designed to shake things up.[18] And we wonder why Rabbinic Judaism and the Jesus movement parted company? Our thoughts can be held prisoner by a long-established image, and when that image is reframed or changed the chains are broken.

Philosopher Nelson Goodman says images are more than world mirroring; they are "ways of worldmaking."[19] If Googlers will take their metaphors seriously, they can change the world for the better. Googlers can succeed where the word-focused Gutenbergers fell short.

3. PREFERRING SOLILOQUY TO COLLOQUY

TGIF Culture is a karaoke culture. Television is a nasty technology from the "late age of print"[20] that interrupted human collaboration and innovation with passive consumption of mass-produced sedatives. Television created a new genre of human whom Jesse Rice calls "screen sucking."[21] Television accelerated the couch-potato lifestyle at home, encouraged pew potatoes in the church, and institutionalized the standardized, lecture-drill-test model of learning. Gutenberger Culture encouraged one-sided events in which spectators pretended to be initiators.

Meanwhile, TGIF Culture is in line not just with *text* as a verb, but also with *life* as a verb. The TGIF world creates interactive people. Googlers can't just sit there and read or watch. They are wired to participate: tweet, blog, post, text, twitpic, and a lot more. In his second book, *Cognitive Surplus,* Internet guru Clay Shirky looks forward to a world where Googlers can spend the time that Gutenbergers wasted on bad TV by using social media for human betterment.[22]

The symbol of this interactive default setting? Google's spare white search screen, which is design intensive in only the six letters (G-O-O-G-L-E) that it customizes for each day. Google's home page is minimalist for three reasons: First, each Googler is encouraged to participate through "add-ons." Google provides an extensive pallette of add-on possibilities so that users have the freedom to customize their own home page.

Second, the Google white screen is a minimalist reaction to Gutenberger mega-ness. Gutenbergers can't get over the idea that to be better, a thing has to be bigger. This mania applies to mega-malls, mega-churches, mega-evangelism, mega-thinking. For the same reason that Ralph Waldo Emerson wanted his essays to get to the "grandly simple," Googler Culture focuses on autonomous agents doing small things well. Simple, sacramental acts of suffering love are at the heart of every spirituality in the Google zeitgeist.

Third, sometimes Googlers don't want more choices. Sheena Iyengar, in her book *The Art of Choosing,* says she began by offering twenty-four different jams for people to taste free of charge. She then reduced the number to six. When she was offering twenty-four choices, 3 percent of the people bought a jar of jam. But when she reduced the selection to six flavors, 30 percent bought some.[23] Too many choices turn people into browsers, not buyers. By the way, the magic number before a person succumbs to cognitive overload is seven. The more à la carte the menus, the more we need a fixed menu once in a while.

> The more equally attractive two alternatives seem, the
> harder it can be to choose between them—no mattter
> that, to the same degree, the choice can only matter less.
> —Edward Fredkin's paradox[24]

Simple Monologue or Complex Interaction?

Having too many options can be overwhelming, which explains why Googlers may choose to retreat to soliloquy over colloquy. One reason the web is so popular is that it accommodates various levels of interactivity. For single participants there are sophisticated video games, visually arresting and geared for just one person. At the other end of the spectrum are simple, short messages that are open to everyone. Someone posts a blog or other item, and the crowd joins the feeding frenzy.

Looking at the same spectrum in mass media, "reality TV" is Hollywood's attempt to make television interactive. When "reality" gets mediated by a third party, however, it is an even more dangerous addiction than watching scripted television. Reality TV is about as connected to real life as is a Gutenberger's addiction to Harlequin romances.

To remain in the soliloquy mode is to choose nonparticipation. But if you are ready to sort through the options and live in the colloquy mode, you can disturb the universe with the truth. The Gutenberger temptation is to acquiesce in soliloquy, which is a pernicious adjunct to business as usual. The Googler temptation is to adhere to colloquy, to pursue border-crossing interaction with large numbers of unseen others. But without the truth, the world will not be changed even in widespread interaction.

The user-generated, free-content culture of the Internet is one of its chief drawbacks, according to Andrew Keen in his *The Cult of the Amateur*. Calling himself a "techno-scold," he claims to be "the leading contemporary critic of the Internet."[25] Keen takes on the Internet, as if it were monolithic. I grew up listening to holiness preachers who stood in the pulpit and took on TV with the same gusto. Keen despises what he sees as the mediocrity, unreliability, and corruption of authority that is endemic to the

Internet, which makes *everyone* an expert. He argues that the Internet's entitlement of everyone to participate spells the triumph of the ephemeral over the epic.

The truth is just the opposite.[26] The democratization that is realized through Googler Culture is a reason for hope, action, and empowerment. Christians should embrace it as a further elaboration of the Reformation doctrine of the priesthood of all believers. Just as the movable-type revolution democratized Scripture by taking it out of the hands of the church, so the Google revolution is democratizing religion by taking it out of the hands of the gatekeepers and enabling more open-source, self-organizing connections with God. This can be for good or ill.

4. Losing the Focus Needed to Bring a Project Home

The Internet makes random the norm and miscellany the model for accessing the world. Googlers surf as much as they settle. They have a thirst for surprise, improvisation, and unpredictability. Googlers fight the gravitational pull of everyday life with randomizing rituals where random means serendipitous perambulation.[27]

Some companies, such as 3M, have institutionalized randomizing rituals under the rubric of "boot-legging policies," also known as the 15 Percent Rule. Employees are encouraged to spend up to 15 percent of their time on pet projects or random undertakings unrelated to their job description. What inspired the 15 Percent Rule was Art Fry's famous invention of Post-it Notes, which came about as a result of serendipitous experiments that had nothing to do with what 3M was paying him to do.

We devalue random connections at our own peril. How else can we break free of our personal concerns to encounter the larger issues in the world? It is hard for a society to have free assembly when there is no place to assemble. Cairo's Tahrir Square is increasingly a rarity in a world of declining public space. The result is that we must seek out those whose experiences differ from ours. We must resist the natural tendency to cling to what is familiar.

The more the Internet enables us to separate and silo our interests, the more we remain isolated from the shared space where democracy thrives. If you live inside an echo chamber, all you hear is your own voice. You are denying yourself the richness of life, and you are denying the world the benefit of hearing what you have to offer. More than ever, we need public space that is random, unplanned, and organic. We need the opportunity to be exposed to people, views, beliefs, and questions that are unlike those we wrestle with. Without such space, polarizing, extremist views gain new credence.[28]

Siloing your life and your interests runs counter to the gospel. But the opposite extreme is no better. Randomness is an insufficient framework on which to grow a life. We don't do very well without some structure, disciplined routines, and a point of focus. We need to be tethered to something that doesn't move. Especially in a TGIF world where the Internet keeps upping the ante, for good or for evil.

5. A Preference for the Wrong Story

Some things aren't worth undertaking, and some are true but impossible for people to believe. Just try to convince a culture warrior that when John Lennon said the Beatles were "more popular than Jesus" in the 1960s, he was not boasting. He was merely saying that something was wrong with a world in which more people would prefer to see the Beatles than the Savior.

And think about our tendency to emphasize the wrong stories. I remember following the story of a heroic Jesuit priest, lawyer, and human-rights activist who became a congressman. In 2007 Robert Drinan died the same week as the horse Barbaro. Guess which story got top billing? Remember Mama T (Mother Teresa)? She died the same week as Princess Diana. Who got top billing?

But sometimes we get the right story and the story right. Pope John Paul II is said to have had the best-attended funeral in history.[29] But the proven ability of stories about child-murdering mothers and exhibitionist members of Congress to capture our imagination should serve as a sober warning. Don't succumb to the WMD stories (a.k.a. Weapons of Mass Distraction).

If our attention is fixed on what is current, no matter its importance or value, then life consists of today and is unaware of yesterday. The worst stories we prefer are scandals, slanders, and scuttlebutt. Philip Gröning's film about the life of Carthusian monks (*Into Great Silence*) reveals that on the rare occasions when the monks are allowed speech, they spend it in competitive gossip about the ascetic practices of other houses in their order. In contrast to this, part of being a Jesus-follower is to be a connoisseur of gossip of the higher kind, the kind that gossips what God is doing behind closed doors in people's lives.

Few foresaw the future as clearly as Marshall McLuhan. One of his most perceptive prophecies was that media would shrink the planet to the size of a small town, what he called a "global village."[30] Today, Google Alert is the village gossip that lets you know what everyone is saying about you.[31] Gossip takes on a sinister face in the conspiracy mills that I have dubbed the BlogisTaliban. If Pierre Bayle was correct in his late-seventeenth-century remark that "the tongue and the pen of one man alone are sometimes more useful for a cause than an army of 40,000 soldiers,"[32] then the Internet has multiplied that army to 40 million soldiers.

> [A celebrity is] a person who works hard all his life to become known, then wears dark glasses to avoid being recognized.
> —HUMORIST FRED ALLEN[33]

Nakedness or Nudity?

The most coveted life in the future? One of obscurity, not celebrity. Sir Antony Jay coined the term *nonebrity* to contrast with the culture of celebrities and celebritocracy.[34] The future belongs to those who can be famous long enough to become invisible. In 1961, Daniel J. Boorstin famously defined a celebrity as "someone who is known for his well-knownness."[35] In the future, the biggest celebrities will be those like J. D. Salinger, who are known for being unknown. The most sought-after path in the future will be to slip back into the shadows and preserve a cordon of privacy. William Faulkner once said with some bitterness that he was "working tooth and nail at [his] lifetime ambition to be the last private individual on earth & expect[ed] every success since apparently there [was] no competition for the place."[36]

Google Earth has yet to learn small-town survival skills. No longer are we naked only at the start and finish of our lives. ("Naked I came from my mother's womb, and naked shall I return there.")[37] Now we stand naked before God (there is nothing more immodest than prayer) *and* we stand naked before each other. On Google Earth we are one people, under surveillance. Through ubiquitous cameras on poles and iPhones, everybody can know everything about everybody at every moment.

In the past, writing promoted inwardness. It was a solitary pursuit. Today, digital culture promotes full-time nakedness, encouraging tell-all exposure in blogs, on Facebook, and in tweets. In the Digital Age, furthermore, manuscripts don't burn. What you say and show will be there forever.

The privacy issue is only going to become more invasive. Google has created a recognition software that lets you take a picture and then search for matching pictures on the Internet. They deliberately didn't include face recognition in the software because it would mean that anyone could take a picture of you and then quickly find out who you are, where you live, and where you spend your time. Such a feature could be abused by stalkers and criminals. Still, it will only be a matter of time before that will be available. Despite our efforts to maintain a private life, our lives will be more and more exposed.

Is such nakedness a kind of return to the Garden of Eden (where we were naked and it was fine)? Or is it unseemly nakedness, what I call nudity? Does ubiquitous exposure become oppressive? Or does it make us a more open and honest people, knowing we can no longer hide, pretending to be who we are not?[38]

> Always be sincere, even if you don't mean it.
> —ATTRIBUTED TO PRESIDENT HARRY TRUMAN[39]

The Scourge of Hidden Critics

At the same time that more of us are exposing more about ourselves, Google makes it easy for people to gossip about those they don't know. Unlike small-town communities where you run into everyone (including the gossips) on a regular basis, Google Age gossipers never have to look their victims in the eye. This anonymity and lack of accountability make gossip one of the most corrupt and reprehensible unintended consequences of TGIF Culture. Gossip edges into slander in scandal-mongering searches, defamatory blogging, and theological cheap shots.

"Woe unto the world because of offences!" Matthew 18:7 (KJV) reads, "for it must needs be that offences come; but woe to that man by whom the offence cometh!" The biblical word for "offend" comes from the root word detailing a "bent twig," a stick used to keep open a trap for an animal. The word means to entrap, trip up, cause to stumble. The English word *scandal* comes from this notion of tempting to sin, enticing to unbelief, setting a trap for "gotcha" snares.

> Every issue facing the church today has a slippery
> Caiaphas, a vacillating Pilate, a betraying Judas, and a
> centurion who will drive the nails because it's his job.
> —LLOYD JOHN OGILVIE[40]

It is one thing to choose not to read Dante because he believed in purgatory, or to shun C. S. Lewis and John R. W. Stott because they were universalists, or to avoid quoting Oscar Wilde or W. H. Auden or anyone else who is gay. It is quite another to ransack someone's statements and writings with a razor blade, in order to assemble isolated quotes to use in raising money to support your hunt against heresy. The honest fund-raising appeal is this: "Send me money so I can protect you from the victims of my slander."

I know personally a handful of highly visible church leaders and best-selling authors who are terrorized by self-appointed heresy hunters. The scenario is always the same: a "well-meaning" Christian hears something about an untoward something that took place some time ago (usually in adolescence, which now extends to the late twenties) and demands "accountability" and an "explanation" from a preacher or Bible teacher.[41] The online inquisitor (driven by unholy curiosity) threatens to launch a nuclear bomb of Internet shaming. There is nothing more evil than a Christian who has been taken over by satanic urges and doesn't know it.

Jesus is not honored when his followers face off across the gutter. Jesus went into gutters, not to throw mud and bile, but to apply salve and bring salvation. I don't believe righteous spiritual instincts will lead you to bring anyone down. They will, however, lead you up a hill; the same direction those instincts led Jesus. Few people understand the cross, which includes being silent when accused as opposed to launching a counter-attack. And because the culture of inquisition is so attractive to so many, few are preaching the humility and sacrifice of the cross. When Jesus is not being lifted up, mean-spirited self-righteousness rears its ugly head.

> The Internet is bringing back
> the Scarlet letter in digital form.
> —DANIEL J. SOLOVE[42]

Researchers at Doñana Biological Station in Seville, Spain, have collaborated with their chief critics, most notably a conservation biologist at the University of Bern in Switzerland, to settle a dispute. Their argument centers on whether Mediterranean bats snatch migrating songbirds out of the night sky in spring and fall, or whether the bird feasts are really bats culling bird feathers that waft down from migrating birds. The debate got so heated that the only resolution seemed to be to work together.

Sure enough, researchers at Doñana turned out to be right. "I was one of the major detractors," says Raphael Arlettaz, the Bern conservation biologist, "but with good evidence, I have now changed my mind completely."[43] Maybe if Christians of different persuasions would work together missionally, the most virulent detractors might become the best defenders. They might even become best friends.

All of us have a favorite story we love to tell. But it's the wrong story if it's not "the story of Jesus and his love."[44] And some of the greatest stories of Jesus and his love are not in a book; they are in a person's life.

Interactives

1. When most evangelical Christians hear the word *infallible,* the next word that comes to mind is *word.* Why not *story*? How would our expressions of faith change if we thought of the Christian life as a "storybook" life?

2. There is a story about two of the great 1960s singers who did leg splits during performances.

> Mitch Ryder (of the Detroit Wheels) was talking to the Godfather of Soul, James Brown, and lamented how his knees were absolutely *shot* because of years of his stage antics. "James," Mitch asked, "I need knee replacements and am in bad shape. How on earth are you able to keep doing those knee drops and splits? You are older, and have been at this longer than I have."
>
> James Brown looked at Ryder and asked, "What kind of kneepads do you use?
>
> Mitch Ryder turned sickly pale and said, "Kneepads?"

   If you are a Gutenberger, how are you mentoring Googler protégées in the secrets you have learned about life? How are you revealing to them the ropes and pulleys behind what you do?

3. Italian novelist Ignazio Silone said that "in the sacred history of man on earth, it is still, alas, Good Friday."[45] Do you agree that the crucifixion is about as far as we have progressed in telling the Jesus story? What is your church doing to move the story toward Easter Sunday?

4. Share with other members of the group the names of some of your favorite storytellers. How good are you at telling stories? What makes your favorite storytellers so good at what they do?

5. Stories told often are not always stories told well, nor are they necessarily true stories. Think of commercials that are repeated on television and ads you see continually on the Internet. Give some examples of great storytellers whose tale is true.

TURNING A TIN EAR TO POETRY

God Crafted Us with an Ear Open to Beauty

> Three equals: a king, a harper, and a poet.
>
> —ANCIENT IRISH SAYING

If you ask your friends about their favorite course in college, you won't hear many stories about the phenomenal poetry class they took. Even Christians, who rhapsodize over the Psalms and the Song of Solomon, have few words to use in praising poetry of a more recent vintage.

I'm aware that my fascination with great poetry is not shared by many. I'm an educator, after all, and when I try to pass on my love of poetry I get either glassy-eyed stares or an argument. Before your eyes glaze over, let me assure you that I won't twist your arm. But I will give you my best arguments for why God is a Poet, and why poetry conveys God's messages in ways no other written or spoken words can. I also will take my best shot at convincing you that a life of faith devoid of poetic sensibilities is a life spent in the valley of dry bones.

The undeniable power of poetry, in spite of its continued discounting, brings to mind a persistent blind spot among Googlers. To mix metaphors, their blind spot involves a literary tin ear. This tendency points out a major reason why Googlers might not be able to instill new vitality and verve into the Western church, which has been hobbled in the prose culture of Gutenberg.

Selective Deafness

The sixth and last reason why Googlers could miss the opportunity to follow the Master Storyteller in changing the world is their tendency to turn a tin ear to poetry. Most of us who took a lit class recall the panic that set in when the textbook shifted from short stories to poetry. A short story, even if it's oblique and open-ended, can be analyzed sufficiently to write a short paper and receive a passing grade. But poetry? It seems designed to bedevil even those who enjoy the written word. Give me an essay, a biography, a memoir, an epic saga—even a play, a dictionary, a telephone directory. But please, spare me the poetry. Or such is the sentiment of most people I talk with.

The systemic aversion to poetry helps explain the tin ear that I associate with Googlers, which is not that different from the tin ear of Gutenbergers. But since it is the Googlers who now have the stage, it is Googlers who need to seize the power of poetry. Here is how it can be done, and it's not even painful.

The poet Matthew Arnold made two predictions. From his hands-on, hear-it-first position as a school inspector looking out on the second half of the nineteenth century, he first predicted that organized religion was rapidly waning. Did he ever get that one right. But what would replace it? Here was his second prediction: more and more, humanity will discover that we have to turn to poetry to interpret life, to console us, to sustain us. Without poetry, our science will appear incomplete; and most of what now passes for religion and philosophy will be replaced by poetry.[1]

Did he ever get that one wrong. But he was not alone in his wrongness about the future of poetic imagination. Another nineteenth-century English art critic and socialist philosopher, John Ruskin, said that "to see clearly is poetry, prophecy, and religion—all in one."[2] "After one has abandoned a belief in god," modernist poet Wallace Stevens wrote, "poetry is that essence which takes its place as life's redemption."[3]

What part does poetry play in your life? A little? At all? In your mind, are poetry and Christian doctrine friends or enemies? As literacy gets augmented with "graphicacy" (communication through visual images) and "videocy" (messages in moving graphics), it appears more and more that poetry is like cursive writing: a casualty of TGIF Culture. Will future generations have as much trouble reading Hiawatha's "By the shores of Gitche Gumee"[4] as they will have deciphering the cursive handwriting in their grandparents' diaries?[5]

What does it mean for our future if religion loses its natural language? What happens when we focus more on the properties and principles of religion than the poetry of religion? What happens to a religion when technicians of thought (philosophers) take over from "technicians of the sacred" (poets)?[6] Do we want to live in communities that can resist (or are oblivious to) the perfection of Emily Dickinson's metaphor for frost— "blond assassin"?[7] Do we want to invest our worship time in the homiletic arts when the preacher can read Robert Frost's line—"Like a piece of ice on a hot stove the poem must ride on its own melting"—and not know that "two roads diverged in a wood" Frost is talking as much about a sermon as a poem?[8]

How atrophied will our imaginations become when we can read the "born again, but stillborn" poem from Geoffrey Hill and not feel a sermon coming on?[9] You can preach till your tongue seizes up about a have-it-your-way culture's infestation of the church with "stillborn" communities while the Holy Spirit is waiting in the wings to turn born-again people into "Have Thine Own Way" dynamic bodies of Christ. Or you can read Geoffrey Hill's poem.

My students hate poetry.[10] Still, I require all doctoral students I mentor to relish a book of poetry. They call it my hazing ritual. (It is one of two. The other is my requirement of Michael Polanyi's *Personal Knowledge*). I argue with them: if you enjoy music, you enjoy poetry, for what are lyrics but poems? But one student who knows more about pop music than any person I've ever met dismissed that argument with "music makes the lyrics non-poetry." I'm incredulous: "You don't call James Taylor a poet?" He's incredulous: "Who's James Taylor?"

> Poetry is a way of singing ourselves out of our trivial
> time with the best that mocks our planning
> —IRISH POET OLIVER ST. JOHN GOGARTY[11]

I continue: if you don't like poetry, then you don't like the Bible, for what is a lot of the Bible but poetry? They counter that biblical poetry such as the songs of Miriam and of Deborah, the oldest poems we have inherited in the West, are meant to be sung. That makes it "non-poetry."

I next try hiding behind Eugene H. Peterson, who in an early essay argued that the last book of the Bible was written by a pastor-poet. Peterson insists St. John was the church's first major poet. "If St. John's Revelation is not read as a poem, it is virtually incomprehensible, which, in fact, is why it is so often uncomprehended. St. John, playful with images and exuberant in metaphor, works his words into vast, rhythmic repetitions."[12]

Peterson then concludes with a zinger I boomerang at my students: "I do not mean that all pastors write poems or speak in rhyme, but that they treat words with reverence, stand in awe before not only the Word, but words, and realize that language itself partakes of the sacred."[13]

For all that fancy footnote footwork, this is the feedback I'm prone to get: "Professor, didn't Martin Luther doubt if the book of Revelation should be in the canon since he could 'in no way detect that the Holy Spirit produced it'?[14] And didn't John Calvin write a commentary on every book of the New Testament except the one written by that apocalyptic pastor-poet you and Peterson like to talk about?"

I then throw a little world history on them: the leader of a quarter of humanity was a poet. Have you ever read *The Poems of Mao Zedong*? And how good was that for humanity, my students counter? How many millions were killed under direct orders of the mass murderer? How many millions more died under his mass-murdering regime that rivaled Stalin and Hitler in its horror? One of my students dredged up the story of Maoist students and teachers from Beijing who traveled to the Confucius Temple at Qufu, near where the sage was supposed to have been born in the sixth century BCE. They then proceeded to destroy 6,618 registered cultural artifacts, including 929 paintings, more than 2,700 books, and 2,000 graves.[15] So much for poetry making us a better person, or corporately, making us a better people.

I try history again, this time making it church history: The incarnation can be expressed in a book, which is what theologians do. But it also can be expressed in a play, a drama, a dance, a musical composition, and a poem, which is also what theologians do but we don't know them as theologians. What is Dante's fourteenth-century epic poem *Divine Comedy* but Thomas Aquinas's medieval synthesis in poetic form? Protestant Reformer Martin Luther believed that theology and poetry have common interests to the point where they rose or fell together: "I am convinced that without knowledge of literature pure theology cannot at all endure...[poets and rhetoricians] are wonderfully fitted for the groping of sacred truth and for handling it skillfully and happily."[16] After hearing these words from Luther, my students ask, "Do you really think Luther would use the word 'groping' if he were writing today? What's the original German word?"

I am getting weary, but I attempt one final theological end-around: What is the Holy Spirit but the greatest Poet of the divine? Many poets liken writing poetry to breathing. D. H. Lawrence separated himself from poets who say their art is a "gift": "Not I, not I, but the wind that blows through me!"[17] It is hard to fit breathy, curved, elliptical theology into oblong, rectangular, boxy spaces. I even quote my students these words of the Nobel Prize–winning Italian poet Salvatore Quasimodo: "Poetry is the revelation of a feeling that the poet believes to be interior and personal but which the reader recognizes as his own."[18] Does that not sound like a definition of the Holy Spirit? Poetry is the gift of "the voice that is great within us"[19] and needs to be let out. My students are undaunted. They come back with, "The Spirit is understandable—even when speaking in unknown tongues there is a translator; poetry isn't easily accessible and comes with no translator."

> Because the Holy Ghost over the bent
> World broods with warm breast
> and with ah! bright wings.
> —GERARD MANLY HOPKINS[20]

As a last resort, I try the biblical trump card. In Ephesians 2:10 we read that we are God's *poiema,* God's artifact and poem, created in Christ Jesus for good works. God is the Divine Poet, and each one of us is an expression of God's poetic creativity, an original poem that exists not for its own sake but for the sake of the world.

> We are His poem, crafted in the heart of Christ Jesus, to live a vibrant expression of His purpose on the Earth, that will serve to establish His kingdom.[21]

This made Christ the Supreme Artist, according to Dutch painter Vincent Van Gogh. In some occasional correspondence two years before his death (1888), Vincent wrote a series of letters to a young friend, Emile Bernard, a French painter and poet who was starting to read the Bible.

> [Christ] lived serenely, as *a greater artist* than all other artists, despising marble and clay as well as color, working in living flesh. That is to say, this matchless artist, hardly to be conceived of by the obtuse instrument of our modern, nervous, stupefied brains, made neither statues nor pictures nor books; he loudly proclaimed that he made...living men, immortals.[22]

You would never know it from inside the church, but scholars contend that in the last one hundred years "we have been living through one of the greatest ages of Christian poetry that has yet occurred."[23] Likewise outside Christianity, poetry is booming. Even those who don't like the poetry being written grudgingly admit it's a "golden age."[24] In the current renaissance of poetry, says US poet laureate Billy Collins, 83 percent of poetry is not worth reading, but he couldn't live without the other 17 percent.[25]

Who Likes Poetry More?

It is more than troubling that the non-Christian world seems more open to poetry than the Christian world. From raps to poetry slams to creative-writing courses to online "poetry generators,"[26] there is a democratization of poetry that has bypassed the church. The thirteenth-century Jalal al-Din Rumi, a Sufi mystic known simply as Rumi, is USAmerica's best-selling poet.

I'm convinced the world needs poetry more than ever. If I were not a Jesus-follower, I would be on the same page with the German philosopher Martin Heidegger. Heidegger believed that the sole hope for the salvation of the human species rested with poets. When he ensconced himself in the Black Forest in what is now known as Heidegger's Hut, he read Sophocles and Holderin.[27] I'm more inclined to read James Wright (if only I could change my preaching style as effortlessly as Wright changed his writing style), Elizabeth Bishop (I still bear scars from her biting critique of Christians), Wallace Stevens (his "Sunday Morning" is truly "one of the great secular-religious poems in any language"[28]), Robert Frost ("No tears in the writer, no tears in the reader"[29]), Denise Levertov (who taught a semester at Drew), Elizabeth Jennings (whose poetry I pair and compare with Waylon Jennings, but that's another story), R. S. Thomas (a legendary grouch), Geoffrey Hill (who leaves images strewn across my soul), Luci Shaw (my favorite Christian poet living today), Wendell Berry (who with reverence celebrates what's right with life), and X. J. Kennedy (who with wit satirizes what's wrong with life).[30]

> Painting is silent poetry and poetry voiced painting.
> —Simonides, quoted by Plutarch[31]

Technology has so embedded itself in our lives that it is no longer considered a separate category, but a part of everything. With that as our reality, we need to be poets more than ever before. Poetry is the art form least influenced by technology, because it is a technology of its own. It is the technology of the sacred. As long as poetry is healthy, "technicians of the sacred" can shape content and beat back the arrogance and overreach of technology.

The more our home pages keep us up-to-the-second on what is happening, and our pundits and blogs keep us up to date on what officially happened, the more we need to be poets. It is poetry that tells us what actually happened or what ought to have happened.[32] "Poetry is always the cat concert under the window of the room in which the official version of reality is being written."[33]

> There is nothing in the world
> that resembles God as much as silence.
> —MEISTER ECKHART[34]

The baggier our prose amidst the plague of oversharing, the more we need to be poets. Poetry is spare, lean, slimming, and silencing. Even heaven needs silence. In the book of Revelation, before the fireworks and trumpet fanfares at the opening of the seventh seal, "there was silence in heaven about the space of half an hour."[35] A poet is a true believer in God's first language of silence but who "could not refrain from speaking" (Ezra Pound).[36] Søren Kierkegaard out-poetized the poets in his definition of a poet as a person whose heart is full of pain "but whose lips are so formed that when a groan or a shriek streams out over them it sounds like beautiful music."[37] Sometimes in life less equals more, especially when that less is the cri de coeur of the soul.

TRAVELING AT GODSPEED

The more this world travels at warp speed, the more we need to be poets and learn Godspeed. All art is finding the time to take time. Pablo Casals practiced for twelve years Bach's six suites for cello before he played them in public. Ansel Adams kept vigil for hours, even days, until the moment of perfect exposure appeared.

Adams is arguably the most famous photographer in USAmerican history. He is known for capturing the grandeur of Yosemite, but he also took photos of the eastern slopes of the Sierras, especially the Owens Valley, where he traveled in 1944. Wallace Stegner, the California writer called "the Dean of Western writers," watched how Adams sat in the desert waiting to take pictures.

> Adams did not grab the image when he came upon it. He studied it, visualizing the finished print. He estimated it as it would appear in various directional lights. Then he went to dinner and to bed. In the chilly predawn blackness of the next morning, he came back. As he waited, clear gray sourceless light grew until it showed him the meadow with its shadowy horses, the mottled foothill, the impressive loom of the Sierra fault block. He

set up the camera and went under the cloth; then he came out and waited. Eventually, the sun, breaking over the White Mountains to the eastward, lit and burned like a laser beam on the highest Sierra peak. He watched the pinkish light flood downward until nearly the whole face of the range was blazing with it. He went under the cloth and came out again, and waited. Then another laser beam slipped past the eastern mountains and tangled itself in the tops of the cottonwoods in the left middle ground. The roll of foothills was still in shadow, the range coldly alight. Nearly at his own level the little smolder of sun grew in the cottonwood branches. He went under the cloth and watched awhile, and came out yet again. By then the light had burst past the leftward cottonwoods and was brightening other trees and a patch of meadow along the creek to the right. There was a horse grazing there. The light pooled behind the horse, turning it into a black cutout. Adams went under the cloth again, waited for the precise instant, and clicked the shutter.[38]

It took poet Ian Hamilton twenty-five years to write fifty poems, proving the contention of one of the world's greatest novelists, Gustave Flaubert, that "Poetry is as exact a science as geometry."[39] It has taken me years to slow my soul down enough to read some Denise Levertov poems. How revealing it is, observed former poet laureate Howard Nemerov, that we praise to the skies the genius who invented the wheel, but never give a thought to the greater genius who invented the brake.[40]

The more we read words and then throw away what we read like peanut shells, the more we need to be poets. Poets read some words repeatedly; poets play with words, petting and stroking them until they purr like a kitten. Poetry is meant to be read like the Scriptures…over and over again. It yields its heart only to those willing to invest time and energy in peeling it, like an artichoke. But there is nothing like "the inevitable solace that right language brings," as Oxford professor and novelist John Bayley has said.[41]

> After a few years of speaking in prose,
> we become prosaic.
> —EUGENE PETERSON[42]

I believe in the well-turned phrase as a defense against chaos, unreason, and kitsch. "Style is not at all a prettification…. It is—like colour with painters—a quality of vision," argued Marcel Proust in his own dazzling stylistic play.[43] The more our words get greasy and sticky from so much fingering, the more we need to be poets. Poetry "rinses the language"[44] and cleanses our imagination. Poetry helps the church rediscover Jesus's beauty and lets the beauty of Jesus be seen in each of us.

The more TGIF Culture "shallows"[45] us, the more we need to be poets and embrace language that helps us go deeper and murkier. In the shallows, everything is clear and exact. In the depths, everything is mysterious and multitudinous.

We are deviled into following those who promise the rectitude of thought, because rectitude leads to certitude. Those who offer the relationships of poetry are not easy to follow, because relationships require blood, sweat, and tears. Relationships compel vulnerability. But the true enemy of faith is certainty. The just shall live by faith, not certainty.

> The opposite of faith is not doubt, but certainty.
> —ANNE LAMOTT'S FAMOUS DICTUM[46]

The more we live in a world where opposites come to light at the same time, but don't contradict each other, the more followers of Jesus need to be poets and inhabit the place of poetry. Not only is poetry a place where contradictions do not fight to the death,[47] but it is the homeplace of paradox—where you can pull the opposite strands tight to get a knot of singular clarity.

The more a culture puts its faith in empirical evidence, that which can be observed and therefore "proven," the more we need to be poets and respect the powers of the invisible—to pray and trust the unseen. According to Samuel Beckett, "All poetry...is prayer."[48] For it is the invisible, unseen spiritual forces that are, in Robert Louis Stevenson's phrase, "the nails and axles of the universe."[49]

The more the engine room of the world economy finds its home in the East, not the West, the more we need to be poets—which can help us feel at home with cultures of the East. Chinese, Japanese, and Vietnamese citizens hold poetry in much higher regard than do citizens of the West. In fact, the Vietnamese and Chinese have the same proverb that makes an appeal to poetry as the final authority: "And there's a poem to prove it too."[50]

The more everything in life is easy access, and the more easy buttons there are to press in order to get "answers," the more we need to be poets and sharpen our souls on things that are hard. Geoffrey Hill has been called the finest British poet of our time. His Christian musings have been called "the major achievement of late twentieth-century verse." Instead of me being the ventriloquist's doll of this Oxford professor's "musings," why don't you check out for yourself his collection "The Triumph of Love," especially his poem on the traceable faults of the moral landscape.[51] Hill responds icily to the charge that his poetry is not "accessible" enough. Public toilets, Hill says, have a duty to be accessible; poetry does not.

> *Accessible* is a perfectly good word if applied to supermarket aisles, art galleries, polling stations and public lavatories, but it has no place in the discussion of poetry and poetics. Human beings are difficult. We're difficult to ourselves; we're difficult to each other and we are mysteries to ourselves; we are mysteries to each other. One encounters in any ordinary day far more real difficulty than one confronts in the most "intellectual" piece of work. Why is it believed that poetry, prose, painting, music should be less than we are? Why does music, why does poetry have to address us in simplified terms, when, if such simplifications were applied to our own inner selves, we would find it demeaning?[52]

Or as he puts it in acerbic form, to demand a great deal of the reader "preserves democracy; you pay respect / to the intelligence of the citizen."[53]

The more we are "information omnivores," the more mindless is our devotion to facts over truths. With that in mind, we need poetic license all the more. Young scholars "can cite anything and construe nothing,"[54] observes one academic. I would not go so far as Nietzsche, who wrote on one of the scraps of paper found on his desk after his death: "There is no such thing as facts, only interpretation." Nietzsche always exaggerated. But the supremacy of poetry to facts and streams of data is best seen in the poet's mission, which is at base a relational one. A poet uses language not to fetch facts and convey information but to form beauty, frame truth, and further goodness in the world.

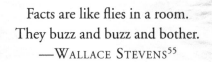

Facts are like flies in a room.
They buzz and buzz and bother.
—WALLACE STEVENS[55]

The more people write their faith story in prose, the more we need to be poets and write our faith story in poetry. Going against the grain is part of the poetic enterprise. The more people "work at it," the more we need to be poets and "play at it." Memory is congealed, and sometimes concealed, in what we "play" at: festivals, rites, rituals, stories, songs. The more TGIF Culture tilts toward the right brain, the more we need to be poets. What better emotional home than poetry, where a culture filled with paradox and ambiguity can live freely and openly? This is why that left-brained "fatso" Plato wanted poets banished from the state. Poets pandered to the heart when people needed to feast on a head-diet of logic and reason, he argued.

In the Welsh tradition, the word for poetry (*Cerdd Dafod*—"tongue craft") is slightly different from the word for music (*Cerdd Dant*—"string craft"). A poem enters through the ear, the Welsh believe, and from the ear to the heart, bypassing the head. Welsh priest / poet R. S. Thomas put a different twist to his Welsh heritage by defining poetry as something "which arrives at the intellect / by way of the heart."[56]

These origins in the heart make it possible for poetry to convey truth before it is comprehended in the head. Emily Dickinson, the solitary Puritan poet, made the right brain the test of whether words were poetry or prose: "If I read a book [and] it makes my whole body so cold no fire ever can warm me I know that is poetry. If I feel physically as if the top of my head were taken off, I know that is poetry."[57] Any atrophy of right-brained knowing cuts us off from much of the New Testament. In 3,874 verses out of 7,957 New Testament verses, the kind of knowing being described (for example, healings, miracles, dreams, visions, images, intuition, discernment, revelation, prophecy, tongues, inward hearings) is the domain of poetry.[58] British theologian David Martin even goes so far as to say that "there is nothing in the Bible remotely resembling a logical sequence or an empirical proposition. It is overwhelmingly narrative, vocative and performative." It revolves around the greatest story lines in the history of humanity: "good and evil, enslavement and liberation, grief and celebration, demand and gift, judgment and grace, alienation and redemption, death and resurrection."[59]

At age twenty Ralph Waldo Emerson decided to attend Harvard Divinity School. He framed his choice of ministry as a career in the context of a "strong imagination" and "keen relish for the beauties of poetry," which were so lopsided that it made his reasoning faculties look "proportionately weak." But Emerson countered that the "highest species of reasoning" came not through left-brained, muscle-bound "reasoning machines" such as John Locke and David Hume, but in the "moral imagination" that is best expressed in the poetry of theology, not the prose of philosophy.[60]

PROTECTION AGAINST CELEBRITY CULTURE

There is one more reason we need to take poetry seriously. Partly because of the image-driven nature of TGIF Culture, there is a rise of "celebrity" that is toxic and dangerous.

TGIFers are obsessed with the cult of the celebrity, and find almost irresistible the "hermeneutic of intimacy" that an actor or sports figure creates with his fans.[61]

Celebrity devours everyone who has the misfortune of becoming one. We love watching the gods fall from the heavens. The cult of the celebrity is chastised by the second commandment: "Thou shalt make no graven image." The more a celebrity culture violates the second commandment and helps fix our gaze on idols, the more we need poets who are masters at showing us how to refocus the floodlights and shine the light on what really matters: truth.

John Ashbery is probably the most critically acclaimed living poet. I have read repeatedly such lines as "I don't understand myself, only segments / of myself that misunderstand each other."[62] But most often when I read a John Ashbery poem I say either, "Is that it? That's all?" or, "What in the world is that about?"

But when I read someone who is writing *about* a John Ashbery poem, I often say, "That was brilliant! Such an incandescent interpretation!"[63] I then return to Ashbery's words with the same attitude as someone once said of Wagner's music: his poetry is better than it sounds. In other words, I am inspired less by John Ashbery than I am by those who are inspired by him. This TGIF world needs inspired people whose excitation and joy excite others to genius and greatness. The community of readers (as the community of faith) all contribute to the poetics of interpretation and inspiration.

> We can put television in its proper light
> by supposing that Gutenberg's great invention had
> been directed at printing only comic books.
> —PHILOSOPHER OF EDUCATION ROBERT MAYNARD HUTCHINS[64]

I admit it: my whole worry about the loss of poetry may be idiosyncratic. I grew up in the strictest of the Wesleyan holiness tradition, which recast every pleasure into a problem or a peril. I spent my first two decades in an almost Puritan household where novels and poetry were dismissed as wastes of time. When behavior is banned, it drives that behavior underground or to a hiding place under the mattress. I knew exactly how many books of poetry or novels (big difference) could be stuffed between the sheets under the mattress without creating any betraying bumps or humps. I also was forbidden to watch more than two hours of television a week. We were punished for listening to non-Christian music, dancing, or playing cards. I became an unwitting teenage biblical scholar in my effort to find out where it said Christians couldn't dance, drink, smoke, or gamble. I never did find the prohibitions.

In that Puritan environment I remember asking God about some of the stupidest things. Conflicted about whether I should kiss a girl I met at a camp meeting, I ran across this poem that eternalized my love for poetry:

Father, Father up above,
should I Kiss
the Girl I love?
Sinner, Sinner, down below
Pucker up
And Let her GO![65]

In response to Puritan charges that poetry was immoral and a waste of time, Sir Philip Sidney wrote *A Defence of Poesy* in 1579, although it wasn't published until 1595.[66] Cited as the first work of literary criticism in English, Sidney's defense was threefold:

1. Poetry has a long and salutary influence in history.
2. Poetry invents the possible and imagines alternatives.
3. Poetry aims, not simply to pander to the emotions, but to bring the heart and head together in order to convict the soul.

Maybe that's all I should have said to my students. Or maybe I should just tell this one story. Richard Rorty, grandson of social-gospel theologian Walter Rauschenbusch and one of the greatest philosophers of the twentieth century, knew he was dying of pancreatic cancer. Just before his death in 2007, he recorded some last thoughts in the journal *Poetry*, which were published posthumously. He reminisced about his life and lifetime of reading, and confessed two regrets. First, he wished he had "made more close friends." Second, he wished he had "spent somewhat more of my life with verse."[67]

Maybe the best way to spend more of life with verse is to read the Bible in some of its more poetic translations. Two translations of the Bible showcase the poetic tapestry of Scriptures on its brightest side. The first is the King James Version, which was mostly cribbed from William Tyndale's Bible of 1537. The irony of this is bloody. Tyndale was killed for making an English translation of the Bible. Yet within one hundred years, nearly 80 percent of his translation was used to produce an "authorized" version.[68]

The Jerusalem Bible came out in the 1960s. It is my favorite Bible for public readings because of its poetic sensibilities. An anonymous committee translated it,[69] although we know the scholar who did the translation of Jonah: J. R. R. Tolkein.[70] I call The Jerusalem Bible the haiku version of the Bible. It is plain, minimalist, unadorned, almost beatific, much like the Beat poets who dominated the 1960s. Here are a few lines from Psalm 29:

The voice of Yahweh over the waters!
Yahweh over the multitudinous waters!

The voice of Yahweh in power!
The voice of Yahweh in splendour!

The voice of Yahweh shatters the cedars,
Yahweh shatters the cedars of Lebanon,
making Lebanon leap like a calf,
Sirion like a young wild bull.

The voice of Yahweh sharpens lightning shafts!

Poetry doesn't try to prove a point. But it does, without trying, point to the truth. And poetic sensibilities are indispensable ingredients in reading well our texts and traditions and times. For Irish poet and playwright Louis MacNeice, this was the prescription for a poet: able-bodied, fond of talking, a reader of news, capable of pity and laughter, informed in economics, appreciative of the other sex, involved in personal relationships, actively interested in politics, susceptible to physical impressions. Can you imagine the body of Christ without these qualities?

Certain things are acquired tastes. Coffee, sushi, bluegrass music. If Googlers don't acquire the taste for poetry, our best hope for reorienting the church in the West and reversing the sundering of society from faith will dim.

Interactives

1. Dr. Susan Greenfield, arguably the leading woman scientist (neuroscience) in the UK, gives a quick tutorial on the brain. She contrasts those who grew up in the world of books with people who are getting much of their information and entertainment from a screen. From a faith perspective, discuss the contrast of the People of the Screen versus People of the Book. (Watch Dr. Greenfield's discussion, beginning at 25:25: http://video .google.com/videoplay?docid=-7355464462502289999#.)

2. Hans Rosling understands the need to convert statistics and data into images. Check out five minutes of history and discuss it. Click on http

://news.yahoo.com/s/yblog_thelookout/watch-200-years-of-history-in-5 -minutes.

3. The word *gospel* comes from "Godspell," which means "God's story." In the four gospels we read the stories of thirty-five people who were healed by Jesus. He healed thousands, but we know the stories of these thirty-five. How many of their stories can you tell?

4. Rachel Naomi Remen's book *My Grandfather's Blessings*[71] tells her story of growing up with nonobservant Jewish parents. One of Dr. Remen's grandparents was an Orthodox rabbi who was forbidden to teach his granddaughter anything about the Jewish faith. This grandfather was a caregiver to Rachel during the week. He agreed that he wouldn't teach her, but he was allowed to tell her stories. So Rachel heard amazing stories about life in a garden, adventures in the desert, boats and floods, little boys fighting giants, and so on. She remembered all those stories and learned about the Jewish faith through them.[72] Do you believe we are designed to be the recipients of stories? How were you told stories? Were they recited, sung, danced, plucked?

5. The Amazon Basin, one of the most important ecosystems on earth, is cradled in Catholic hands. Mary Colwell raises this question: What if the pope "would say Mass in the middle of the smoking ruins of a cleared area of forest"?[73] What environmental effect do you think that would have?

PART IV

iPhones

THE ADVANTAGES OF WHOLE FRUIT

God Brings Things Together;
People Insist on Separating the Parts

[Printers] fill the world with pamphlets and books…[that are] foolish, ignorant, malignant, libelous, mad, impious, and subversive; and such is the flood that even things that might have done some good lose all their goodness.

—RENAISSANCE HUMANIST DESIDERIUS ERASMUS,
WRITING IN THE EARLY SIXTEENTH CENTURY

One way you can tell Gutenbergers from Googlers? Check their wrists. Googlers rarely wear a watch. "Why would you want a device that only does one thing?" one of them replied when I asked, "Where's your watch?" They have iPhones, iPads, Androids, mobiles, and BlackBerries that put the equivalent of a newsstand, a library, a shopping mall, a jukebox, a video camera, and a high-tech communications center at their fingertips. Soon a handheld device also will double as your wallet, credit card, keys, bank, remote control, airline ticket, video conferencing center, and a thousand other nonvoice uses.[1] Gutenbergers use technology, often reluctantly. Googlers live technology.

Every day the number of text messages sent and received exceeds the population of planet Earth. Every day, two-thirds of the people on this planet use their cell phones in some way, including rag dealers driving goat carts in Senegal and a homeless person in Marion, Iowa, who called the weather station to see if he needed to find warm and protective shelter for the night.[2] In fact, cell-phone technology has played a major role in reducing the number of people who live on less than a dollar a day from 29 percent in 1990 to 18 percent in 2004.[3] Soon access to a mobile phone will approach 100 percent penetration of the population. Marshall McLuhan said that the telephone is an extension of the ear. If only he could have lived to see our earbuds and blinking-blue lobes.

Virginia Woolf famously remarked, "On or about December, 1910, human character changed."[4] No one has ever been able to figure out what there was about December 1910 that inspired Virginia to make this statement. But there is another calendar date about which we surely can say that something human changed. On or about April 1973 there was an irreversible, unstoppable, revolutionary shift in the course of history. For on the third of April 1973, Martin Cooper invented the cell phone. Cooper placed the first call to his rival at Bell Labs on a street corner near the Manhattan Hilton. The mobile device has become the fastest diffusion of any technology in history, even faster than electrification of homes[5] or the distribution of the Salk vaccine.

Another way you can tell a Gutenberger from a Googler? Ask if they have a landline. Googlers have cut the landline cords permanently. Landlines are family phones or communal communications. Cell phones are personal, highly individual artifacts. They have replaced the automobile as the major way young people create their own identity separate from parents and outside the control of adult dictation.[6] Digital culture doesn't think "drive first"; it thinks TGIF first.[7]

I remember well how eager I was to turn sixteen so I could get a driver's license. My kids chomped at the bit waiting for their thirteenth birthday so they could get a cell phone. When they turned sixteen, I had to pressure them to go take the driving test for a license. "But Dad, you get fined or arrested if you text while driving!" One of the most far-reaching but least observed changes taking place in the TGIF generations is this move away from car culture.

Soon you'll be able to tell a Gutenberger from a Googler by whether they have a laptop. Laptops are letdowns to Googlers, dinosaurs in the land of Androids, PDAs, iPhones, and iPads. When you pick up an iPhone, you are holding a supercomputer. You also are holding a Tower Records store, except in this online version of the now-defunct retail store you choose your song, which comes to you unmediated: no packaging, no sales pitch, no marketing. The cell is your covenant with life; the cell is your convent in life.

Googlers at Play

But the surest way to tell a Googler from a Gutenberger is their enjoyably gamey approach to life. In other words, see if they're playing Angry Birds or some other hot cellphone game.

When Gutenbergers think of Finnish corporations, they think of Nokia. But Nokia has been so slow in competing with Google and Apple (its cell-phone platform has been called a "turkey" by its own CEO) that it slipped to 1.6 percent of Finland's GDP in 2009. In 2011 it announced a last-gasp global partnership with Microsoft. Ask a Googler about a corporation from Finland and they will tell you about egg-stealing pigs under attack by irate birds.[8]

The world's half billion gamers spend three billion hours a week playing online games. The online wiki for World of Warcraft is the second-largest wiki in the world (second only to Wikipedia), with more than eighty thousand articles. Almost one-third of entertainment dollars are spent on video games. In a 2009 survey, 63 percent of USAmericans indicated they had played a video game in the past six months, whereas only 53 percent had been to a movie.[9] In terms of market power, every year video games sweep Hollywood off the red carpet. What's more, video games have proven themselves recession-proof.

Frequent users of electronic games do not fall into a single demographic group. The average age of a gamer in USAmerica? Thirty-six.[10] Almost 30 percent are older than fifty. Females make up 40 percent of gamers in USAmerica.[11] Almost 70 percent of American households have members that play video games.[12]

Brain researchers already tout the training advantages of video games to heighten sensitivity to one's environment, sharpen cognitive skills, make good decisions faster, and develop life skills as diverse as driving, reading small print, navigating, and social networking.[13] Video games take users into highly complex, imaginative worlds and demand logic and quick reflexes on the part of a successful gamer.

The military is ecstatic over new recruits who have been response-time-quickened by growing up on computer games with virtual persona that are, in a way, "more real than reality," as French psychotherapist Jacques Lacan put it. For the last two decades, when more people were playing increasingly violent video games, violent crime in

USAmerica and the European Union declined, in contrast to what the critics predicted.[14] Jane McGonigal, director at Game Research and Development at the Institute
for the Future, says Googlers have been shaped by video games in these four areas:

1. "urgent optimism": Gamers don't procrastinate and overplan before
   they go on a "world-saving mission."
2. "weaving a tight social fabric": Gamers have learned to build bonds
   of trust and cooperation that enable collaboration and teamwork.
3. "blissful productivity": Gamers work hard and can stay on task for
   hours.
4. "epic meaning": Video games inspire big dreams and "planetary scale
   stories."[15]

GOOGLERS APPROACH LIFE AS A WHOLE

But perhaps more important than all this, Googlers are holistic thinkers.

One of my students tried an epic version of the standard "passing the peace." Instead of shaking hands with everyone, he asked his people to go outside and pick a
flower from the bushes and fields around the church, and to bring the flower back into
the sanctuary. When everyone had reassembled, he then asked people to bring their
flowers up front, place them on the altar, and return to their seats.

Even before the rustling stopped, he started talking about the different parts of a
flower as he used the congregational bouquet as an object lesson. Picking up one flower
after another, he showed the difference between the pistil and the stamen. Then he
pulled off the petal, exposing the stigma, which he punched open to get to the ovary and
then further inside the ovule with embryo sac. The sepal, receptacle, and peduncle were
then separated from another flower. When he had finished exploring the beautiful complexity and elegance of a flower, he looked down and all he had on the altar was dis-
sected blooms.

Dozens of murdered flowers marked the crime scene. The pastor looked at his people and asked, "Now what do we do? We no longer have any flowers." The sanctuary got
quiet for a moment, but then a kid's voice was heard: "Go back to the bush." Googlers
are returning to the bush and picking fresh flowers, not to analyze and dissect them so
much as to enjoy and smell them. *Analyze* means literally "to dissolve." *Dissect* means
"functionally to kill."

The primary image for learning is the apple. If you wanted to get on the good side
of your teacher, you didn't bring in a banana or a grapefruit. So powerfully embedded

as a knowledge symbol is the apple that a certain information-industry company, which functions more like a cult than a corporation, has made its primary logo an apple with a bite taken out of it.

I repeat, Apple is a cult. Don't believe me? When the iPad first was introduced in 2009, it was greeted by Apple afficionados as "the Jesus tablet," so second-comingish was the excitement.

DISCIPLES OF A DEVICE

Almost every day brings new evidence that Apple is a cult. The most photographed site in New York City? The Apple store. Dedicated Apple users have brain activity that mimics that of religious piety. The opening of new Apple stores has been likened to a prayer meeting. But perhaps nothing proves the cultishness of Apple more than "Antenna-gate," so dubbed by the late St. Jobs. As soon as Apple released iPhone 4 on June 24, 2010, it was apparent that the phone dropped calls when users touched the lower left corner. At first, Apple shrugged it off.

Between June 24 and July 16, when Steve Jobs went public with the problem, Apple sold three million reception-challenged devices. After *Consumer Reports* magazine made its devastating non-buy recommendation on July 12, there still were two- to three-week waiting lists and lottery systems for the "winning buyers" of the iPhone 4.

Even after Antenna-gate, "They Still Believe in Steve" was the title of an article that explained why people were buying defective phones. "For many people, Apple is what makes them happy. Its products make their lives easier, and provide some entertainment, at a time when people don't feel good about a lot of other things in their lives. It sounds silly, but it's not that far from the truth."[16]

Apple later redesigned its Verizon iPhone slightly, shifting around the antennas so the "death grip" problem (when you hold the phone a certain way you lose bars) is no longer an issue. The downside is that the Ringer Off switch is slightly askew for those using an older iPhone case, forcing you to buy a new case. But hey, you can't have everything.

COMPARING APPLES TO ORANGES

We should have been giving oranges to teachers, rather than apples. Gutenberger Culture upset the apple cart. It turned everything it touched into a fruit as flashy in color as the unrhymable-in-sound orange.[17] The orange is the most popular fruit in USAmerica.[18]

At its core, what is the primary difference between oranges and apples?

You eat an apple whole. You pick it up and bite into it without first altering it. Depending on how big your mouth is, you can taste the whole organism: skin, meat, core, seeds. Eating an apple is an organic, holistic experience. It involves a unified approach to and account of the apple.

But what of the orange? You don't eat an orange until after you have manipulated it. It has to be taken apart. You peel it, separate the skin, section it, and sometimes even remove the meat from the membranes. This is eating a fruit according to the scientific method, a mechanical approach. It replicates a mechanical explanation of existence that leads to quantitative scorecards and the disciplinary organization of knowledge. Premodern cultures could handle degrees of chaos, but not so in the Gutenberg world. We partitioned everything and created a "disciplinary society," which focused on the distinctiveness of each segment, not on the unity of the whole.[19] Even the Bible got partitioned and became the sum of its chapters and verses, not the summit of experiences and relations between its stories and songs, histories, and letters.

> Fragments are the only form I trust.
> —FLASH FICTION WRITER DONALD BARTHELME[20]

Scholars of the Torah are still biting the apple, even though they could be peeling the orange. If you get a PhD in Hebrew Bible, your final exam could be on any passage in the Torah. You are inducted into the line of ancient interpreters of the Hebrew Scriptures who spoke of the "seventy sides" (Shivim Panim) of the Torah. But if you get a PhD in New Testament, your final exam will be on your specialization (for example, Philippians or Titus) or even on a shorter periscope located within a gospel or epistle. In treating the Bible like an orange more than an apple, Christian-oriented biblical scholars have lost the sense of the Bible as a living organism. When Jesus the Jew taught in the Nazareth synagogue on the Sabbath, he approached the Scriptures as an apple. In a holistic and imaginative reading of the Scriptures, surprising interconnections and unexpected parallels are constantly being discovered. You miss those insights and connections when you piece out the Bible as if you were separating an orange.

The Gutenberg world marked the triumph of the orange over the apple. Books are the most antisocial technology ever invented. Books separate people from one another, siloing them off in a corner and making them submit to a distant, invisible, print-bound authority. How ironic that Gutenbergers attack social media for not being relational.

It was the Gutenberg world that invented the subjectivity of the self, which we know as "the individual." The free-standing, autonomous, sovereign self was defined as the sum of its choices. We have forgotten that *autobiography* is a nineteenth-century term. Earlier centuries were not preoccupied with individuality or interior life. When they told life stories, it was not to explore their selfhood but for didactic or propaedeutic purposes.

Everything Gutenbergers touched (including people) they turned into an orange. They took a subject apart, critiqued it, categorized and cataloged it. Today scholars know no other way of making a living than revising one another. Similarly, this is how theologians make a living.

For the last five hundred years, anything that was not well-suited to dissection and analysis was suspect. Even the father of psychoanalysis, neurologist Sigmund Freud, worried that an enterprise rooted in telling stories would lack "the serious stamp of science," and well he might worry. In the orange world of the Gutenbergers, we were

Fruitful Adventures

Have you ever wondered why St. Paul used "fruit" as the image of God's character (see Galatians 5:22–23)? In Paul's "fruit of the Spirit" metaphor, we see what God is like and how we are to live. But what fruit is this, an apple or an orange?

Can you parcel out the attributes of God and work on living out just one a week? If so, that would make the fruit of the Spirit more like an orange. If you prefer to think of becoming an imitator of God piece by piece, orange-like, you are thinking like a Gutenberger.

If, however, you picture the fruit of the Spirit as an apple, all of a piece, you lean more Googler. An apple is not at all like a checklist, but more like a striped beach ball. You can't bat around a beach ball by pulling apart the striped segments. You inflate it and the entire multicolored ball gets round. It has to be used all together.

Likewise, following God is more similar to an apple than an orange. It is an all-or-nothing proposition—a way of life, not a to-do list. An apple is unified, skin and meat and seeds and core taken together. An apple symbolizes Googler spirituality.

guided by "objectivity," which hitched itself to "truth" to hide objectivity's self-propelled supremacy. Truth showed where arguments must end; objectivity showed how arguments should begin and proceed, promising us freedom from bias and partisanship (right!). But objectivity and subjectivity are like convex and concave curves: they bend the same body part. There is a type of wisdom that comes from judging and criticizing. But wonder and appreciation are great wisdom too.

The difference between an apple world and an orange world can be seen in the difference between a medieval village and a modern city. I make this contrast partly because Christianity is urban-friendly. It placed itself in the public square and evangelized cities. In fact, when monks went to the deserts it was most often to ready them to return to the cities. In a medieval village, everything and everyone is interlocked within a shared system of values. Your economic, religious, political, and business interactions are related, and there is no escape from the network of relationships that converged on the village commons. A medieval village enjoyed an overarching value system and moral universe.

The modern city is organized very differently, with its key feature the differentiation of sectors. Everything and everyone gets pulled into their own sectors. Educational system, health-care system, professional system, religious system: each sector stands free of the values of the others. When you go to work, your values are efficiency, productivity. When you go to the health club, your body is everything and your mind means nothing. When you go to a prayer meeting, your body means virtually nothing but your soul means everything.

> It [Philosophy] wasn't a subject to Plato; it was a way.
> —OWEN BARFIELD TALKING TO C. S. LEWIS[21]

Gutenbergers move from one situation to another, one sector to another, and become somewhat different people in each one. When each sector goes its own way, and different values dominate in each domain, there is a dissociation and disintegration that pulls people apart. The word *individual* is a misnomer, because the so-called individual in this system is actually a multi-vidual, a different person depending on which sector she is occupying at the moment. What results is fragmentation, both of societies and of individuals. Everyone is on his own: there is no overarching worldview, no community to fall back on. Just me, on my own, conforming to the sector I happen to find myself in.

"Homes are no longer warm islands of intimacy among the fast-cooling seas of privacy. Homes have turned from shared playgrounds of love and friendship into the sites of territorial skirmishes, and from building sites of togetherness into the assemblies of fortified bunkers. 'We have stepped into our separate houses and closed the door, and then stepped into our separate rooms and closed the door.... The home becomes a multi-purpose leisure centre where household members can live, as it were, separately side by side.'"[22]

Hence the "social construction" of individuals. With nothing to robustly resist these sectors' values, I become socially constructed and defined by external constructs. I become not one individual but a concatenation of individuals. There is the business me, the health-club me, the sports me, the religious me, and the home me. Soon there is no longer an "individual." We are an assemblage of individuals, an assortment of selves, an ensemble of identities,[23] each human being a psychophysical unit that interacts with its sector as a sovereign self without any overarching psychophysical social unities. The modern theologian is self-confined to an academic ghetto, walled round with technical jargon and insulated from any impact on life outside the lecture hall.

It didn't used to be this way. In pre-Gutenberg times we were whole people.

Connected Community vs. Partitioned Individuals

Resurrection, from a biblical perspective, is not about the raising up of individuals, but the resurrection of the community. Of course, that entails the resurrection of its individual members who have been incorporated into the body of Christ. Biblical identity is bound up with the community. Yahweh's covenant was with the people, not just with individuals. The promise of resurrection is to the body of Christ, which is the church, not just to individuals.

The Gutenberg world has trouble with such apple thinking. It is far more comfortable considering a single component (a section of orange) than trying to take into account the whole (biting into an apple). Like the scientist who explained kissing as a craving for salt, an orange thinks of the world not as a mystery but as a machine. Whether it was a body of knowledge or a Bible, the orange privileged the critical method of slice and dice. The orange created a *Good Housekeeping* world where one of its most fundamental principles was "a place for everything and everything in its place." The shift from mechanical to organic involves more than just enriching theological language with biological borrowings. It is a completely different way of living.

In the Gutenberg world, knowledge became more and more orangish: specialized, segmented, reduced to thinner and tinier slices. Every specialty came to boast its own subspecialty, each with its own vocabulary, professional society, body of literature. A physicist, who is a specialist of a scientist, now has innumerable subspecializations such as "astrophysicist" or "plasma physicist" or "superstring physicist." Each specialization creates a world of discrete subspecialties, silo pits where you end up talking to other people in your subspecialty. The isolation of cubby holes, cubicles, disciplines, and specializations is so severe, so searing to the soul, that it renders hollow all protests against social media that accuse it of being pretend, virtual, or self-involved. Before a Gutenberger can criticize a Googler for networking with scores of people who are never seen, he needs first to climb out of his superspecialized silo.

Silos serve to keep people separate from those who are different from them. Silos lead to the false belief that to be acceptable you must be similar. But history has shown that building and maintaining silos at the expense of connection and community does far more harm than good. Wrongs committed by one society against another are still being avenged hundreds of years later, as siloed ethnic groups stoke the fires of memory and hatred toward other siloed groups. Religious factions war against one another. And a lot of us turn off the television in the weeks leading up to an election, to avoid the constant venom released against political opponents.

St. Paul went to great length to establish the metaphor of a body as the church of Christ, the representative of Christ on earth after he ascended. A body is interconnected, interrelated, of a piece. It has component parts with specific functions, to be sure. But the parts are all in touch with one another.

The body of Christ is much closer to resembling an apple than an orange.

Interactives

1. One of the brain's most stunning innovations is its ability to look deeply into the future. But it's only a very small part of the brain that does this, and a largely unused one. How good are you at the knack of treating the future as the present? Who in your church or community is good at this?

2. One of the raps on TGIF Culture is that if a Googler doesn't like something, then it's not true. In other words, it has to be true "for me." Is this a fair criticism? Why or why not? How do we help people understand that some things can be beautiful, good, and true, although they might think of them as ugly, bad, and lies, and vice versa?

3. The intimate relationship between technology and nature was revealed in a comment by an executive of TWA who was a passionate environmentalist.

He also was a pilot who made somewhat of a name for himself because of his skill at flying. On a solo flight over the Rocky Mountains in 1938, Charles Lindbergh mused about his reaction: "I owned the world that hour as I rode over it…free of the earth, free of the mountains, free of the clouds—yet how inseparably I was bound to them."[24]

4. Whether you are a Googler or a Gutenberger, there are times when you are living cross-culturally. So it's handy to be able to speak a second language. If you are a Gutenberger, invite some Googlers to your group and see what Gutenberger expressions and assumptions they are familiar with. Ask if they know how to use a slide rule, if the acronyms VHF and UHF mean anything to them, or if they know the origin of the expression "to dial a phone." See if they ever have listened to music on an AM radio or an eight-track tape, and how they respond to these idioms: "his needle is stuck in a deep groove" and "please turn in your hymnal to…" If you are a Googler, invite some Gutenbergers to your group and try them out on social-media terminology, such as Interwebs, hashtag, epic fail, FTW, Rickroll, pwned, and "It's Facebook official."

Trading the Orange for an Apple

Why Settle for a Partitioned Existence When You Can Enjoy a Life That Is Whole?

The best thing to do is to make the puzzle bigger.

—Dutch writer Harry Mulisch

Social media is a term that means "community." We have focused so orangishly on the component parts that we've given little attention to connections and couplings. And the whole has all but been forgotten. Silvia Thrupp, in a 1958 editorial that launched the journal *Comparative Studies in Society and History,* wrote these words: "Confronted by a choice between possible error through insularity, and probable superficiality through spreading his operations, a sound scholar would prefer to stay in his corner."[1] Albert Einstein liked to say that if you can't solve a problem, make it bigger, not smaller. In other words, think more holistically, think larger, think more organically, and obtain more perspectives. When God gets bigger, life's problems get smaller.

Jesus is mystery, not equation. Add him up, and you still don't have it. He didn't come to earth so you could use him to prove a point. He is the point.

Gutenbergers often missed the point. The Gutenberg world couldn't see the forest for the branches. They failed to see that when you chop up wildlife areas, you are destroying the animals that depend on whole ecosystems for life. They failed to see that when you chop up the sixth-century 450x90-foot hand-knotted Bahârestân Persian carpet of Khosrow into thirty pieces (as the Arabs did in the seventh century as special trophies of victory), you don't have thirty masterpiece carpets, but thirty fraying, decaying fragments.[2] We became so orangish that we couldn't even eat an apple whole, but needed an apple slicer-corer that did its best work when it turned an apple into an orange.

The orange world (and the orange church) produced people who were denatured and denurtured, with disconnected selves, compartmentalized psyches, and an acute case of versitis. Say something I disagree with and I'll quote a verse that proves you wrong. An orange world (and church) segmented everything and lived in separate silos—and never the grain shall meet.

But Googlers have no interest in silos, or in proving you're wrong so they can feel right, or in basing their identity on how they are different from someone else. Googlers are moving beyond silo-based, or what I call "silo-solo" learning, and are yearning for an apple church that is whole again with cross-hemisphere interaction.

Oranges That Have Navels

One of the greatest gifts of Brazil to the world, besides the Samba, bossa nova, the Amazon rainforest, and beautiful beaches is a fruit-borne navel. Every navel orange plant in existence comes from genetic clones of a single 1820 mutation in a Brazilian monastery's orchard. Every navel orange also is a conjoined twin. The protruding navel is part of the shriveled dead twin that had its life sucked out of it by the surviving twin. The stillborn twin is a testimony to the cost of what makes navel oranges our favorites: they are super sweet, easily separated, and seedless.

Navel-gazing was the favorite pastime of the Gutenberger church. Self-love became the subject of faith. Church was a place to go to get one's needs met; Jesus was a person who helped us discover ourselves; religion became self talking to itself. Gutenberg-era technology enabled us to quote ourselves quoting ourselves. Conversion became less metamorphosis than endomorphosis: an interior, sealed-up-inside experience, focused on self and projecting self. Conversion to Jesus meant less that lives are expanding outward to touch others and more a process of lives circling inward to embrace themselves. The "principle mission" of the church became "to foster the conditions for the self-realization and fulfillment of each and every person and for the full flowering of nature."[3] Intimacy turned into what the word becomes when you break it down: "into me I see."[4] In a navel church, like a navel world, there is no world beyond itself.

Five Orange Fallacies

The problem with navel-orange churches is the same problem that navel oranges have. Or I should say, the same five problems.

First, they are so sweet they can create sugar highs and diabetic comas. Gutenbergers loved the sweetness so much that they froze it into concentrate, which condensed so much sugar in high doses that a big glass of orange juice is no longer seen as healthy. It's time for the church to look up from its navel, past its narcissism, and cast its eye over God's mission in the world. (A van driver once told me he could no longer attend what he called "lollipop churches.")

Second, the cost of super-sweetness is high: the lives of family and friends. When you're concerned only about yourself, and you place yourself in the center of the universe, the cost on those around you is enormous. I often talk about the cultural movement beyond narcissism to solipsism. The ancients had another way of portraying it. There is a movement in Greek tragedy from *koros* (pride in oneself) to *hubris* (fixation on oneself) to *ate* (identifying oneself with God). *Ate* is a character's final fatal flaw.

A hill-walker was impressed on noticing several circles on trees with a bullet hole dead center. Meeting the marksman, he commented on his skill. "It's easy," said the man. "I just shoot and then paint the circle." We judge ourselves by our own standards, and then marvel at how wonderful we are.

Third, without seeds navel oranges and navel churches can't reproduce. And the worst crisis any species can have is a reproduction crisis. Orange churches teach people to have faith in themselves, when it's faith in God and who God is that lies at the heart of the good news. You can't reproduce faith in yourself. Jesus didn't say, "Your self-esteem has made you well."

William James popularized the term *self-esteem* in his book *The Principles of Psychology* (1890).[5] James's thesis was simple: the more you achieve your goals, the more your self-esteem rises; the less you achieve your goals, the more your self-esteem drops. We have reversed that meaning. Now the belief is that the higher our self-esteem, the more we think we will achieve our goals, and vice versa. We are *so* far from the original concept of self-esteem, which was a measurement of the reality of our professional life.

There is another reason navel-love can't reproduce. Orange churches are stunted grown-ups or "grups."[6] Stunted orange churches have never reached puberty. They have not feasted on a strong enough diet to mature and procreate. British broadcaster Michael

Bywater has made the case that baby boomers are still babies living in spoiled babyhood. "Birth rates…have been falling for years…[because] we are so well entrenched in our infantilised self-obsession that we surely have no room for real babies."[7] In 1865 a Methodist minister named Rev. A. McKechnie wrote a tract called "Sugar Plums for Big Babies." Here is how it began: "There are more big babies in the world than those who are wrapped in swaddling clothes, rocked in cradles, carried in arms, or dandled on nurses' knees. To be a man does not consist merely in being a full grown body."[8]

Fourth, the cost of compartmentalization is to make Christianity into something "spiritual." Christianity is in truth the least spiritual of all religions. It is not something one can compartmentalize into the sexy "spiritual" category alongside intellectual, moral, philosophical, and social. Christian spirituality is totalitarian.[9] Jesus asks for *all* of our lives, not just a "spiritual" segment. Catholic historian Robert Orsi makes this case forcefully:

> So "spirituality," in authoritative singular like "religion," often presents itself as discovery and recovery while it functions in fact to fabricate particular forms of "traditional" religious practice tolerable to modern religious sensibilities, liberal or conservative. Paying homage to history on one level (who in these historicist days would simply dismiss the relevance of historical setting?) "spirituality" severs religious idioms from their precise locations in the past, then posits an essential identity among these deracinated "spiritual" forms, on the one hand, and between the present and the past, on the other, obliterating difference. "Spirituality" does so without giving an account of the reasons for its selections, moreover, masking the fact that it is making any selections at all, authorizing a new canon while pretending to be surveying an established "tradition." I applaud the work of scholars of Western spirituality in challenging such claims to the authority and prestige of a fictitious past.[10]

Fifth, navel churches have trouble reproducing, in part, due to the prevalence of versitis. This is an ailment that causes Gutenbergers to think of Scripture as a long series of verses, and to consider each verse as a stand-alone statement. They fail to adequately weigh the broader themes being dealt with. In plucking verses, they often miss the bigger meaning of Scripture.

English translations of the Bible are almost always subdivided and numbered into chapters and verses, breaking the flow of the narrative. Of course, there is a place for verse. I have said already that I love poetry and regret that Googlers are not more attuned to it. There are arguably two finalists for the title "Finest Poem of the First World War." Both were written in the trenches by British soldiers later killed in combat just months before the war ended. The most famous of the two was penned by Wilfred Owen, whose *"dulce et decorum est"* begins with two lines that have inspired thousands of students' essays: "Bent double, like old beggars under sacks, / Knock-kneed, coughing like hags, we cursed through sludge."[11]

> World is crazier and more of it than we think....
> The drunkenness of things being various.
> —LOUIS MACNEICE[12]

The second candidate was written by Isaac Rosenberg, whose "Break of Day in the Trenches" would get my vote.[13] Rosenberg was an artist and an engraver as well as a poet. Beyond his famous poem, a statement he made to a friend might shed more light on the navel-orange church than any other personal admission. He confided: "I often find bibles in dead men's clothes and I tear the parts out I want and carry them about with me."[14]

This is exactly what the navel church did to the Bible (and to life). We turned the Bible into an orange. We cut it up into manageable bites called chapter and verse, and this became the alien template on which we feasted on the Word. But the Bible wasn't written in chapters and verses. That's what King James did to the Scriptures. (Okay, really John Calvin. But that's another story.) The Bible was written in songs, poems, letters, stories, histories. Sadly, Gutenberger Christians were not given a chance to learn the Bible as it was written but only as verse-length segments.

When you lift out a musical phrase from its context and play it, musicologists like to call this "bleeding chunks." Because of our orangish obsessions, when Gutenbergers picked up the Bible they less picked up a corpus of truth than bleeding chunks. In an orange world, to verify is to versify, and to versify is to pin down and silo God's Spirit. Gutenbergers were taught to read "against the text" in a laudable attempt to place the Scriptures in their social, economic, and historical context. But when you play deity and devil and all you do is read against the grain, you break the text's power over the reader. In other words, in seeking to unmask its face and empty its authors' bag of tricks, you treat the Bible more as an object than a subject. Most of my biblical study in seminary was in service to the cause of canonical unmaskings and interpretive interests.

D. H. Lawrence wrote something about the novel that applies more to the Scriptures: "The novel is the highest example of subtle inter-relatedness that man has discovered.... If you try to nail anything down, in the novel, either it kills the novel, or the novel gets up and walks away with the nail."[15] The Bible has been walking away with our nails ever since we began trying to "nail it down."

It is time to do some apple theology, and to bring apples and oranges back into relationship. It's time we rediscovered the whole of the apple. You bite into an apple and taste skin, meat, seeds, core. Our future depends on our rediscovery of an apple approach to life without leaving behind our orangish accomplishments.

After all, orange and apple are roommates in our brain. Learning, like archaeology, may or may not involve digging things up or taking things apart. Even Albert Einstein admitted: "My understanding of the fundamental laws of the universe did not come out of my rational mind [i.e., left brain]."[16] An orange world was left-brain dominant. In an orange world, the right brain was about as welcome as a pork chop at Passover. In fact, the church learned to play whack-a-mole with any sign of right-brained activity. Wallop that intuition and initiative! Wham those emotions! Anesthetize those aesthetics!

And we wonder, *Where have all the artists gone?*

What Gutenbergers think is a no-brainer is really a half-brainer. The cleavage in the head is a cleavage in the heart as well. There is a schism within every Gutenberg soul. But it's also a schism in the soul of the Gutenberg church. If the church has only half a brain, I have to say it's the wrong half. Jesus is more right-brained than left-brained; he's more artist than engineer, more storyteller than didact, more global thinker than hairsplitter. The church's failure to tell stories in a culture that talks in stories is a story in its own right.

As much as the past belonged to left-brainers, the future belongs to right-brained people. Neil Cole, Joe Myers, Robert Dale, Frank Viola, Alan Hirsch, Wolfgang Simson, Bob Roberts, and many others are giving a twenty-first-century church the conceptual tools by which to dream into being organic communities. But they are not the first to show Christians how to see the church as an organic, developing body within an organic, changing society. Just read Thomas Cranmer or Richard Hooker, the sixteenth-century founders of Anglicanism.

It is important to end this chapter with a reminder that God gave us two brains for a reason. Hear the words of historian Iain McGilchrist, who wrote the definitive book on this subject: "I do not wish to leave the impression that it might be a good thing if the entire population had a left-hemisphere stroke."[17] God designed us to live out of both sides of our brain, just as Jesus did.

Socrates (469–399 BCE) was known for speaking what was on his heart and mind, for bringing the apple and the orange together. Socrates's student Plato, with his ideal types, divorced the left brain from its marriage with the right and accelerated the orange assault on the apple that has had such an insidious influence in history. Jesus combated the orange-dominant way of thinking both in his life and his teaching. And Socrates, using plain, unvarnished language that everyone could understand, moved the human soul by telling the whole truth.

Here are the charges leveled at Socrates by the political establishment for upsetting the apple cart and telling the truth in rational and logical—but passionate—terms: "Socrates, you are disloyal to the state, you are corrupting the minds of the young, irreligious, a complete atheist because the things we call gods you say are no gods, like the sun and the moon."[18]

Socrates was given a choice: turn down his heat and compromise the truth; mix some of the truth of God with the lies of the system. Then he could survive till a ripe old age. But Socrates replied with this speech:

> Men of Athens, I honor and love you, but I shall obey God rather than you and while I have life and strength I shall never cease from the practice and teaching of philosophy, exhorting anyone whom I meet.... I believe that no greater good has ever happened in the state than my service to God. I would have you know that if you kill a person like me, you will be injuring your-selves more than you can injure me.[19]

The whole-brained life has its challenges and challengers. But if you want the whole Truth, you invest in it, no matter the cost. Lifting up of mere truths can kill the spirit. But lifting up of Truth draws us to God and gives life to the soul.

Jesus was not more apple than orange because he was employing a strategy, like Paul's, to be all things to all people. Nor was he more apple because he lived on earth in premodern times, when the worldview and life-ways were holistic. Nor did he adopt the pattern of his culture and era in order to "relate to the masses," or to better convey truth to his audiences.

He was Truth, the Reality behind all realities, and he conveyed God's kingdom by being God incarnate. The Last Adam was what the First Adam failed to be: whole, perfect, complete, mature. Jesus, "the human one" (best translation of *the Son of Man*), was the human that God created us to be before the stain of sin and rebellion rendered us flawed and incomplete.

Jesus was both apple and orange. The "mind of Christ" is whole-brained, just as the soul of Christ is whole-souled. The church needs both brains if it is to personate Christ in a world of impersonation and impersonators. My burden in this book is for Gutenbergers to release the reins of power so that Googlers will not be forced to find God outside the orange world of partitioned faith. It is time to unite the two so long divided—for orange to be wed with apple. Until and unless that happens, I hold out little hope for vital, organic, growing Christianity in the Western church.

Interactives

1. Max Beerbohm once said of Oxford and the tenaciousness of its traditions, it's "that curious little city where nothing is ever born nor anything ever quite dies."[20] Does this sound like your church? What is being born? What is dying? What are your church's most tenacious traditions?

2. Discuss the portrayal of "new media" by Dan Brown, available at www.youtube.com/watch?v=RXdVa87CKXY.

3. The president of USAmerica had this to say about certain technology: "With iPods and iPads; and Xboxes and PlayStations—none of which I know how to work—information becomes a distraction, a diversion, a form of entertainment, rather than a tool of empowerment, rather than the means of emancipation."[21] Discuss President Barack Obama's dismissal of social media, as stated in his Hampton University commencement address. How does it fit with his embrace of social media in his presidential campaign?

4. Digital technology lets us click, drag, cut, paste, and post, shoring fragments instantly and frictionlessly. We all are electronic collagists now. Where else in Googler Culture do you see evidence of this collage phenomenon?

5. Why is old wisdom constantly being rediscovered rather than reinforced and forwarded? Is wisdom less something we inherit than something we must discover for ourselves? If so, why can't we learn from other people's journeys? Is there nothing that can spare us from the pain of having to learn everything from scratch? Discuss.

PART V

—

Facebook

12

CLOUD AND FIRE

God Appears Day and Night
but Not Always the Same Way

Technology…the knack of so arranging the world that you
don't have to experience it.

—SWISS PLAYWRIGHT AND NOVELIST MAX FRISCH

When God appears, clouds roll in and fire breaks out. The cloud and the fire are symbols of the permeability between this world and the next.

The cloud was present at the dedication of the Jerusalem temple, and on Mount Sinai, and while Moses (and God) led the Exodus. It was there at Mount Tabor during the Transfiguration. Isaiah said that when the Messiah comes, "God will bring back the ancient pillar of cloud."[1]

In our day, The Cloud is the future of IT (information technology). Or more accurately, The Cloud is a technology tornado that will alter the landscape of human life. When your digital device connects to The Cloud, it can boast near-infinite resources and storage. To try to quantify this, think of your cell phone as the Library of Congress.

Long before The Cloud was even imagined, we were given cloud power. It's called the "great cloud of witnesses,"[2] the "communion of saints," the solidarity of souls, the wisdom of the ancients. When we live in that cloud environment, that cloud of knowing and unknowing, and when we connect to that cloud cycle, we have an almost unlimited supply of riches and resources to help us move into the future.

Most Gutenbergers think of the cloud of witnesses either as theoretical (an interesting idea, and it's in the Bible so they try to believe it) or as immediate and physical (watch what you do and say, folks from your church are sure to find out). Neither approach is helpful or accurate. If the witnesses exist only in theory, what's the point? And if they exist only in the same church sanctuary with you, what makes it a great, ancestral, longstanding, time-spanning cloud? It's just you and your fellow Methodists or Presbyterians or Lutherans sitting around on a Sunday morning. It could just as easily be the Kiwanis.

Googlers don't approach the "cloud of witnesses" truth as an interesting idea or novel theory. They apply it to their lives, nearly every waking moment. How? Through social networking. Facebook can be a digital form of the "great cloud of witnesses."

HOLY FIRE OR UNHOLY ZEAL?

But remember, in God's dealings with people, the pillar of cloud by day came with the pillar of fire by night. Like the cloud, fire is a universal symbol of divine energy and divine presence. Try to find a religious tradition that does not grant sacred significance to fire. In Christian tradition, John baptized with water, but Jesus baptized with fire: "He shall baptize you with the Holy Ghost, and with fire."[3] The Holy Spirit is the Fire-Giver, the Fire-Starter who fires up the church when it falls asleep or slips into a stupor. Every culture needs a baptism of fire and a continual salting of life with fire.

One of the most important tasks of life? Keep the fire burning.

In ancient cultures, the most important thing a household did was to never let the fire go cold. In rural Korean cultures the same ancestral fire burned for centuries, and when they moved they took the fire of the forefathers with them. When your fire went out, it was thought, you lost your connection with heaven. Would that Christians were as careful about tending spiritual fire as these ancients were careful about natural fire. We are to nourish the spiritual fire, and we do that by prayer, obedience, mission, devotion, and study.

Holy fire is warming. In the words of the nineteenth-century New England poet Lucy Larcom: "If the world seems cold to you, / Kindle fires to warm it."[4] How many fires will you kindle today with the flint of faith? How many will you douse with a wet blanket of reluctance and dead doctrine? Or will you be selfish with your fire like Peter, who sat by the fire warming himself?[5] Holy fire is not the fire that devours everything in its path, but fire that draws people in closer to get warm and to find more light.

But too many churches have been reduced to rubble by the wrong fire, by fires that leave behind charred walls and blackened stumps and scorched souls. Check out the websites of self-proclaimed "watchtowers" (a.k.a. ODMs). You will see how many Christians are using social media to stoke fires with a form of zeal Christ will not own.

Every well-known Christian author or speaker on the conference circuit is harassed by hate sites. In fact, it's now almost a badge of distinction among speakers. "How many hate sites do you have?" These hate sites operate out of a culture of complaint that is

Adventures in Googler Orthodoxy

Jesus recruited participants, not observers. He said to James and John, "Follow me," not, "Come, follow my teachings." I don't discount orthodoxy, but orthodoxy without orthopraxy requires orthopedics. There is a reason there are no bleachers in the kingdom of God.

Here are three suggestions for making your faith move with a musculo-skeletal system:

1. Be truthful. Truth informs and inspires, then faith acts. Find a truth from a biblical metaphor or story that you will enact this week. Afterward, discuss the outcome with a friend. God's truth moves, and it moves us.

2. Be intuitive. Exercise your muscles of intuition. Trust the leading of the Holy Spirit as much as you trust the well-thought-out plan. Ask God to give you direction with Jesus as your compass. If the intelligence of nature can bring a bird across six thousand miles of land and sea to arrive at the mission of San Juan Capistrano every March 19, think what the intelligence of the divine can do. When you feel a nudge, act in accordance and move in that direction. Even if it feels awkward.

3. Be helpful. Nothing says "authentic Christian" more loudly to a cynical world than a disciple who goes out of her way to help someone in need.

firmly set in the "fault" default. When ODM bloggers find a phrase that is used in a way they don't approve of, or catch an author quoting a person they don't agree with, that is sufficient reason for launching an online attack. It's as if the writer or speaker were a swarming invasion of Amalekites. "Utterly destroy all that they have, and spare them not; but slay both man and woman, infant and suckling, ox and sheep"[6]

I call the ODMs "online doctrine mafia" since they act in ways that make even the book of Judges look like a Sunday school picnic. Of course, a no-fault default setting, which holds no one accountable, is almost as bad as a fault default. There needs to be critique and correction and discrimination in the body of Christ. We need to air and debate our disagreements over both ideas and actions. But when we critique brothers and sisters in the body of Christ, it ought to be done in a spirit of gentleness, meekness, integrity, and humility. Perhaps we need a mercy default where we cringe when criticizing others, where we get quickly tired of finding fault, and where we focus more on what we can learn from people we disagree with than what divides us. There is danger in a world where everyone feels entitled to wear the badge of the doctrine police. It is the fear of ridicule and accusation that can prevent Christians from listening for God. There can fall over the body of Christ a chilling of creativity, a shunning of partnerships, and a pall of clichéd repetition.

How We Know God's Fire

Holy fire is enlightening. You see things and understand things better than ever before. One of the greatest things you see is yourself. In some areas, you are much worse than you thought; in others, you're much better than anyone knows or thinks you are.

Holy fire is cleansing. The Holy Spirit's baptism is the purifying fire that burns up the chaff of sin, pride, and selfishness. The Holy Spirit's power either blesses or burns. The Holy Spirit baptizes the wheat, but the fire burns the chaff. The aspects that don't show life, that have dried out, are what burns. And what is good and green with life-bearing fruit and wet with the water of repentance doesn't burn.

But how do you know when you're green enough? How much life is enough life?

In Old Norse poetry of the Viking Age, a "skald" was a member of a group of poets from Iceland or Scandinavia who specialized in heroic verse, especially as it related to the exploits of the king. The skaldic term for gold was "fire in the water." Even though Facebook brings up the rear in the TGIF acronym, it is the golden thread, the "fire in the water," the liquid fire that ties Googler Culture together. It is the gold standard of social media.

Facebook is a digital form of fresh fire that can help make fire again in a world drowning in fizz and froth. It is hard to see how anyone can stir up a spiritual firestorm in the culture without being struck by bolts of Facebook lightning. Can you imagine doing ministry the last five hundred years and getting away with "Sorry, I don't do books"? Can you imagine doing ministry in the next five years and getting away with "Sorry, I don't do Facebook"?

> I'd rather have a rectal examination on live TV by a
> fellow with cold hands than have a Facebook page.
> —Actor George Clooney[7]

Facebook might also be named Flatbook. It has the capability of flattening the world.[8] Facebook can burn to the ground the barriers that keep people apart. The 800 million people (and counting) who use Facebook are not there to recruit members to their silo; they are there to connect with a diverse, international, democratic array of individuals. Sure, there are interest groups and pages that relay news on musicians, authors, movements, and a lot more. But check a person's list of interests and you will see a startlingly diverse array of connections.

Nowhere else on earth can you connect with this many people, this many hobbies and causes and things you are curious about or fully committed to. Could God be using Facebook to make the high places low and the low places flat? Might God use Facebook to set the world on fire and to light the revival fires?

The Facebook Cloud

It can almost be said: if you're online, you're on Facebook. Like learning to play the cymbals, it's not so much *how* as *when*.

Ford Motors revealed its 2011 models on Facebook. It didn't happen first at an auto show; it happened online. It appeared not in a cavernous convention center, but on your cell phone or computer screen. The most popular site on the Internet is no longer Google; it's Facebook. Were Facebook a nation, it would be the third-largest country in the world.

I have a youth-ministry friend who claims that almost overnight, Facebook has become "the most important tool that I own." He may have a couple dozen kids show up on Sunday evening. But during the week he will have Facebook conversations with two or three times that number of kids. He told me about a chat window pop-up from one of his kids who was having trouble at home. "Mom and dad are getting divorced." Suddenly the student's older sister, who was away at college, popped up and joined the conversation. Then my friend realized the parents were about to finalize their decision on the divorce *at that moment*. They were in the other room hashing it out.

This story takes a tragic turn.

The youth-group kid recounted the screaming of the word *divorce* in the next room. The youth-group leader had both sisters online—one who wanted to be at home to help her little sister, the other who couldn't get away from the screaming. When he closed the chat windows after ministering to two kids in the midst of crisis, his text ring went off. A girl was texting him from her car because her best friend's dad had just killed himself. She was driving to the friend's house while asking the youth-group leader, "What do I say?"

A couple hundred million people log on to Facebook each day, 70 percent of whom live outside USAmerica.[9] I predict that soon, every USAmerican citizen at birth will be given a social-media name along with a Social Security number. With social media such as Facebook,[10] our social universe has changed. Compare the social environment of a child born in 1950, or even 1960, or even 1970, with the social environment of a child born today. We're not even on the same planet. As little as ten years ago, half of humanity had never made a phone call and only 20 percent of humanity had regular access to high-speed communications. Today cell phone coverage is available over 90 percent of the globe, and almost 77 percent of the earth's population has a cell phone.[11]

If change is the only certainty, the future looks to be less La-Z-Boy recliner and more adrenaline-pumping roller-coaster ride.

> So far humans have created 500,000 different movies and about one million TV episodes. At least 11 million different songs have been recorded. Chemists have cataloged 50 million different chemicals.... If the current rates of inventiveness continue, in 2060 there will be 1.1 billion unique songs and 12 billion different kinds of products for sale.
> —KEVIN KELLY[12]

For the first time in history, the majority of humanity is connected. In a world of hyperconnectivity, when three-quarters of humanity may be connected by mobile communications by the time you read these words (2012 or later), the amplification of resources and capabilities is exponential. In the words of Australian futurist Mark Pesce, "Hyperconnectivity begets hypermimesis begets hyperempowerment." Or in more accessible language, "After the arms race comes the war."[13]

In other words, the more we use Facebook, the more we find ourselves in the faces of each other and the more we find God in face-to-face interface. French philosopher Jean-Paul Sartre is famous for saying, "L'enfer, c'est les autres" ("Hell is other people").[14] But walking through Sartre's hell (being fully engaged in relationships) is the key that unlocks the gates of heaven. When we don't need each other, we don't need God. If we can't connect with a person who is right here with us, how can we seek out the God whom we cannot see?

Facebook limits me to 5,000 connections, or "friends." But the size of my neocortex, according to Dunbar's number, limits me even more—to only 150 friends. Oxford University anthropologist Robin Dunbar studied social groupings in a variety of contexts, from neolithic villages to modern office environments to Facebook. While social-networking sites allow us to amass more and more relationships, his studies reveal that the number of meaningful friendships is the same as it has been throughout history.[15] People self-organize in groups of around 150 for good reason. This is the optimal number of people you can care about enough to contact at least once a year, and this is the maximum-sized social network where you can know how each friend relates to every other friend.

I can hear the Gutenbergers repeating their claims that social media creates false relationships and imaginary friends, and produces little more than lists of self-obsessed collectors of names in place of real friendship. Gutenbergers don't hesitate to say that virtual relationships are self-deceiving and not just virtually meaningless, but unapologetically, completely without meaning.

Does Facebook create a false notion of friendship? To answer that question, I'll first introduce you to Travis. Then we'll look closely at the concept of paradox.

FACEBOOK FRIEND TRAVIS

I never met Travis, but I think of him as a friend. Maybe he wasn't part of my Dunbar's number, but Gideon Travis Addington was a valued theological sparring partner. I knew his story and tracked his pilgrimage with attention and prayer, especially as he prepared for his first year at seminary. As a smells-bells-chants evangelical Episcopalian with monastic leanings, Travis decided to attend General Theological Seminary (GTS), the oldest seminary of the Episcopal Church. He was nervous about the rigors of graduate school and especially its outmoded learning models. But I assured him that his spiritual appetites and intellectual agility would find in a seminary community the ideal weather for growing a soul.

On December 10, 2009, Travis posted on his Facebook page that he was going to Outback for a steak. (*Unusual for a vegetarian,* I thought.) Anyone who wished to come along was invited to join him. A little later he posted on his blog the song "Here Comes the Sun," the Nina Simone version.[16] He invited people to listen to the song. "Enjoy" was the last word of his blog.

The next day my Facebook friend was one of the ninety people a day who take their own life. One person every fifteen minutes kills him- or herself.[17] For reasons no one fully understands, in the past three decades the number of suicides committed by people age fifteen to twenty-four has tripled. Travis was age thirty demographically, but psychographically he was part of a younger group. There is a cultural syndrome where more teenagers and twentysomethings are dying from suicide than from cancer, heart disease, AIDS, the effects of birth defects, stroke, and chronic lung diseases combined. In a world that seems out of control, suicide is the ultimate act of being in control.

The promise and peril of living in TGIF Culture both come alive in the story of Gideon Travis Addington. Because he was active on Twitter, and was a blogger and Facebook user, I came to know and like him. If it had not been for social media, my life would not have been enriched and enlivened by his presence. Yet for all his Facebooking and tweeting and conversing, there was no evidence of a problem. He never shared with any of his Facebook friends that his heart was breaking, and that inside he was a wreck.

Studies have shown that it takes only *one* friend to stop a suicide. You don't need a dozen friends to come to your rescue. Just one will suffice to speak a word of hope to counter the four biggest reasons for committing suicide, as reflected in suicide notes:

1. unlovability ("I'm worthless.")
2. helplessness ("I'm in over my head"; "My problems are unsolvable.")
3. poor distress tolerance ("I can't stand the way I feel.")
4. perceived burdensomeness ("Everyone would be better off if I were dead." This is the most fatal of the four feelings.)[18]

To my knowledge, not one friend has come forward to say they accepted Travis's invitation to meet at Outback for a steak dinner.

Was I a fake friend to Travis, or does the concept of friendship now include being an influencer or a connector? The CEO of Facebook, Mark Zuckerberg, was also *Time* magazine's 2010 "Person of the Year." This is how he explains the success of Facebook: "The message you get…is actually less important than whom you get it from…. If you get it from someone you trust, you'll listen to it. Whereas if you get it from someone you don't trust, you might actually believe the opposite of what they said."[19] Is he right?

> I believe what happens online is connection—
> not community. People can be vulnerable and
> honest online. At times these online connections
> can be more life-giving than our offline
> relationships, but they are not the same.
> —AUTHOR AND BLOGGER ANNE JACKSON[20]

I recently asked a group of students, "Do you prefer to talk to someone face to face, or on someone's Facebook wall, or over the phone, or by text message?" The overwhelming majority ranked texting at the top of the list, Facebook second, with "face to face" at the bottom. This has massive ramifications for the 90 percent of communication (the nonverbal aspects) that gets lost in a text or post.[21]

FACEBOOK OR FACE TO FACE?

In a Facebook world full of social friends, maybe we need face-to-face personal friends all the more, not less. Maybe the more we use Facebook, the more we hunger for face time and even in-your-face connections. I don't know about you, but pictures of food make me hungry. Someone pointed out that trying to slake your hunger for relationships through social networking is like eating rabbit food (celery, lettuce, carrots) when you're really hungry. You'll feel better in the short term, but hungrier for the real thing in the long run. Sherry Turkle's study of Internet and computer-mediated connectivity concludes that virtual relationships are rather "thin gruel," unsatisfying substitutes for the flesh and blood of the real thing.[22]

But who doesn't like some appetizers on the way to the meat course? Maybe it's both/and, even and/also, not either/or. That is why after Travis died, I made a resolution that I would put a face to every contact in my Microsoft Outlook. This has not been easy or done overnight. I am approaching ten thousand names in my personal Outlook. But to help prevent another tragedy and to turn my contacts into true connections and from there into community, I have in the course of a year made it a personal spiritual discipline to find faces for as many of my contacts as is possible. When each one is downloaded, I breathe a prayer for that person and offer gratitude for his or her presence in my life.

What is sure is this: social media is all about connections.

For much of my Gutenberger life, I have been engaged in the antisocial activity known as reading. There are few pursuits that are more isolating. In a Googler world, being isolated is not a sought-after state of being. Instead, the best way to get ahead in life is through relationships and sociability. Of course, humans have always been social beings. But we are now learning how to be hyper-social beings: connected to (almost) everyone else instantaneously, globally, 24/7.

With the near-omnipresence of social media, our social universe has changed. Most of the world is connected and thankful for it. It's time for Gutenbergers to get over their conviction that relationships are real only when they exist face to face in the physical world. Online relationships may be a different kind of real, but they can be as veritable and valuable in their own way as off-screen, on-site relationships.

It is time for a relationship recalibration.

Interactives

1. How might your church develop a greater sense of the "local"? Efforts are well-known to shop locally and buy locally grown goods. How might you extend "locavore" to more than food: encouraging and learning from local authors, local poets, local musicians, local artists and artisans?

2. Eighty-two percent of people who use the Internet say they go online to socialize. Thirty-one percent use the Internet to shop. More than twice as many users report that socializing—not commerce—is the top reason for going online.[23] Knowing the strength of the urge to acquire and accumulate things, what do these findings tell us about the power of the human drive to connect with other people?

3. Have members of your group share their online habits. Do the findings on Internet use (see question 2) reflect your own use of the Internet? How would you compare your online usage patterns with the following top-ten responses: passing time, educating one's self, connecting with others, researching, sharing, seeking entertainment, staying informed, discussing issues, being part of a community, getting work done?

4. One of the most common criticisms against Facebook is that it feeds narcissism. Has this been your experience? Give examples.

ME AND WE IN THE TGIF WORLD

Is This Really Community
or Just Too Much Information?

The connecting is the thinking.

—PHILOSOPHER WILLIAM JAMES

One of Martin Luther's favorite Latin phrases was *Crux probat omnia,* "the cross is the test of everything"[1] that deserves to be called Christian. Luther's signature symbol, which is ubiquitous in Germany, was a black cross embedded in a red heart surrounded by a white rose. When you make the sign of the cross, which brings together the vertical with the horizontal, you are symbolizing the paradoxy of orthodoxy, the union of all opposites.

It is inaccurate to imply that Christian theology comes to light in a steady unveiling and shows itself to be a straight-line revelation of truth. The far more accurate image is that Christian theology is a parabolic, harmonious oscillation of truth. The stone that the builders rejected has become the chief cornerstone.[2] The Bible brings opposites together in parabolic fashion. It is heaven and earth, God and humanity, light amid the darkness, easy yokes and light burdens. This is not a completely rational, linear process of thinking. You might even call it, as some have done, "thinking in circles."[3] Paradox is the unique essence of Christian thought.

Along with Walt Whitman, Christians can comfortably hold in the mind a series of ideas that would appear to contradict one another. For example, in the fourth century there were two competing Christs. The Antiocheans stressed a human Jesus, "tempted as we are"; while the Alexandrians believed in a divine Jesus, majestic and transcendent. Which one was right? Christian theology says both.

The paradoxical nature of TGIF Culture is reflected in the triumph of the well curve over the bell curve.[4] Instead of the massification of culture into big middles, there is a mitosis of the middle and a bimodal distribution toward both ends. "The big get bigger, the small survive, and the mid-sized are squeezed out."[5] For the past couple of decades, the market in the middle has almost vanished. Mass media, mass audiences, and mass-market entertainment are vanishing.

> [Our] impatience with debate, conflict, ambivalence,
> polysemy, paradox…is at heart an impatience with
> learning, and with learning about our learning.
> —ARCHBISHOP OF CANTERBURY ROWAN WILLIAMS[6]

In fact, in book after book and classroom after classroom, I have argued that every Christian must learn how to put on the spectacles of paradox and become a paradoxalist. It's precisely this paradoxy that has been the generator of creative tensions in Christian faith. We have inward (conscience) and outward (lawful obedience), humility and honor, forgiveness and retribution, giving of oneself in love and giving of oneself in defense of one's neighbor. All creativity is the colliding and docking of diverse ideas into stable combinations.

In the Gutenberg world, falsehood was defined as a logical contradiction. A false assertion was not categorized as something that denied God and God's truth. Instead, it was an assertion that violated human logic. The offended party was not God but humanity. It was widely believed, especially in the West, that A cannot equal both B and C without A first being altered in the process. Water cannot be both steam and ice. An egg cannot be both an aspiring chicken and breakfast.

This is an area where the contrast is clear between Gutenbergers and Googlers. In the TGIF world, the understanding of a truth demands that it be a logical contradiction. To stay spiritually aloft, you have to be as grounded as possible. Only those rooted deep grow tall. To fly and be free, you need to be like a kite, tethered to your Maker. Just as a swing is propelled by two simultaneous actions—leaning back and kicking forward—so TGIF Culture swings by the leaning back of *ressourcement* (a return to the sources) and the kicking forward of *aggiornamento* (updating).

JESUS, THE FIRST GOOGLER?

The early working title for this book, or I should say the playing title, was *Googlier Than Thou*. If you are a native to TGIF Culture, you almost certainly are much more a Googler than I am. You probably have more followers on Twitter than I do, and more people who "like" your Facebook page, and more comments on your latest blog post. This is not a race or a contest. But if it were, Jesus would be the winner. He was very possibly the first Googler. Think about the paradox of truth in TGIF Culture. Jesus was God incarnate, a perfect human living in the stench of earth. Fully human, fully God.

Jesus's life illustrates that the sweet spot is not in the middle, but in holding both extremes together. The goal is not to balance competing opposites, but to make opposites dance with one another. Jesus did it again and again: Lion/Lamb, Alpha/Omega, come live/come die, first/last, Prince of Peace/wields sword, emptying/filling, exalted/humbled, saint/sinner, One/Three, transcendence/immanence, dove (innocence)/serpent (wisdom), East (intuition)/West (reason). If you're not hearing Jesus in surround sound, you're not hearing Jesus.

Digital technologies are intrinsically both/and, or more accurately, and/also. Technologies throw us together, Shane Hipps has argued, but at the same time they can divide and disembody us.[7]

> Christianity is strange. It bids man to recognise
> that he is vile, and even abominable, and bids
> him want to be like God. Without such a
> counterweight, his exhaltation would make him
> horribly vain or his abasement horribly abject.
> —PASCAL'S *Pensées*[8]

If you want to see what happens when you deprive your kids of social media, ask deposed Egyptian president Hosni Mubarak. Egyptian kids with cell phones and keyboards brought down a dictator in just eighteen days.[9] The Jasmine Revolution of 2011 might one day be called the TGIF Revolution. The TGIF generation has found its voice, and the Arab world is awakening. The protesters used social networks to communicate with one another. And beyond that, they used social media to provide the world with an apologetic for revolution and to tell their story before big governments and government-controlled or -regulated media could spin the story.

"Facebook and Twitter pulled the Internet trigger that turned out hundreds of thousands of protesters in Egypt and the Middle East and tens of thousands in Wisconsin and our Midwest," wrote the founder of *USA Today,* Al Neuharth.[10] The Arab Spring assault on (and even collapse of) a number of Middle Eastern and North African regimes is in part a product of the growing gap between the antiquated worldviews of Gutenbergers and the cosmopolitan outlooks of Googlers. "We were always looking at photos, but were never in the picture. Now the photo is us," claimed Egyptian protester Walid Rashed.[11]

The TGIF Revolution in the Middle East and the Japanese earthquake/tsunami are cases in point as to how media mediate meaning. When the Red Cross announced it would no longer be able to accept inquiries to locate missing or displaced family and friends in Japan, Google set up its People Finder page to allow anyone to type in the name of a person they were looking for in the wake of the tsunami. Posts and connections on Facebook walls fueled the desire for change in the Middle East. But the lasting images were crowded faces in Cairo's Tahrir Square, all played out in the world of social media before traditional news outlets broadcast the story. Global citizens increasingly turn to Twitter for fast-breaking news, Google for pictures and information, iPhones for contacts, and Facebook for answers to questions.

"The greatest invention of the nineteenth century," according to English mathematician and philosopher Alfred North Whitehead, "was the invention of the method of invention."[12] Whitehead was right in his thought but wrong in his valuation of what that "invention" was, which he thought was organized research and development. The real method of invention is the bringing together of opposites. Every study of creativity ends at the same place: in a loop. The secret of creative thought is for the mind to go parabolic by juxtaposing difference. As Matt Ridley put it, "at some point in human history, ideas began to meet and mate, to have sex with each other."[13] Ideas—especially contrasting ones—appear in several places at once. They're in the air and they breed virally. The key is to create a feedback loop that can shape their development.[14]

PARADOXICAL FAITH

The freedom for creative space to form in the midst of opposites is the secret weapon of Christianity. Where is Jesus to be found? "In the midst." To paraphrase a familiar text, where two or three different people or different ideas are gathered together, there is the divine in the midst of them. Creativity is at core a linking of unrelated things, which is why creative types (poets, musicians, writers, artists) are six to seven times more likely to experience synesthesia than others. Social networks such as Facebook help to trigger creativity mash-ups by randomizing our lives so that conceptual collisions can occur. TGIF Culture is generative because it is constantly jarring us with the introduction of contradictions, oppositions, and exposure to unrelated concepts.

And where does that leave the church and its mission? The intense imagining of new social links is the R&D of the church. But first there must be a spirit of freedom that invites an openness to new combinations and jarring juxtapositions. Both Facebook and Twitter have birthed third-party ecosystems of apps and services that help shoulder the load of innovation. In other words, TGIF Culture creates an ecosystem of imagination and improvement and cultivates collective intelligence.

> The creative person is not a special type of being;
> every being is a special type of creator.
> —ATTRIBUTED TO ERFURT MYSTIC MEISTER ECKHART

Every week I receive thousands of texts and e-mails and sometimes even a letter in the mail. Hardly ever does a week pass when someone doesn't ask me to join them in denouncing something. Why do so many people support campaigns to oppose things, to smear a preacher or teacher or a teaching? Or even a person's offhand comment? In doing these things, the critics indirectly are attempting to destroy the person and his ministry. These people see TGIF Culture as a ripe field of battle for defeating the opposition. The problem is, the "opposition" is almost always a fellow Christian.

The attack mentality is Gutenberger. TGIF Culture, at least as it is captured in Facebook, is in favor of "liking" something. It has no built-in template for "disliking." Facebook is on record as being against against. It has said no to negativity.

FROM COMMON SENSE TO COMMONS-SENSE THINKING

TGIF Culture may be returning us to commons-sense thinking after centuries of reliance on common sense. If so, there will be a whole new understanding of what it means to be a body of believers and the "body of Christ."

The democratic notion that every person is born with common sense that can be trusted and put to use is of relatively recent vintage. In fact, the notion of individual common sense is dependent on the acceptance of the concept of individuals existing.

As stated earlier, this was largely a Gutenberg-era invention, with credit given to the King James Bible. The word *self* may have a pedigree dating back to the tenth century, but it didn't convey the meaning it does today. The self as a separate, isolated being grew out of an eighteenth-century idea, when *self* signified what a person was at a particular time—one's nature, character, core identity.

> A simple layman armed with Scripture
> is greater than the mightiest Pope without it.
> —MARTIN LUTHER[15]

Admittedly, the Abrahamic principle of the sanctity of the person was a huge step away from the herd and hive. The next leap forward came with the apostle Paul, whose letters created the frame for the Western portrait of the individual human being, unconditionally precious to God and entitled to love and protection.[16] But even though the individual poked its head periodically above the group from Paul onward, the determining unit of the ancient social order was the family. You cannot find, in fiction or even in diaries from premodern times, the notion of individual human agency and conscience.[17] Families and groups, bound by kinship and covenants, acted as units. The notion of an individual separate from the group, a person with rights and choices in pursuit of a unique identity and cultivating an inner life, is present only in the most elementary ways.

Here's what I mean. John Locke's classic *An Essay Concerning Human Understanding* (1690) defines *self* this way:

> Every one is to himself that which he calls self.... For...consciousness always
> accompanies thinking, and it is that which makes every one to be what he
> calls self, and thereby distinguishes himself from all other thinking beings;...
> it is by the consciousness it has of its present thoughts and actions, that it is
> self to it self now, and so will be the same self, as far as the same consciousness
> can extend to actions past or to come.[18]

See how Locke's thinking on the "self" clarifies the matter? Neither do I.

If the unit of the premodern world was the family, the unit of the Gutenberg world was the individual. The technology of printing fostered the notion of a separate self, making difference desirable, as Rousseau's *Confessions* made clear: "I venture to believe that I am not made like any of those who are in existence. If I am not better, at least I am different."[19] Martin Luther's "Here I Stand" individualism led theology to dig down *doctrinally* on the whys of suffering rather than take the hows path of being with one another in our suffering.[20] In the eighteenth century the Scottish Realism movement, or what became known as "common sense philosophy," reassembled the rational Humpty-Dumpty that David Hume had knocked down and assured the individual that there was something God-given inside that could be trusted even more than book learning. The new true north was common sense.

But ever since, individuals have been learning to follow their bliss. And ever since the birth in the West of individualism, the disease of depression (a.k.a. melancholia) lurked in the shadows and spread through Western Europe. (This dates as far back as CE 1600.)[21] One of the great insights of superstar nurse Florence Nightingale was her opposition to private rooms, not on socioeconomic grounds but on psychological ones. In single rooms, patients didn't need to interact with others and could languish alone and unseen. In fact, she proved that patients assigned to single rooms had three times more accidents than those in her Nightingale wards. Without a social community in which to get well, people die, if not of the disease itself then of despair and depression.

TGIF Culture Introduces a New Social Unit

If the unit of the premodern world was the family, and the unit of the Gutenberg world was the individual, the unit of the TGIF world is the network. At its best, this means a rediscovery of our being-in-common, the sense of the village square or town commons. This gets at the new commons-based thinking that moves from the individualism of common sense to the holism of "commons" sense, a sensitivity to our common life together and the things that produce what is good for the village. The Apostles' Creed begins with "I believe." The Nicene Creed begins with "We believe." We need both.

All identity comes from relationship. The notion of a "separate identity" is oxymoronic. I love Ayn Rand's famous slogan: "INDIVIDUALISTS OF THE WORLD, UNITE!"[22] One wonders if this libertarian ever saw the ironic, even comic component to her mantra. We are incomplete in and of ourselves. In the Latin expression *dumitria in incognito,* there is the recognition that to come to complete truth is to know oneself as incomplete, half of a pair. It is only the coming together of the whole, the uniting of the individual parts, that encompasses integrity and truth.

People such as the quantum physicist David Bohm and his implicate theory, or the Hungarian novelist Arthur Koestler and his holon theory, posit levels of reality beyond our thoughts and experiences. If everything is both a whole and a part, if the whole is enfolded within each fragment of space and time, then everything in the universe affects everything else because all are part of the same unbroken whole. Thomas Merton said it another way: "There is in all visible things…a hidden whole-ness."[23] Martin Luther King Jr. described it this way: "Whatever affects one directly, affects all indirectly."[24] Jesus put it like this: "Inasmuch as you did it to one of the least of these…you did it to Me."[25]

> As long as we are on earth, the love that unites
> us will bring us suffering by our very contact
> with one another, because this love is the
> resetting of a Body of broken bones.
> —THOMAS MERTON[26]

In TGIF Culture the "me" is being flipped over (not tossed aside) and read from right to left to rediscover the "we." Indeed, TGIF may be forcing the *me* to discover that it needs the *we* to *be*—to exist and thrive. In his book *The Wisdom of Crowds,* James Surowiecki contends that me's make better decisions when informed by we's than when they make "me" decisions in isolation. This is true even when the decision-making in-dividual is an expert on the matter.[27] As proof that the family can be made stronger by TGIF Culture, a study of college students in Norway found that they get in touch with their parents ten times a week thanks to Skype and social-networking sites. Surprisingly, kids today feel closer to their parents than was true of any generation in the twentieth century.[28] Facebook and other TGIF media do more to build and broaden family ties than quash them.

Unfortunately, the reciprocity and mutuality of we and me is not proving to be an easy rediscovery. The English language is notoriously weak in any "we" words and con-cepts. For example, "we" in Kwaio, a language spoken in the Solomon Islands, has two forms: we as "me and you" and we as "me and someone else other than you." Kwaio has not just singular and plural, but dual and paucal too. English has just "we," but Kwaio has "we two," "we few," and "we many." Each of these has two forms—one inclusive ("we including you") and one exclusive ("we without you"). This level of nuance is impossible in English.

You see the flipping-upside-down of the "me" in three trends in office design, all revolving around a new understanding of "we": (1) open-space offices, (2) nonterrito-riality, and (3) communal meeting areas. The private office is becoming history. Once-coveted exterior offices with panoramic vistas are being converted to common space for meetings, team building, and socializing. Cisco Systems wiped out the cubicles and replaced them with living rooms, lounges, and cafes. Hewlett-Packard (HP) offers employees different themed "neighborhoods" on different floors—a mix of private spaces, small and large conference rooms, lounges, small libraries, quiet zones, and cafes. Depending on the project, HP employees are assigned to a neighborhood instead of an office or cubicle.

To be sure, there are voices that warn that the networked "we" could wipe out the "me." After all, how long have humans struggled with the question, What does it mean to be human? Jaron Lanier's manifesto *You Are Not a Gadget* rails against the anonymizing forces of the web and impugns the collectivism in web culture as a danger to the creative agency of the individual. Once a celebrated pioneer of virtual-reality technology who still defends VR as "the first medium to come along that doesn't narrow the human spirit,"[29] Lanier now has turned on social media to warn of its "hive mind" dangers. For him, the "fake friendship" of Facebook "is just bait laid by the lords of the clouds to lure hypothetical advertisers." For Lanier there is no wisdom of crowds, only groupthink, a cruel mob he dubs "digital Maoism." He wrote: "Anonymous blog comments, vapid video pranks, and lightweight mashups may seem trivial and harmless, but as a whole, this widespread practice of fragmentary, impersonal communication has demeaned interpersonal interaction."[30]

What might all of this mean for the organized church in the West? In her CNN blog, Lisa Miller wrote that she sees digital technology putting an end to church as we know it: "With Scripture on iPhones and iPads, believers can bypass constraining religious structures—otherwise known as 'church'—in favor of a more individual connection with God."[31] Whatever sense of "church home" remains, it is argued, will be a "we" that reflects the interests and causes of the "me."

There are elements of truth in Miller's critique. In the nineteenth century Henry Adams called politics "hatreds"[32] when politics should be a means of securing the common good. TGIF Culture, by making it easy for an isolated individual to communicate with the masses, holds out the possibility of living your entire life in the convenience and comfort of your bubble-wrapped hatreds and causes. It's a lot easier to skewer your opponents when you don't have to risk a face-to-face encounter. In premodern times, village life put you in contact with friends, neighbors, enemies, and critics. You could not avoid the person you owed money to, for instance. A danger of TGIF Culture is its promise of communal life while enabling participants to limit it to a unidimensional "community." But if I never encounter anyone who disagrees with me, I am far from living in a community.

Faith and Finding Who You Are

Christian personhood differs from other understandings of what it means to be a person. A biblical person is a continuum that reaches back into the past and throws forward into the future while extending into the present to embrace people of difference, not just of likeness. A biblical person is both unitive and communitive, to somewhat alter Emil Brunner's useful distinction. The Christian looks for union with God without losing her individual spirit in the divine Spirit. (Michelangelo's God isn't touching Adam, as Brunner liked to point out to distinguish the communionists from the unitists.) But Christians look for a communion with the divine in which individual identity is altered and changed to be more like that of Christ. While there is no sucking of the soul into an undifferentiated divinity, there is a metamorphosis of the me into the image and shape of the triune We.

What I see happening is this: The old concept of a church home is disappearing. It is becoming more personalized and particularized while at the same time more distributed. Individualization and personalization are proceeding apace with globalization. The world's global systems are growing more interconnected as nation-state borders are crumbling, and as new borders based on interests, causes, and personalized content are forming. For example, the highly individualized paper[33] creates a personalized newspaper just for you based on your Twitter followers and what they said was significant, based on the number of their retweets.

The Well That Never Runs Dry

I grew up in the sixties and seventies, a world of superstar orchestra conductors with supersized egos. Two of my favorites were close in name and geography: Leonard Bernstein (New York City) and Leopold Stokowski (Philadelphia). I loved Bernstein for his mane and magic; I loved Stokowski for his flamboyance and daring alterations of the great masters.

One of the Stokowski stories I'll never forget is the time when he was conducting Beethoven's Leonore Overture No. 3, which calls for an off-stage trumpet solo just before the whirlwind coda. Before a standing-room-only audience, Stokowski flawlessly conducted the Philadelphia Orchestra. But when the time came for the off-stage musician to play, there was silence. The back of Stokowski's neck reddened, but he kept on conducting until it was time once again for the off-stage trumpeter to play. Again, only silence. Now Stokowski's face had turned as red as his neck.

When the piece ended, the maestro threw his baton down and charged into the wings. With mayhem in his eyes he looked for the trumpet player. And there he was, where he was supposed to be. But the musician had his arms pinned to his side by a burly security guard who was saying to him, "You can't play that horn here. There's a concert going on!"[34]

God is conducting the orchestra of creation. Each of us has been given an indispensable instrument to play and a song to sing. And how many of us are pinned to the wall, missing in action, because we have allowed guardians of mediocrity and the status quo to silence us?

When my wife and I purchased our home on Orcas Island, there was an old well that was used for outdoor watering. The water was cold and the pipe never failed to bring up water from the shallow but strong aquifer. Then we read a news report about a child from the South falling into an old well, so we decided that while our children were young we would cover our well.

Twenty years passed, and recently we thought it would be good to start drawing water from the well. But when we uncapped it and sucked on the straw, nothing came up. The well was bone dry. It had been fed by underground rivulets that had continued to supply water as long as there was a use for it. But when the well was not used, the rivulets rerouted the water in another direction. We had a dry well not because there was no water, but because the water had not been drawn.

If we do not draw 365 days a year from the Living Water of God's love, our souls will become like a dried-up well. We need to always gather with family and friends to drink it in. Don't cover up the well head of your soul. Taste and see that the Lord is good. Your soul need never run dry.

BLOGATURE AND BLOGARRHEA

The power behind the creation of the universe is the power behind all creativity. TGIF Culture is a hotbed of creativity. The question is, what will benefit most from our newfound creativity? The average mobile phone has more computing capacity than *Apollo 13* had. What moons and stars are we reaching for? The average mobile phone opens doors to the equivalent of the Library of Congress. What masterwork will we produce?

The democratization of social media advances everything from citizen journalism to citizen diplomacy to citizen architecture. What used to be called "the vulgar herd" are now power brokers. The greatest impact of the democratization of TGIF technology, however, may be the amateurization of expertise. *Amateur* comes from the Latin word for "lover" (*amo, amare*). An amateur is someone who engages in a study or sport for the sheer love of it. Love is building an open-source, wiki world out of passion and participation.

> To believe in a God means to see that the facts
> of the world are not the end of the matter.
> —LUDWIG WITTGENSTEIN[35]

Our help is in the name of the Lord…and the hands of amateurs, not professional bureaucrats. After every disaster, hope is inspired by the work of self-organizing samaritans: volunteers, passersby, spontaneous intervention by heroic civilians. Like Deamonte Love, the six-year-old boy who led five toddlers and a baby out of the Katrina flood zone, and Jabbar Gibson, the young man who commandeered an abandoned school bus, drove it to Houston with seventy people crowded aboard, and arrived well in advance of the official convoy.[36]

In many ways, the creativity that empowers amateurs is a return to more premodern modes and models. For example, Augustine, Western Christianity's preeminent Doctor of the Church, was an amateur theologian. He had no training in philosophy or theology, demonstrated horrible Greek language skills, and displayed minimal knowledge of Plato or Aristotle. The difference today is in scale. Airplanes fly only a little faster than they did forty years ago, but everyone is flying. The Internet sends signals a little quicker than a nineteenth-century telegraph, but everyone is Googling. TGIF Culture has leveled every playing field.

In the not-too-distant past, academics had a virtual monopoly on knowledge and professionals had cornered the market on credentialed expertise. A scholar would research a topic, find something to say that no other scholar had said, and write a definitive tome that staked the topic as his intellectual property. A professional would get credentialed in an area of expertise (law, religion, plumbing), and then expect to get hired because of the credentials. It didn't matter that thousands of other people were thinking and saying the same things as the academic, or were as capable of doing the work of the "expert." As long as the outsiders lacked a certain academic degree or the authorized credential, their work wasn't taken seriously.

TGIF has changed that, making everyone an author, a publisher, an expert. Some 175,000 new blogs are posted every day. Blogs expanded from about 50 in 1999 to more than 50 million by July 2006. There were 1 billion blogs worldwide by 2010, which includes 400 million active English-language blogs. All this blogging has generated a new disorder called CBD (compulsive blogger disorder), the urge to express definitive opinions on all subjects whether or not one has even a modicum of knowledge in the area. The web's encouragement of "the wisdom of crowds" challenges the print-based, institutional authority of libraries, encyclopedias, professors, and hierarchies.

TGIF Culture makes everyone a creator. But that also can be the equivalent of saying there are no more artists, only painters; no more musicians, only soloists. True artists become a concentrated oddity, a marginalized niche instead of the opposite. To find them in the sea of painters becomes an art in itself.

The peril is that the same technology that promises ubiquitous access to books also hampers our ability to read those books with discernment and diligence. Just because you can find anything at your fingertips doesn't mean you can pick up the wisdom or even pick it apart. A writer can fail readers. But the reverse is also true: readers fail writers when they confuse glitterati for literati or look only for confirmation that the world is exactly how they prefer to see it. In its current form, TGIF does not bode well for the future of literary culture.

Two people who have issued warnings of amputations from social media and the dangers of some new addictions are Shane Hipps and Nicholas Carr. They join a distinguished roster of those who have trashed new technologies and cultural change. In the *Phaedrus,* Socrates predicted dire atrophy to the human memory because of the innovation of writing. In the early days of Gutenberg, defenders of handwritten manuscripts warned that printed texts would vulgarize the culture and put bad ideas into the minds of the masses. Franz Kafka's work revolves around the fear of the spectre of technology, especially letter writing, which he deemed particularly diabolical and destructive of authentic relationship. When someone asked Henry David Thoreau if he did not consider the railroad a great improvement over the stagecoach, he said dryly: "Provided it carries better people. Otherwise it's only meanness going faster."[37]

> I've almost given up making an effort
> to remember anything, because I can instantly
> retrieve the information online.
> —*Wired* WRITER CLIVE THOMPSON[38]

Shane Hipps has done the most to warn of the Faustian bargains of social networking as it changes the way we live. Like diet shapes our body, Hipps insists, media shapes our mind "without our permission."[39] By media he means (à la McLuhan) "any extension of ourselves." For Hipps, the expression "Out with lines. In with webs" is shorthand for "Out with hard, slow, laborious rationality. In with flexible, fast intuition."[40] His article "What's [Actually] On Your Mind?" begins with a burst to the Internet bubble: "If you make it to the end of this article, you are an impressive and rare breed of human—an intellectual Navy SEAL, an elite mind, trained with an ability most people just don't have anymore: the ability to sustain concentration over long periods of time."[41]

Nicholas Carr, former *Harvard Business Review* editor, wrote in *The Shallows* about the birth of a new civilization that has lost the literary mind-set.[42] During 2007, he became aware that "the very way my brain worked seemed to be changing.... I began worrying about my inability to pay attention to one thing for more than a couple minutes.... My brain, I realized...was hungry. It was demanding to be fed the way the Net fed it.... I yearned to check e-mail, click links, do some googling."

Today's student and tomorrow's leader "lacks the mental circuitry required to read beyond a few sentences" and "is incapable of reflection or contemplation and doesn't care to remember much."[43] The name I have coined for the type of writing practiced and prized by bloggers is "blogature." Blogature dominates the blogosphere and is a harbinger of the massive shift in reading habits. Blogature tends to be presentistic, almost diaristic, dominated by personal pronouns, barren of the discipline of historical context, but with a high esteem for immediacy, irony, spontaneity, and story. Blogature processes information quickly and efficiently, but is temperamentally allergic to subordinate clauses, complex sentences, the third person, word play, and sustained use of metaphors.

To be sure, some call blogging a "new journalism." But journalists knew they weren't writing literature. They worked in a genre all its own. However, journalists honored the power of language and what language can do even though they were writing columns.[44] The stark and dark contrast between journalism and most blogging explains why I so often have bouts of "blogarrhea"—a condition associated with too much exposure to blogs.

Blogature is mostly insensitive to marvels of style, vivid language, and literary verve. There is no need to worry anymore that we will hear shrieks of "Hurry up, it stinks of literature in here."[45] Rather than preserve style and honor complexity, blogature flattens writing under the weight of immediacy and relevancy.

THE LOG AND THE LONG OF IT

I suspect the TGIF world is not so much promoting short-form thinking at the expense of long, sustained, and complex thinking, but that it's leading to either short or long—with no middle size. Either we need the terse LOG—short text messages, tweets, status updates; or we need the LONG take, the big blog, even the big book. But author/ marketing maven Joan Ball may be right in her assessment of where the blog fits in:

> I find it helpful to think about the relationship between Twitter, blogging and longer forms like essays, books and films in terms of the title, abstract, body format used in research papers and proposals. As with a proposal title, a well-constructed Tweet offers a compelling distillation of the core essence of a larger idea that is meant to intrigue and prompt the reader to want more. Then, as with an abstract or executive summary, the blog post develops the idea further and provides the reader with just enough meat on the bone to prompt a question that is critical in our fast-moving culture: Is this idea worth spending my time in conversation or further reading? Of course, if the answer is yes, books, essays, films and other longer-form communication tools provide space for a more in-depth treatment of an idea that has already been deemed by the reader to be worth their time.[46]

Another question is worth considering, and this one is even more important: Does this blog, idea, kernel, or personal revelation not only offer more to chew on but also point to something much bigger? In the nineteenth century, diaristic literature, written primarily but not entirely by women, pointed to a redefinition of what—or who—is important in life. Jesus tells us that God cares even for the sparrow's fall. Today, each tweet is a symbol of that sparrow's call for validation, purpose, and meaning. The right to know and be known is a basic human need. The hunger not just for relationality but for the valuing of all relationships within a community could be the fodder of revival, a new Great Awakening.

Diaristic literature created a sense of common identity and a loyalty to an imagined community. These writers heard each other and herded to each other—and pointed to something bigger than themselves. Like the nineteenth-century diarists, TGIF bloggers yearn for a taste of something bigger. Whether the nineteenth century's "imagined" community or the twenty-first century's "virtual" community, even those who are expressing mundane thoughts reveal a hunger for the ties of relationship. And more important, they expose the undeniable longing for the bigger sacred something that lies beyond the semiotic of "somethingness."

All of this bears more than a passing resemblance to honest biblical faith. An organic and vital faith gives us the ability to make imagined into real, virtuality into actuality. And what else is revival if not the willingness to see what God wants to do and then heading off in that direction? The TGIF world could be the impetus for an infectious epidemic of monumental proportions. In the nineteenth century, we saw what resulted from such viral-like phenomena: nationalism, revolution, and revival. In the twenty-first century we are seeing a search for a new national identity, a TGIF revolution, and soon, revival.

Interactives

1. Check out John Newton's poem "The Kite; or, Pride Must Have a Fall." The kite dreamed of being cut free from its string:

   Were I but free, I'd take a flight,
   And pierce the clouds beyond their sight,
   But, ah! like a poor pris'ner bound,
   My string confines me near the ground.[47]

   The kite finally manages to tug itself free, but instead of soaring higher it crashes into the sea. The kite couldn't get past its resentment toward the string. What strings constrain you? Discuss your reactions to this statement: the things that make us feel tied down are the things God uses to hold us up.

2. Discuss: "The paradox is there from the beginning. For example, when Jesus hounded the money-changers out of the temple, he wanted people to respect God's house—even as he proposed to replace it. Churches can be confining and deadening—and churches may liberate and enliven. Buildings are unnecessary—but needed. Churches remain—but they remain in order to keep alive a message that is all about movement, about hope and change. In short, a Christian church seems to be—and quite consciously is—a contradiction."[48] Do you think this commentator is missing the point about Jesus and the money-changers? If so, in what way?

3. John Habgood, Anglican archbishop of York, liked to compare knowing God with getting the "point" of a joke—"you can't actually

explain it, and to try to removes the humour."[49] Does his analogy work? If so, why? If not, why not?

4. What do you think? "We are living through a revolution. It is not a political upheaval but rather a massive change in the beliefs on which people base their understanding of life."[50] How do you react to Phil Hill's assessment? Do you largely agree or disagree, and why?

5. It was reported that a Korean couple took care of their virtual baby in an online platform called Prius to the exclusion of caring for their real baby, to the point that their real baby starved to death.[51] This is an extreme and tragic example, of course. But do you sometimes get the feeling that we are more invested in virtual relationships than our face-to-face ones?

6. Social-media critic Shane Hipps says of the virtual community: "It's virtual, but it ain't community." Watch "Shane Hipps on Virtual Community" at www.findingrhythm.com/blog/?p=1638. Hipps has said any "disembodied" encounter cannot be considered or called "community." Does online community really satisfy our relational needs? Can there be an experience of authentic community without face-to-face interaction? What about the "communion of saints"? Is our relationship with those who have gone on before us a legitimate form of community? Why or why not?

7. Shane Hipps has argued that "the more connected in terms of content," the "less connected" we are "in terms of relationship."[52] Further, he has said: "The electronic age has this natural bias to disembody us, to discarnate us and to leave us operating primarily in the realm of content."[53] What say you?

8. Discuss this quote from blogger Jesse Rice:

> The core of the issue: Younger generations…would say relating in the "real" world is not an experience of either "higher" or "lower" quality, it is simply another way of relating. After all, they have mostly experienced relationships as always having contained a strong online component. Theirs is a world where an intimate conversation is just as likely to take place over email (or each other's Facebook walls) as in the locker room or a coffee house

or a church building.… "Community" is not understood as a dichotomy between "real" or "online" relationships but as a composite of *both*. This growing reality forces us to adapt the way we think about community. It is no longer enough to define community in either good or bad terms, to debate whether one brand of relating ("real") is better than another ("online"), though…there is certainly a qualitative difference between the two. A more inclusive definition is needed, one that takes into account the fact that the always-on do not make traditional distinctions between real and online relationships.[54]

Do you agree with the younger generations cited by Rice, who do not believe that relating in the real world is either of higher or lower quality, but simply a different way of relating? Explain. Do you agree that online relationships are just as valid as face-to-face encounters? Why or why not?

PART VI

—

Googlers:
A Culture of Revival

AN INFECTIOUS FAITH

The TGIF Revolution and the Coming Viral Revival

Life doesn't imitate art, it imitates bad television.

—WOODY ALLEN

Here are the natural advantages of tweets or blogs: they are fast, furious, and infectious. For Googlers, the real stuff of life is revealed within mundacity, and it is shared obsessively. It is the TGIF version of a neighborly talk over the back fence, a brief conversation while waiting in line for coffee, sharing gossip in the lunch line, or an introvert's diary. Except now, the diary is available tout de suite online.

The Googler recasting of a previous generation's casual chat in a grocery store aisle engages us, and not casually. TGIF modes of sharing are provocative, even addictive. They reveal something about the irresistible mundacity of everyday life. Movies such as *Napoleon Dynamite, Bridget Jones's Diary,* Woody Allen's *Matchpoint,* or Sacha Baron Cohen's *Bruno* fit this category. As does the brilliance of *Seinfeld* (a television series about nothing) or any number of reality TV shows. We have more than enough evidence to verify our unbridled fascination with the mundane and the ordinary.

Follow a friend's tweets or read status updates on Facebook. We describe a good meal, an inspiring movie, the breakup of a relationship, our pet's bathroom habits. And notice the imaginative ways people express the ordinary. There are passion, avid glee, and clever aphorisms. The most memorable tweets, YouTube videos, blogs, and quotes become the wheat of our proverbial and "provisual" field. Despite the inevitable chaff, the glorious and mundane amber waves of grain feed our need to connect, propagate, and grow in a communal environment.

Our everydayness is sacred to us. And the ways we tend our relational gardens reveal more than a little about our natural proclivities, which favor a wildflower over a cultivated rose. From whole foods to "buy local," globalization to tribalization, we are more interested in planting a microcosm of the universe (rampant global diversity) than we are in attaining a macrocosm for all people (strategic, syncretistic, inter- [or intra-] culturalism).

Googlers are the folk artists of God's creation, and TGIF Culture provides the communal creating place. We might even call it The Village Palette, the new village commons. The invitation to play—to express ourselves—is infectious. Although it may be hard sometimes to find an artist in a sea of painters, you also discover more artists by giving everyone an opportunity to paint.

But what kinds of artists are these? What do we do with gardens of ordinary words and "sky is the limit" images that don't fit conventional ideas of what a good garden should include? And perhaps more important, why do I believe that the Googler Generation could trigger a spiritual revival of epidemic proportions from out of such a commonplace, mundane garden?

In order to answer that, I need to go back to Jesus.

Jesus was a master Storyteller, but he wasn't a contriver of fantasies for kings and queens, or even temple authorities. He was a crafter of parables for the artists of everyday life, who grew things and created joy out of next to nothing. For these "weeds" of society, he created the parables of the mustard seed and the leaven of yeast.

Jesus's parable of the mustard seed is better named the parable of the mustard weed. Pliny the Elder, a first-century historian, wrote in his *Natural History* about the mustard weed: "It will grow without cultivation.... It is extremely difficult to rid the soil of it when once sown there, the seed when it falls germinating immediately."[1] Jesus used the metaphor of the mustard weed to describe the impact, discipleship, and evangelism of his ministry. He decided not to use the image of a neatly planted flower or the majestic monarchs of the forest (such as the Cedars of Lebanon, which were used to symbolize past and future kings). Instead, he called attention to a relentless, unstoppable, invasive, self-germinating infestation. (Think dandelion, only worse!)

The subversive mustard weed is nearly impossible to get rid of. Once it takes root, it takes over and invites every insect, pest, and rodent to live within its leaves. It spreads quickly and can grow and thrive almost anywhere.

And what about his parables involving leaven? When yeast or leaven comes in contact with water, even the smallest amount of the germ quickly expands throughout the dough, creating a multitude of food from a minimum of ingredients. The mustard weed and leaven both are common, everyday increments of life. They represent God's kingdom, which is filled with the "germ" of Jesus himself. The incarnational and natural qualities of their propagation and identity define Jesus's "kingdom of God" on earth and serve as images for the same types of spiritual *"vivre"* or "revival" seen in the Pentecostal (in)flammation and, much later, the Great Awakening.

Jesus spoke to an agricultural community about agricultural imagery. I am convinced that if Jesus were incarnated within today's culture and took part in the advances of the biological world, as well as the technological revolution, he would be using images such as the virus and the tweet to describe a kingdom without containment.

What does infectious faith look like? It erupts in amazing beauty and resilient brilliance. It pricks with an occasional thorny thistle. It incites passion, spreads love, breeds kindness, generates compassion. While it infests the mind and heart with Jesus, it revives the body with the Holy Spirit.

Nobody does sacred like Jesus.

The Virality of the TGIF Revolution

A virus always begins in relationship. The origins of a virus are difficult to pin down, because in essence viruses evolve and develop out of the mundane and routine elements of life. It can be the air we breathe, the food we eat, or the happenstance that one cell meets another and forms an unexpected and provocative union, which then mutates into something new. The manifest complexity of life allows for a multitude of possibilities, and out of this mystery of complexity, the cells of life emerge. Once a virus breathes its first breath, it replicates itself, much like the yeast in a loaf of bread, and a movement is born.

The Jesus movement began virally, and "viral" was the Jesus way of living. Like any life-beginning and life-affirming process, the Jesus movement revives itself again and again with a period first of incubation, then relationality, replication, and a bursting forth of multiplication that cannot be contained. But how does this relate to the TGIF revolution? Or rather, how does the TGIF revolution relate to a Jesus revival?

In a sense, Googlers are the ultimate lab rats, creating an entire community of virtual replications. Born in the insular environment of virtuality, every tweet, blog, keyword, and image is a trailblazer, creating a breeding ground of experimental ideas and connections. This virtual incubator cannot remain in the technological petri dish. It takes on a life of its own and can erupt and emerge triumphantly from the "culture" of the lab and into the culture of the world. Sometimes these eruptions can be random moments of inspiration or a synthesis for individual growth. Other times, breaking out of virtual space can mean a life-changing or revolutionary communal phenomenon. But no matter how you look at it, breakouts are inevitable and infectious. Before you know it, a viral epidemic takes root and spreads from lab to world.

The Nature of TGIF Evangelism

Jesus was a master of stories and, as we know, a healer of the body. The body, as a holistic blend of mind/heart, soul, and physical body, constitutes the entire living organism that is a human being. For Christians, the body also is the communal, living, breathing embodiment of Christ. The secret to Jesus's virality is in his self-healing and self-replicating presence. Jesus was and is the body. Any resurgence of life to that body, we call a revival. A revival is a resuscitation or fresh infusion of life. Since all life comes from Jesus, the incarnational presence of Jesus is in essence the virality of life itself.

From the beginning of time, God granted humankind the sexual gift of propagation: "be fruitful and multiply" was the command, and lineage became the ultimate Abrahamic sign of the covenant. In Jesus, as a part of his body, we all are rooted in the lineage of God. Our identity, our genus, our germ (if you will) is not merely biological but holistic—in mind, heart, and spirit a Christ-filled signifier.

TGIF evangelism is, in its purest form, discipleship: a recognition of being part of a body bigger than ourselves and an organic way of behaving within it.[2] Viruses are not bacterial. They cannot be simply eliminated by antibiotics. Likewise, a TGIF community, if driven by faith in Christ, cannot be easily prevented. By nature, its all-inclusive, nonrestrictive leveling of the field allows for a nonhierarchical and nonpretentious spread of the Jesus story and the Jesus life.

But whom and what will be revived? A TGIF revival is not a revival of an institution or a tradition, but a revival of the body of Christ as it reconstitutes itself and breathes virality into an already present organism. The question of the day, then, is whether the church can survive this new viral mutation—this infectious, fast-spreading, life-giving virality of Christ. The TGIF revolution will be a spiritual revival of Christ's body within the world. It will be a new strain that resists evil, heals its wounds, and sustains in the face of a changing cultural paradigm. God's capital-C Church will endure and prosper. Christ is alive and moving in all generations and cultures, whether or not our immune systems can handle a new breakthrough.

Which leaves us with a question for every individual member, whether person or community: Will you be part of it?

FROGS, KISSES, AND
THE KINGDOM OF GOD

In Western cultures, a favorite symbol of hospitality is the pineapple. In Eastern cultures, it's the frog. That's why entrances to homes and front gardens feature welcoming frogs as a symbol of blessing and prosperity.

I wrote this book while looking at a cast-iron frog. The frog represents this book because they're amphibians, able to live in the water and on land. In this tale of two cultures, the overlap of Gutenbergers and Googlers, we need individuals and communities that can live in both worlds. For the sake of conversation I have grievously (some will say egregiously) simplified the two cultures. But the fact remains that if we are to move into the future, we need to practice not cultural apartheid, but cultural amphibianship.

Another reason why I chose the frog as the totem for this book is because I often feel like a frog, and no more so than when I was writing this book. Frogs feel slow, low, clammy, and bumpy. I get that frog feeling when I want to be Googler but feel Gutenberger. I'm a frog when I want to grasp the new culture, but feel it slip through my fingers. I'm froggish when I want to be big in hope, but realize how small my dreams actually are, and when I want to be fast and first in embracing new technology without missing a beat, but most of the time feel flatfooted and gimpy unless I'm holding my kids' hands. I get the frog feeling when I want to swagger like Abel but walk with Cain; when I want to be bright, but feel duh!

This book has been the lily pad on which I've floated down the TGIF rapids, frightened and bewildered but too froggish to budge.

A fairy tale: Once upon a time there was a frog. But he wasn't a frog; he was really a king who looked like a frog. A wicked witch had cast a spell on him and only the kiss of a beautiful maiden could save him. But since when do cute chicks kiss frogs? So there he sat, an unkissed king in frog form.

But miracles do happen. One day a beautiful maiden grabbed him up and gave him a big kiss. *Crash! Boom! Zap!* There he was, a handsome king again. And you know the rest: they lived happily ever after. That's shorthand for another story ready for the telling.

So what is the task of the church? To kiss frogs, of course. Whether Gutenberger or Googler.

HOW GUTENBERGERS
CAN LEARN FROM GOOGLERS

Church leaders and supporters, members and pastors all are concerned about the generation that is not present on Sunday mornings. To take necessary steps toward opening the doors to those who are missing, here are some ideas for your church.

GET A CAMPFIRE STORY

Every church needs its own campfire story and campfire rituals. This is another way of saying that your church needs to become more tribal, more local, more pedestrian, more artisanal. Artisan cheeses differ markedly from mild, mass-produced cheeses, partly because they are handcrafted, aged, and ripened to reflect the story of where they were made. In the same way, artisanal churches have a flavor, texture, and aesthetics that are uniquely their own.

The more global the world gets, the more we will see tribal identity being prized. Think of premodern times when individualism was not the norm, or in many cultures even acknowledged. Up until the start of the Gutenberg era, one's identity was tied closely to one's tribe. It was not a personal identity but a tribal identity where one didn't learn to "fit in" but to "fit together." This was true as well in Hebrew culture in biblical times.

All this changed in the early sixteenth century when Martin Luther's "Here I

Stand" brought the *I* to the fore. We have no appreciation for how recent the word *I* is, nor do we recognize the revolutionary power of that perpendicular. *I* meaning "self" has a pedigree dating back to the tenth century at the earliest, but *I* didn't carry the meaning it does today until the eighteenth century. At that point, it signified what a person is at a particular time—one's nature, character, and appearance—the person's core.[1]

I is the best friend of humanity. *I* is the worst enemy of humanity. Draw from the well of common human experience while showing each person and community how to add her own flavor to the water. Decontextualize the global; contextualize the local and make it tribal. The church must love and live its zip code.

Mean the Meaning

Googlers can find facts faster than ever, but they also lose the meaning of those facts faster than ever. There are three basic, recurrent philosophical attitudes that run through the history of philosophy:

1. materialism: the world is devoid of meaning.
2. objective idealism (or classical liberalism): the world is meaningful in and of itself.
3. subjective idealism (or idealism of freedom): the world receives its meaning from outside itself—a transcendental deity.

Christians believe God is the source of all meaning. It's time to skip the "information" and supply meaning. Googlers hunger for something more than they are, a meaning beyond themselves, the Reality behind all realities. In this culture, it is more important than ever to mean the meaning. Humanity has excelled at technological progress, but failed at moral progress.

Give Up the Controller

Before Google, success belonged to those who controlled content. The rest of us had to get it from the controllers.

After Google, success belongs to those who give away content: we'll give you what you need to succeed.

Yahoo! is a Gutenberg dinosaur in twenty-first century clothing. It markets to bring people in, controls content, shows ads. Google builds networks and platforms to help people succeed in whatever they're doing.

Gutenberg Culture was a society hooked on control. It's time to surrender our control and trust and obey God's Spirit. Think about it: Do the best things in life happen when you're in control? Do you fall in love when you are "in control"?

The only institutions that can look forward to a future are those that transition from regulation to resource. The Gutenberg church sought to regulate its people. Behavioral conformity was prized (that's part of a manufacturing mind-set), affirming a statement of faith was required, lists and rules were emphasized and enforced. This is consistent with an assembly-line mind-set (the industrial model, which is prized by Gutenbergers). Parts are interchangeable, efficiency is prized, quality control is impossible without strict standards and specifications. For purposes of record-keeping and charting growth, you need a clear definition of who's in and who's out. Who's one of us and who isn't.

But in a Google world, no one wants to be measured, quantified, or regulated. Instead, Googlers seek resources that will help them in their journey toward the things they value, hunger for, and seek after. They want to be resourced. Effective ministry and mission will resource the user to help create the meaning he is seeking.

To effectively resource Googlers, you have to take into account their learning style and learn to contextualize your own. A book is at its root an antisocial medium. It is individualist and isolating. A book is enjoyed best in privacy. In fact, in a social setting if you pull out a book and start reading, it's considered rude. A book is not like a photo album, a deck of cards, or even video of your last vacation—all of which invite group participation. A book shuts out the distraction of other people. So when you're getting nostalgic about "the book," think of the antisocial negatives that came with it.

We don't have space here to introduce the new teaching styles that must attend the new learning methods of TGIF Culture. But it begins with authority figures who no longer control access to information, but instead help students assess and process information. Suffice it to say that in a Google world, you don't standardize, you customize.

Set Jesus Free from the Page

Just as the Protestant Reformation was a revolution in reading among Europeans, especially how they read the Bible, so the TGIF revolution will entail a whole new reading of the Bible that exegetes images and stories as much as words and points. The Word of God is primarily Jesus Christ, not the Bible. It is Person, not print.

Of course, three things cannot be separated: the Holy Spirit, Jesus, and the Scriptures. When one is missing from the braid of truth, it all comes unraveled. But Jesus did not rise from the dead for us to entomb him again in a book. Jesus is alive and living his resurrection presence in our world. The Scriptures point us to him, as we then point others to what the Scriptures point us to.

Living lives that "arise, shine, for your light has come" is the essence of evangelism.

From Teaching to Participation

Social media is inherently interactive. You can choose to make church interactive, or you can resign yourself to seeing a generation missing for decades to come. By "interactive" I mean someone's participation has the ability to shape the content of the experience itself.

Googlers function with a twofold test of participation: (1) Am I learning something? (2) Am I contributing something? If the answer to either question is no, they get out of there quick.

Learning and participation must have free rein. I approach my Facebook page not as a conversation so much as a party. My posts invite friends over, and I greet them with a theological cocktail that starts the conversation. Then I let them take it from there, and learn, learn, learn from their every post.

Mess Up

One of the most creative things you and I can do in these times of disruption and destruction is to fail fast. Get some failures behind you; that way you won't be afraid of things going wrong as you try out new ways of doing things.

Tell Stories

Tell stories as though your life depended on it…because it does. But storytelling needs to explore new venues. Like Second Life, where you enter a virtual 3-D world in the guise of an avatar. Webkins is another example of this virtual world. In any system, you connect with your audience through an interface. For TGIF Culture, the interface is EPIC (experiential, participatory, image-rich, and connective). But what is the content that we transfer through the EPIC interface? The content is Truth.

Bless Others with God's Strength, Found in Your Weakness

Jean Vanier, the founder of L'Arche community, built his mission on this key insight: "society can ultimately be healed only by those whom it rejects. The disabled are a part of the 'poor' with whom God has chosen to identify himself, shaming the wise and the strong in their illusory self-sufficiency. Reaching out to them becomes a means of being led—by God, to God." [2]

It was Vanier who convinced Pope John Paul II of this truth. At breakfast with the (then fit and healthy) pope in 1987, Vanier found that John Paul II had difficulty understanding what he meant by a disabled person having a healing presence. When the pope got sick, however, "a deep bond arose between us," wrote Vanier, who had a leading role in the pope's 2004 visit to Lourdes where Vanier read these words standing a few feet from the pope: "Our Pope is poor. He is fragile, but he is the glory of God. God manifests himself in him." [3] More than anyone else, it was Vanier's influence that convinced Pope John Paul II not to hide his physical deterioration from the rest of the world because God's strength is made perfect in our weakness. [4]

Notes

Acknowledgments

1. Charlie Chaplin, *My Autobiography* (New York: Simon & Schuster, 1964), 211.

Introduction

1. W. H. Auden, quoted in Josephine Hart, ed., *Catching Life by the Throat: How to Read Poetry and Why: Poems from Eight Great Poets* (New York: W. W. Norton, 2008), 11.
2. It should be noted, however, that China's woodblock printing industry antedates Gutenberg's technological advances by five hundred years.
3. "I'm Bound for the Promised Land," lyrics written by Samuel Stennett, 1787. Public Domain.
4. See Jeremiah 29:11–13.
5. Ecclesiastes 3:11: "He has made everything beautiful in its time. He has also set eternity in the hearts of men; yet they cannot fathom what God has done from beginning to end."
6. This story came from Al Caldwell, a retired librarian at Garrett-Evangelical Theological Seminary and a longtime friend of my friend Elmer O'Brien.
7. See Eamon Duffy, *Walking to Emmaus* (New York: Burns & Oates, 2006), 52.

Chapter 1

The chapter epigraph is taken from a variation of Blaise Pascal, *Pensées: The Provincial Letters* (New York: Modern Library, 1941), 48: "All the unhappiness of men arises from one single fact, that they cannot stay quietly in their own chamber."

1. See Acts 1:14, NKJV.
2. Keith Richards, quoted in Stanley Booth, *Keith* (New York: St. Martin's, 1995), 38.
3. "The Net reroutes our vital [neural] paths and diminishes our capacity for contemplation...altering the depth of our emotions as well as our thoughts." Thus Nicholas Carr summarizes the literature in *The Shallows: What the Internet Is Doing to Our Brains* (New York: Norton, 2011), 221. See also *Is the Internet Changing the Way You Think? The Net's Impact on Our Minds and Future,* ed. John Brockman (New York: Harper Perennial, 2011).
4. Zygmunt Bauman, *Liquid Love: On the Frailty of Human Bonds* (Cambridge, UK: Polity, 2003), 62.
5. The actual question is "Where did we miss the person and get the point instead?" See Leonard Sweet, *Out of the Question Into the Mystery: Getting Lost in the Godlife Relationship* (Colorado Springs, CO: WaterBrook, 2004).

6. Marshall McLuhan and Quentin Fiore, *The Medium Is the Message* (New York: Random House, 1967).

7. John 1:14, ESV.

8. Sir Arthur Stanley Eddington, *The Nature of the Physical World* (New York: Cambridge University Press, 1953), 291.

9. Check out http://touchpress.com/titles/thewasteland.

10. Marianne Sawicki, *Seeing the Lord: Resurrection and Early Christian Practices* (Minneapolis: Fortress, 1994), 310.

Chapter 2

The chapter epigraph is taken from the first stanza of Charles Wesley's 1762 hymn "A Charge to Keep I Have," *The United Methodist Hymnal: Book of United Methodist Worship* (Nashville: United Methodist Publishing, 1989), 413.

1. Stephen Stills, "Love the One You're With" (1970), www.suitelorraine.com/suitelorraine/Pages/ltoyw.html. You can hear the song on YouTube at www.youtube.com/watch?v=HH3ruuml-R4.

2. This is the second stanza of Charles Wesley's 1762 hymn, "A Charge to Keep I Have," *The United Methodist Hymnal,* 413.

3. These are the opening lines of the first two stanzas of Charles Wesley's 1762 hymn, "A Charge to Keep I Have," *The United Methodist Hymnal,* 413.

4. Esther 4:14, NRSV.

5. Jude 1:3, ESV.

6. Genesis 6:9, NRSV.

7. Woody Allen, quoted in Jim Holt, "Smarter, Happier, More Productive," *London Review of Books,* March 3, 2011, 9.

8. This is the third stanza of Charles Wesley's 1762 hymn, "A Charge to Keep I Have," *The United Methodist Hymnal,* 413.

9. Alan Hirsch, *The Forgotten Ways: Reactivating the Missional Church* (Grand Rapids: Brazos, 2007), 122–23.

10. Albert Einstein, quoted in "Einstein and Faith," *Time,* April 5, 2007.

11. Graham Greene, interviewed by John Cornwell in *The Tablet,* September 1989.

Chapter 3

The chapter epigraph is taken from W. H. Auden, *The Age of Anxiety: A Baroque Eclogue* (London: Faber and Faber, 1948), 123.

1. Kathleen Norris, *Acedia & Me: A Marriage, Monks, and a Writer's Life* (New York: Riverhead, 2008), 131. Norris is quoting from Wendy Wasserstein, *Sloth* (New York: Oxford University Press, 2005). Wasserstein uses this term extensively throughout her book.

2. John Wesley and Charles Wesley resisted the entrenched ritual and distanced application of faith in England's state church. They insisted that faith be

active and engaged in everyday existence. In contrast to the rational formalism of Anglican tradition, the Wesleys fashioned a heart-head-hand missional spirituality to address the cultural issues of their day. These Methodists started a revolution that went from England to America and then across the world.

3. This is the second stanza of Ray Palmer's 1875 hymn "My Faith Looks Up to Thee," *The United Methodist Hymnal: Book of United Methodist Worship* (Nashville: United Methodist Publishing, 1989), 452.

4. Søren Kierkegaard, *Kierkegaard's Concluding Unscientific Postscript* (Princeton, NJ: Princeton University Press, 1941), 30.

5. The chorus of Ginny Owens's "I Wanna Be Moved," www.stlyrics.com/songs /g/ginnyowens1650/iwannabemoved78319.html.

6. St. Bernard, "Sermon 79," in *On the Song of Songs, IV,* trans. Irene Edmonds (Kalamazoo, MI: Cistercian, 1980), 4:138.

7. William Sloane Coffin, quoted in Studs Terkel, *Touch and Go: A Memoir* (New York: New Press, 2007), 253.

8. See 1 Corinthians 2:16.

9. See Luke 1:29.

10. Eric Shinseki, quoted in the *Congressional Quarterly Weekly* 59 (2001), 2751.

11. St. Teresa of Avila, quoted in Donald B. Bloesch, *The Church: Sacraments, Worship, Ministry, Mission* (Downers Grove, IL: InterVarsity, 2002), 61.

12. For more on this, see Frank E. Manuel, *The Religion of Isaac Newton* (Oxford: Clarendon, 1974), 120.

13. Ruth Knafo Setton, "The Rubble Women," in *To Mend the World: Women Reflect on 9/11,* ed. Marjorie Agosin and Betty Jean Craige (Buffalo, NY: White Pine, 2002), 186–87.

14. John Maynard Smith and Eörs Szathmáry, *The Major Transitions in Evolution* (New York: Oxford University Press, 1999), 81. I love the metaphoric partnership of the authors' names—one simple, one complex, at least to an English mind.

15. See Matthew 22:37–40.

16. 1 Thessalonians 4:14, ESV.

17. Romans 4:24, NRSV.

18. With thanks to Dan Anderson-Little for help in this elaboration.

19. cf. "Thy mercies are new [fresh] every morning." See Lamentations 3:22–23.

20. These are the closing words of David M. Smick, *The World Is Curved: Hidden Dangers to the Global Economy* (New York: Portfolio, 2008), 275.

21. "WordBuzz: Complexipacity," *The Futurist,* November/December 2009, 2.

22. "The Nicene Creed" as found, for example, in *The United Methodist Hymnal: Book of United Methodist Worship* (Nashville: United Methodist Publishing, 1989), 880. Or in *The Lutheran Book of Worship* (Minneapolis: Augsburg, 1978), 64.

23. Clifford Longley, "It Has 1969 Stamped All Over It—Except Even the Beatles Were Writing Better English," *The Tablet*, January 23, 2010, 12.

24. See 1 Thessalonians 5:16–24, especially v. 23.

25. Francis Bacon, "Of Truth," in *Essays, Moral, Economical, and Political* (New York: Harper, 1847), 44.

26. Quoted in Paul N. Anderson, *The Riddles of the Fourth Gospel: An Introduction to John* (Minneapolis: Fortress, 2011), 1. "Attributed both to Augustine and Pope Gregory the Great, who describe Scripture as 'a stream in which the elephant may swim and the lamb may wade.' A recent application of this imagery to the gospel of John is made by Paul F. Brackman, who said, 'Someone has described the remarkable character of this Gospel by saying that it is a book in which a child can wade and an elephant can swim'" ("The Gospel According to John," *Interpretation* 6, 1952, 63).

27. The first quote is John 10:30 and the second, John 14:28.

28. John 3:17; 12:37.

29. John 9:39.

30. C. K. Barrett says John is a "dialectical theologian" in "The Dialectical Theology of St. John," *New Testament Essays* (London: SPCK, 1972), 49–69. For a superb recent exploration of John in this vein, see Paul N. Anderson, "The Cognitive Origins of John's Unitive and Disunitive Christology," in *Psychology and the Bible: A New Way to Read the Scriptures,* ed. J. Harold Ellens and Wayne G. Rollins (Westport, CT: Praeger, 2004), 3:127–48: "The most distinctive aspect of John's Christology is not that it is the highest in the New Testament, nor that it is the lowest; that the Son is one with the Father or subordinate to the Father; that eschatology is present or futuristic; that Jesus knows what is going to happen or that he anguishes in pathos; that the signs are embellished or that they are existentialized. The most distinctive aspect of John's Christology is that *both* parts of these polarities, and others, are held together in dynamic tension within the Johannine narrative" (127).

31. See Proverbs 23:23; Wisdom of Solomon 6:22, KJV; John 14:6.

32. John 10:16, DRB.

33. William Shakespeare, *Hamlet*, Act 3, Scene 2.

34. Reg Saner, *The Dawn Collector: On My Way to the Natural World* (Santa Fe, NM: Center for American Places, 2006), vi.

35. Parker J. Palmer, *The Courage to Teach: Exploring the Inner Landscape of a Teacher's Life* (San Francisco: Jossey-Bass, 1998), 95.

36. Private remark to George Weigel, as referenced in *The Tablet*, June 11, 2011, 35.

Chapter 4

1. This is the fourth stanza of Charles Wesley's 1762 hymn, "A Charge to Keep I Have," *The United Methodist Hymnal: Book of United Methodist Worship* (Nashville: United Methodist Publishing, 1989), 413.

2. The apostle Paul was not the only one "untimely born" (1 Corinthians 15:8, ESV).

3. As was mentioned previously, TGIF is an acronym used to identify the Twitter, Google, iPhone, Facebook culture. TGIF is another way of talking about post-modern culture. Admittedly, the postmodern label has fallen out of favor, and it is hard to know what to call this period, this project that we're now in. At times I wonder if it would be better to not give a name to a new culture, since so much of our conversation is devoted to what we mean when we use the culture's designated label.

4. James Ellroy, *The Hilliker Curse: My Pursuit of Women* (New York: A. A. Knopf, 2010), 120.

5. Jeffrey Cole directs the Center for the Digital Future at the University of Southern California Annenberg School for Communication & Journalism. Cole made this statement to participants on April 10, 2010, at a plenary session of the Religion Communication Congress 2010 in Chicago, quoted in Chris Herlinger, "The Future? Think Mobile, Mobile, Mobile, Says Digital Expert," www.rccongress2010.org/news/jeffcoleplenary.shtml.

6. See Seth Weinbraub, "The Numbers Don't Lie: Mobile Devices Overtake PCs," August 11, 2010, CNN Money, http://tech.fortune.cnn.com/2010/08/11 /the-great-game-mobile-devices-overtaking-pcs/?hpt=Sbin.

7. Quoted in Oliver Burkeman, "SXSW 2011: The Internet is Over," *The Guardian,* 14 May 2011, www.guardian.co.uk/technology/2011/mar/15 /sxsw-2011-internet-online.

8. The polysemous family means basically that any combination of self-defined or self-selected "family members" suffices. By this definition, a family could be a single woman, her cat, and her Bible study group.

9. Check out RightStuffDating.com, designed for people who can prove that they've graduated from or are on the faculty of Harvard, Yale, MIT, Cornell, Northwestern, Duke, Emory, Vassar, and other select schools. Try FarmersOnly .com for people with "good old-fashioned traditional values"; and plentyoffish .com for people with matching "chemistries."

10. See Arnold Brown, "Relationships, Community, and Identity in the New Virtual Society," *The Futurist,* March/April 2011, 29–34.

11. Jon Zogby, *The Way We'll Be* (New York: Random House, 2008), 107.

12. Kevin Kelly, "Understanding Technological Evolution and Diversity," *The Futurist,* March/April 2011, 46, www.allbusiness.com/trends-events /trends/15523683-1.html. See also Kevin Kelly, *What Technology Wants* (New York: Viking, 2010), 288.

13. Bernard J. F. Lonergan, *Insight: A Study of Human Understanding* (New York: Harper & Row, 1978), 191.

14. W. G. Hoskins, quoted in Alfred Leslie Rowse, *Portraits and Views, Literary and Historical* (London: Macmillan, 1979), 141.

15. See John 17.

16. Marshall McLuhan, *War and Peace in the Global Village* (New York: McGraw-Hill, 1968), 73. This statement often is misquoted (with verifications) as "there is no augmentation without an amputation." For more on this, see websites such as http://larsrood.com/2011/04/12/there-is-no-augmentation-without-an-amputation-mcluhan.

17. Shane Hipps, quoted in Jennifer Bradbury, "Tuned In, Turned Off: The YWJ Youth Culture and Technology Roundtable," *YouthWorker Journal,* January/February 2011, 4, www.youthworker.com/youth-ministry-resources-ideas/youth-ministry/11640986/page-4.

18. See David E. Nye, *When the Lights Went Out: A History of Blackouts in America* (Cambridge, MA: MIT Press, 2010), 205.

19. Dean Kamen, quoted in "Mr. Segway's Difficult Path," *The Economist,* June 10, 2010, 25, www.economist.com/node/16295592.

20. Edward Tenner, *Why Things Bite Back: Technology and the Revenge of Unintended Consequences* (New York: Vintage, 1997).

21. The *Jeopardy* "Man vs. Machine" episodes were first broadcast February 14–16, 2011.

22. Evgeny Morozov, *The Net Delusion: The Dark Side of Internet Freedom* (New York: Public Affairs, 2011), 63–65, quote on 64.

23. Oliver Burkeman, "SXSW 2011: The Internet Is Over," *Guardian,* March 15, 2011, www.guardian.co.uk/technology/2011/mar/15/sxsw-2011-internet-online.

24. Brendan Greeley, "The Fallacy of Facebook Diplomacy," *Bloomberg Businessweek,* 07-13 February 2011, 8–9.

25. For more on this, see Morozov, "Why the KGB Wants You to Join Facebook," in *The Net Delusion,* 142–88.

26. Morozov, *The Net Delusion,* 156.

27. This well-known quote appears in many different forms.

28. T. S. Eliot, "Murder in the Cathedral" in *The Complete Poems and Plays 1909–1950* (New York: Harcourt, Brace & World, 1962), 211.

29. Charlie Peacock, *New Way to Be Human: A Provocative Look at What It Means to Follow Jesus* (Colorado Springs, CO: WaterBrook, 2004), 9.

30. For more on this, see Joseph Horowitz, *Classical Music in America: A History of Its Rise and Fall* (New York: Norton, 2005).

31. Quoted in Jon Spayde, "James D. Hodgson," *Utne Reader,* May/June 2003, 152.

32. Bradbury, "Tuned In, Turned Off: The YWJ Youth Culture and Technology Roundtable," *YouthWorker Journal,* 22–24.

33. Paul Asay, "KidTech: How Technology Is Changing the Way Young People Work, Play and Live," *YouthWorker Journal,* January/February 2011, 33–34.

Chapter 5

The chapter epigraph is taken from F. T. Marinetti, "Destruction of Syntax—Wireless Imagination—Words of Freedom," in *Stung by Salt and War: Creative Texts of the Italian Avant-Gardist F. T. Marinetti* (New York: Lang, 1987), 47.

1. Bonnie Rochman, "Twittering in Church, with the Pastor's O.K.," May 3, 2009, www.time.com/time/business/article/0,8599,1895463,00.html. See also Bonnie Rochman, "Twittering in Church," *Time,* June 1, 2009, 51–52.

2. Because many Arabs do not like the phrase "Jasmine Revolution" because it appears "too passive, too perfumed," I suspect that the phrase "Arab Spring" will win out. See Jonathan Steele, "Half a Revolution," *London Review of Books,* March 17, 2011, 36. See also, for example, Jonathan Steele, "Iraq's Own Arab Spring," *Guardian,* April 25, 2011, www.guardian.co.uk/commentisfree/2011 /apr/25/united-states-troop-presence-iraq-long-term.

3. Dovid Zaklikowski, "The Rebbe and President Ronald Reagan," www.chabad .org/therebbe/article_cdo/aid/142535/jewish/The-Rebbe-and-President-Reagan .htm.

4. Beth Snyder Bulik, "What Your Favorite Social Net Says about You," *Advertising Age,* July 13, 2009, 6.

5. Lyrics from the fourth stanza of Charles Wesley, "And Can It Be That I Should Gain," *The United Methodist Hymnal: Book of United Methodist Worship* (Nashville: United Methodist Publishing, 1989), 363.

6. Quoted in Robert Andrews, *Columbia Dictionary of Quotations* (New York: Columbia University Press, 1993), 186, where it is cited as originally quoted in *Q Magazine,* January 1980, and spoken on stage in Syracuse, New York, May 1980.

7. See John 6:66–67. "From this time many of his disciples turned back and no longer followed him. 'You do not want to leave too, do you?' Jesus asked the Twelve."

8. For more on this, see Leonard Sweet and Frank Viola, *Jesus Manifesto: Restoring the Supremacy and Sovereignty of Jesus Christ* (Nashville: Thomas Nelson, 2010).

9. Matthew 4:18–20.

10. David D. Kirkparick and David E. Sanger, "A Tunisian-Egyptian Link That Shook Arab History," *New York Times,* 13 February 2011, www .nytimes.com/2011/02/14/world/middleeast/14egypt-tunisia-protests .html?pagewanted=all.

11. See Acts 11:26.

12. See 1 Corinthians 11:1.

13. Dan Fehrenbacher, quoted in Richard Carwardine, "The Lincoln Enigma (Book Review)," *TLS: Times Literary Supplement,* September 7, 2001, 32.

14. Every day I have what I call "soul moment blessings" from the participation of people on Twitter and Facebook. For example, I posted stories from Elie Wiesel's

book *Souls on Fire* (89–112) where he elaborates how Hebrews have a way of talking with God that is unvarnished and unafraid: "Levi-Yitzhak of Berditchev told God one day that unless he began to answer his prayers, he would refuse to say them any more. He warned God that if he did not improve [at running the universe], then God would be in for a tough time at the Last Judgement! When people criticized him for 'impious' words, he said that as a child of Israel, one may say anything." Immediately after I posted this, I got all sorts of replies, including this one: "I can almost hear Morgan Freeman (as God) saying, 'That's fine, Levi. Just be sure to smile when you say that.'"

15. See Al Ries, "The TGIF 'Revolution' Is Nothing Without a Marketing Strategy," *Advertising Age,* November 9, 2009, 22, http://adage.com/article/al-ries /marketing-social-media-save-a-weak-brand/140353.

16. In John Bunyan's writing, according to T. Babbington Macauley, "the vocabulary is the vocabulary of the common people." You can read for pages and there will be no word with more than one or two syllables. See T. Babbington Macauley, "Southey's Edition of the Pilgrim's Progress," *Edinburgh Review,* 1831, in *Critical and Miscellaneous Essays* (Boston: Weeks, Jordan, 1840), 1:443.

17. Macauley, "Southey's Edition of the Pilgrim's Progress," *Edinburgh Review,* 1:444.

18. Samuel Taylor Coleridge, "Lecture 3," (1818) in *Lectures 1808–1919: On Literature,* ed. R. A. Foakes, *The Collected Works* 5 (Princeton, NJ: Princeton University Press, 1987), 2:103.

19. As noted in such unexpected places as "Some Choice Books Which Ought to Be in Every Household," *Gleanings in Bee Culture,* November 15, 1895, 833.

20. James Boswell, *The Life of Samuel Johnson, Including a Journal of a Tour to the Hebrides* (New York: Harper, 1859), 2:258.

21. Louise Glück, "March," in *A Village Life* (New York: Farrar, Straus and Giroux, 2009), 37.

22. Mother Teresa, *Love: The Words and Inspiration of Mother Teresa* (Boulder, CO: Blue Mountain, 2007), 72–73.

23. Quoted in Martin Kreuzer and Lorenzo Robbieno, *Computational Communative Algebra* (Berlin: Springer, 2005), 2:100.

24. See "Phil., ii. 5-11 (Rheims, 1582)" in George Milligan, *The English Bible: A Sketch of Its History* (London: A. & C. Black, 1895), 101.

25. Note the change in punctuation and emphasis as found in John 13:34: "Love one another. As I have loved you, so you must love one another."

26. Favorite Robert Runcie quote of the Right Reverends Peter and Michael Ball, as recorded in Deborah Cassidi, *Favourite Wisdom: Chosen by People from All Walks of Life* (New York: Continuum, 2003), x.

27. I have searched to find the primary source of this quote. If you are aware of where it is documented, please send it to me.

28. Terry Tempest Williams, *Finding Beauty in a Broken World* (New York: Pantheon, 2008), 29.

29. Raskolnikov in Fyodor Dostoevsky, *Crime and Punishment,* trans. Constance Garnett (New York: Modern Library, 1994), 4.

30. John Franklin, *Narrative of a Journey to the Shores of the Polar Sea, in the Years 1819, 20, 21, & 22* (Philadelphia: H. O. Carey & I. Lea, 1824), 311.

31. E. V. Knox, quoted in C. H. Rolph (a.k.a. Cecil Rolph Hewitt), *London Particulars* (New York: Oxford University Press, 1980), 132.

32. For the argument that "pluralism cannot avoid being tinged with exclusivism unless it is to collapse into meaninglessness," see Roger Trigg's *Rationality and Religion: Does Faith Need Reason?* (Malden, MA: Blackwell, 1998), 58.

33. For more on this, see Sergie Lobanov-Rostovsky, "The Politics of Metaphor," *Kenyon Review* (blog), July 27, 2009, http://kenyonreview.org/blog/?p =4550.

34. See John 17:20–21.

35. W. H. Auden, Epigram to *The Orators: An English Study,* in *The English Auden: Poems, Essays, and Dramatic Writings, 1929–1939* (New York: Random House, 1977), 59.

36. For more on this, contact They at therealthey@yahoo.com.

37. Tony Schwartz, quoted in Oliver Burkeman, "XSW 2011: The Internet Is Over," *The Guardian,* March 15, 2011, www.guardian.co.uk/technology/2011 /mar/15/sxsw-2011-internet-online?INTCMP=SRCH.

Chapter 6

The chapter epigraph is taken from C. K. Barrett, *The Gospel According to St. John* (Philadelphia: Westminster, 1978), 181.

1. The average Londoner may be monitored by three hundred surveillance cameras a day.

2. See Daniel J. Solove's thesis in *The Future of Reputation: Gossip, Rumor, and Privacy on the Internet* (New Haven: Yale University Press, 2007), 2.

3. Marshall McLuhan, *The Gutenberg Galaxy: The Making of Typographic Man* (Toronto, ON: University of Toronto Press, 1962), 31.

4. This is the thesis of philosopher Genevieve Lloyd in *Providence Lost* (Cambridge, MA: Harvard University Press, 2008). She argues that a purposive understanding of history dropped out of the philosophical scene after Hegel (11). But what about Karl Marx? What about Francis Fukuyama?

5. Paul Ginsborg, *The Politics of Everyday Life: Making Choices, Changing Lives* (New Haven: Yale University Press, 2005), 54.

6. For more on this, see Robyn Griggs Lawrence, "Wabi-Sabi: The Art of Imperfection," *Utne Reader,* September/October 2001, 48, www.utne.com /2001-09-01/Wabi-Sabi.aspx.

7. See Lawrence, "Wabi-Sabi: The Art of Imperfection," *Utne Reader,* 48, www
.utne.com/2001-09-01/Wabi-Sabi.aspx.

8. See Allen S. Weiss's short essay on Japanese sake cups, "Ingestion/Guinomi,"
Cabinet 30 (Summer 2008), www.cabinetmagazine.org/issues/30/weiss.php. See
also Allen S. Weiss, "Guinomi," *Gastronomica: The Journal of Food and Culture*
10 (Winter 2010), 136–42.

9. Deyan Sudjic, *The Language of Things: Understanding the World of Desirable
Objects* (New York: Norton, 2008), 110.

10. This tale is retold in Alex Kerr, *Dogs and Demons: Tales from the Dark Side of
Japan* (New York: Hill & Wang, 2001), 10.

11. Samuel Butler, *Unconscious Memory* (Whitefish, MT: Kessinger, 2004 [reprint]),
116.

12. Cicero, quoted in Mark Staniforth and Michael Nash, *Maritime Archaeology:
Australian Approaches* (New York: Springer, 2006), 109. An older translation
is found in "The Orator of M. T. Cicero," XXXIV, in *The Orations of Marcus
Tullius Cicero,* trans. C. D. Yonge (London: G. Bell, 1890), 4:416.

13. Bernard of Chartres, quoted in C. S. Baldwin, *Medieval Rhetoric and Poetic (to
1400) Interpreted from Representative Works* (New York: Macmillan, 1928), 168.

14. Robert Greenleaf, "Servant-Leadership," in *Insights on Leadership: Service,
Stewardship, Spirit, and Servant-Leadership,* ed. Larry C. Spears (New York:
Wiley, 1998), 17., or earlier in *The Leader's Companion: Insights on Leadership
Through the Ages,* ed. J. Thomas Wren (New York: Simon and Schuster, 1995),
20.

15. Brad Meltzer, *The Book of Lies* (New York: Grand Central, 2008), 329–30.

16. *Birth:* Ah, the miracle of birth, filled with joy, wonder, screaming, and blood.
And yet, Carmen Leilani tweeted it all. As she notes in her blog, "Some people think it's insane that I was updating my Twitter stream throughout my
childbirth/labor experience—as in during my contractions, from the hospital
bed, through my water breaking, my epidural, and immediately after pushing
out the Pod," http://carmenleilani.blogs.com/transmutation/2007/08/i-twitterd
-my-e.html. What's worse? Obsessively announcing how many centimeters
you're dilated, or referring to your newborn as "the Pod"?

    Death: Reporter Bernie Morson of the *Rocky Mountain News* probably
thought he was being cutting-edge when he tweeted the funeral of a three-
year-old boy, but it was just morbid. Let's hope we never have to read "family
members shovel earth into grave" on Twitter again (http://twitter.com/#!/
RMN_Berny/status/916669713).

    Therapy: In September 2008, licensed clinical hypnotherapist Wendi
Friesen launched "hypno-Twitter," which she says "will use my hypnosis skills
to give my tweeples an instant hypnotic boost of confidence, stress relief, focus,
and mental toughness during their day." Right now, we are feeling sleepy, very

sleepy. Soon we will submit to being called "tweeples." Wendi Friesen, quoted in Dan Tynan, "8 Ways Twitter Will Change Your Life," *Computer World,* October 29, 2008, www.computerworld.com/s/article/print/9118441/8_ways_Twitter _will_change_your_life?taxonomyName=E-business&taxonomyId=71.

17. E. W. Blandy, "Where He Leads Me," written in 1890. Public Domain.

18. Michelle A. Vu, "'Twitter Bible' Converts Scripture into Mini Messages," *The Christian Post,* October 16, 2009, http://in.christiantoday.com/articles/witter -bible-converts-scripture-into-mini-messages/4637.htm.

19. Released in 2009 at the Frankfurt Book Fair, *And God Decided to Chill* is a German-language book that compiled tweets by more than 3,000 German Christians who participated in a church project that summarized 3,906 Bible sections into 140-character messages. For more on this, see Michelle A. Vu, "'Twitter Bible' Converts Scripture into Mini Messages," *The Christian Post,* October 15, 2009, www.christianpost.com/article/20091015/-Twitter-bible -converts-scripture-into-4-000-short-messages/index.html.

20. Simon Dumenco, "Twitter: A Vampire That Can Legally Suck the Life Out of You," *Advertising Age,* September 21, 2009, 42, http://adage.com/mediaworks /article?article_id=139133. See also Rory Cellan-Jones, "My Life Online–Time to Delete?" November 5, 2009, www.bbc.co.uk/blogs/technology/2009/11 /my_life_online_time_to_delete.html.

Chapter 7

1. See Luke 12:41–48.

2. A. Bartlett Giamatti, *A Free and Ordered Space: The Real World of the University* (New York: Norton, 1990), 18.

3. Google, "Our philosophy," www.google.com/corporate/tenthings.html. See Ken Aulette, *Googled: The End of the World as We Know It* (New York: Penguin, 2010) for the best background to how Google came up with these slogans.

4. BBC News, "Pope Sends First E-Mail Apology," Friday, November 23, 2001, http://news.bbc.co.uk/2/hi/europe/1671540.stm.

5. The matter at issue was the lifting of the excommunication of the Holocaust-denying Lefebvrist Bishop Richard Williamson. See "Letter of His Holiness Pope Benedict XVI to the Bishops of the Catholic Church Concerning the Remission of the Excommunication of the Four Bishops Consecrated by Archbishop Lefebvre," www.vatican.va/holy_father/benedict_xvi/letters/2009 /documents/hf_ben-xvi_let_20090310_remissione-scomunica_en.html. See also Pope Benedict XVI, *Light of the World: the Pope, the Church, and the Signs of the Times: A Conversation with Peter Seewald,* trans. Michael J. Miller and Adrian J. Walker (San Francisco, CA: Ignatius, 2010), 121. His statement: "Unfortunately, though, none of us went on the internet to find out what sort of person we were dealing with."

6. Anthony Grafton, *Worlds Made by Words: Scholarship and Community in the Modern West* (Cambridge, MA: Harvard University Press, 2009), 299.

7. T. G. Jackson, "The Libraries of the Middle Ages," *Journal of the Royal Institute of British Architects* 5 (1898): 376.

8. Robert Darnton, *The Case for Books: Past, Present, and Future* (New York: Public Affairs, 2009).

9. Grafton, *Worlds Made by Words*, 300.

10. Grafton, *Worlds Made by Words*, 311.

11. See Seth Weintraub, "The Numbers Don't Lie: Mobile Devices Overtaking PCs," August 11, 2010, http://tech.fortune.cnn.com/2010/08/11/the-great -game-mobile-devices-overtaking-pcs. Here is some of what Weintraub wrote: "In a nutshell, what we are seeing in smartphones is bigger than anything that has come before it.... The numbers are really big.... The billion-plus phones sold per year. The number of active subscriptions, which is greater than half of the human population. The number of new Android devices that check in with Google every day.... Smartphones, or Mobile devices, will soon become the dominant computing platform for humanity."

12. Ken Dulaney, quoted in Jason Nolte, "6 Endangered Tech Species," http ://finance.yahoo.com/family-home/article/110304/6-endangered-tech-species. Thanks to Russell Kirby for this reference.

13. See the Google website's Corporate Information at www.google.com/about /corporate/company.

14. Five hundred billion words have been put online, or 4 percent of the total. See the Ngram Viewer at www.ngrams.googlelabs.com and play some "Culturomics."

15. Nicholas Negroponte, quoted in *TechCrunch*, M. G. Siegler, "Nicholas Negroponte: The Physical Book Is Dead in 5 Years," August 6, 2010, http ://techcrunch.com/2010/08/06/physical-book-dead.

16. This is the phrase first used by Alan Greenspan to describe the dot-com economy. See Alan Greenspan, "The Challenge of Central Banking in a Democratic Society," Annual Dinner and Francis Boyer Lecture, The American Enterprise Institute for Public Policy Research, Washington, D.C., December 5, 1996, www.federalreserve.gov/boarddocs/speeches/1996/19961205.htm.

17. Christopher Mims, "Predicting the Death of Print," August 23, 2010, www .technologyreview.com/blog/mimssbits/25642.

18. I would argue that www.codexsinaiticus.org is one of the most magnificent achievements of the Google world. The printed version of these digitized photographs is soon to come. But in the meantime, check online the original Codex Sinaiticus. At the end of the manuscript there are two early Christian writings, *The Epistle of Barnabas* and *The Shepherd of Hermas*.

19. Grafton, *Worlds Made by Words*, 324.

20. Tim Gautreaux, "The Pine Oil Writers' Conference," in *Welding with Children* (New York: Macmillan, 2009), 105.

21. The closing words of Misia Landau, *Narratives of Human Evolution* (New Haven: Yale University Press, 1993), 185.

22. Thomas McGrath, excerpt from *Letter to an Imaginary Friend* (Port Townsend, WA: Copper Canyon, 1997), 155, copyright © 1997 by Thomas McGrath. Reprinted with the permission of The Permissions Company Inc. on behalf of Copper Canyon Press, www.coppercanyonpress.org.

23. National Museum of the American Indian, "Lone Dog's Winter Count: Keeping History Alive," www.nmai.si.edu/education/files/poster_lone_dog_final.pdf. See also Diane Glancy, *Lone Dog's Winter Count* (Albuquerque, NM: West End, 1991).

24. Flannery O'Connor, "Writing Short Stories," in *Mystery and Manners: Occasional Prose,* ed. Sally and Robert Fitzgerald (New York: Macmillan, 1969), 96.

25. One of many quotable, but unsubstantiated, anecdotes about George Bernard Shaw.

26. E. O. Wilson, *The Creation: An Appeal to Save Life on Earth* (New York: Norton, 2006), 10.

27. David Martin, *Christian Language in the Secular City* (Aldershot, Hants, England: Ashgate, 2002), 200.

Chapter 8

The chapter epigraph is taken from Groucho Marx, quoted in David Horspool, "He Saw What He Could Do," *TLS: Times Literary Supplement,* September 18, 2009, 17.

1. Google Wave, for example, enables shared space where people can interact and shape the story in real-time conversations.

2. C. H. Dodd, *Parables of the Kingdom,* rev. ed. (New York: Charles Scribner's Sons, 1961), 5.

3. *Manual of Style: Being a Compilation of the Typographical Rules in Force at the University of Chicago Press* (Chicago, IL: University of Chicago Press, 1906), v.

4. As advertized in "What's New in the 16th edition," Chicago Manual of Style Online, www.chicagomanualofstyle.org/about16.html. It is interesting to note that the 201-page first edition has grown to include 1,026 pages of regulations and yet, while the text has become more complex, the title has been simplified.

5. John Scotus Eriugena, *The Voice of the Eagle: Homily on the Prologue to the Gospel of St. John,* trans., with an introduction and reflection by Christopher Bamford (Hudson, NY: Lindisfarne, 1990), 73.

6. Quoted on the back cover of Martin Luther, *Table Talk,* updated and revised by William Hazlitt (Gainsville, FL: Bridge Logos, 2004).

7. Justus Lipsius, quoted in Anthony Grafton, *Worlds Made by Words: Scholarship*

and Community in the Modern World (Cambridge, MA: Harvard University Press, 2009), 16.

8. See Leonard Sweet and Frank Viola, *Jesus Manifesto: Restoring the Supremacy and Sovereignty of Jesus Christ* (Nashville: Thomas Nelson, 2010).

9. Bob Dylan, "It's Alright, Ma (I'm Only Bleeding)," 1965, www.bobdylan.com /songs/its-alright-ma-im-only-bleeding.

10. Marina Warner, *Signs & Wonders: Essays on Literature and Culture* (London: Chatto & Windus, 2003), 380.

11. W. H. Auden, "A Shilling Life Will Give You All the Facts," in *Selected Poems,* expanded 2nd ed., ed. Edward Mendelson (New York: Vintage, 2007), 33.

12. William Carlos Williams, "Author's Introduction to *The Wedge*," in *Selected Essays of William Carlos Williams* (New York: New Directions, 1969), 256.

13. See Gail T. Fairhurst and Robert A. Sarr, *The Art of Framing: Managing the Language of Leadership* (San Francisco: Jossey-Bass, 1996). Fairhurst and Sarr reference Lakoff's work on the "skill" and "power" of framing.

14. George Lakoff, *Don't Think of an Elephant: Know Your Values and Frame the Debate* (White River Junction, VT: Chelsea Green, 2004), xv.

15. Alan Deutschmann, "Change or Die," *FastCompany,* May 2005, www .fastcompany.com/magazine/94/open_change-or-die.html.

16. Michel Serres, writing in *Rameaux* (Le Pommier, 2005), approaches "languages and myths as 'formatting' cultural and ethical life," sometimes on a religious grid, sometimes on a scientific grid, and sometimes on a "meshed amalgam," quoted in Frederic Raphael, "*TLS* Books of the Year," *TLS: Times Literary Supplement,* December 2, 2005, 11. See also the French original: Michel Serres, *Rameaux* (Paris: Editions Le Pommier, 2004).

17. Archibald Macleish, "Hypocrite Auteur (2)," in *Collected Poems, 1917–1982* (Boston: Houghton Mifflin, 1985), 415.

18. See, for instance, Matthew 10:34.

19. Nelson Goodman, *Ways of Worldmaking* (Indianapolis, IN: Hackett, 1978).

20. To borrow a phrase from David Bolter, quoted in David Harsanyi, "The Amateurs' Hour: Is the Internet Destroying Our Culture, or Is It Just Annoying Our Snobs?" *Reason,* January 2008, 66, www.reason.com/news/show/123523 .html. See also Andrew Keen, *The Cult of the Amateur: How Today's Internet Is Killing Our Culture* (New York: Doubleday/Currency, 2007).

21. Jesse Rice, *The Church of Facebook: How the Hyperconnected Are Redefining Community* (Colorado Springs, CO: David C. Cook 2009), 192.

22. See Clay Shirky, *Cognitive Surplus: Creativity and Generosity in a Connected Age* (New York: Penguin, 2010).

23. Sheena Iyengar, *The Art of Choosing* (New York: Twelve, 2010), 185–87.

24. Quoted by Edward Fredkin's associate, Marvin Minsky, in *The Society of Mind* (New York: Simon & Schuster, 1988), 52.

25. Andrew Keen, quoted in Harsanyi, "The Amateurs' Hour," *Reason*, 66, www .reason.com/news/show/123523.html. See also Keen, *The Cult of the Amateur*.

26. For my exploration of the EPIC interface to TGIF Culture, see Leonard Sweet, *Postmodern Pilgrims: First Century Passion for the 21st Century World* (Nashville: Broadman & Holman, 2000) and Leonard Sweet, *The Gospel According to Starbucks* (Colorado Springs, CO: WaterBrook, 2007).

27. For more on randomizing rituals, see Leonard Sweet, *Nudge: Awakening Each Other to the God Who's Already There* (Colorado Springs, CO: David C. Cook, 2010).

28. Cass R. Sunstein, *Republic.Com 2.0* (Princeton, NJ: Princeton University Press, 2007), 100, 150. See also Jon Garvie, "Off the Board," *TLS: Times Literary Supplement*, May 2, 2008, 8–9.

29. Found on the final page of Harold James, *The Roman Predicament: How the Rules of International Order Create the Politics of Empire* (Princeton, NJ: Princeton University Press, 2006), 149.

30. This concept is developed in Marshall McLuhan and Bruce R. Powers, *The Global Village: Transformations in World Life and Media in the 21st Century* (New York: Oxford University Press, 1989).

31. Even in Jane Austen's time gossip was the lubrication that kept the wheels of village life turning. In a village, everything is observed and everything is assigned a meaning. As John Broderick put it so beautifully in his novel *The Pilgrimage*, "The city dweller who passes through a country town, and imagines it sleepy and apathetic is very far from the truth; it is as watchful as the jungle" (Dublin: Lilliput, 2004, 134, quoted in Sam Thompson, "Perversely Cured," *TLS: Times Literary Supplement*, December 17, 2004, 21).

32. Quoted in Robert Darnton, *The Devil in the Holy Water or the Art of Slander from Louis XIV to Napoleon* (Philadelphia: University of Pennsylvania Press, 2010), 259.

33. Fred Allen, quoted in Orville Gilbert Brim, *Look at Me! The Fame Motive from Childhood to Death* (Ann Arbor, MI: University of Michigan Press, 2009), 108.

34. Antony Jay, quoted in Peter Hennessay, "Britain's Post-War Thaw, *TLS: Times Literary Supplement*, 6 May 2009, http://entertainment.timesonline.co.uk/tol /arts_and_entertainment/the_tls/article6232707.ece.

35. Daniel J. Boorstin, *The Image, or What Happened to the American Dream* (New York: Atheneum, 1952), 57.

36. William Faulkner, "To Hamilton Basso, 23 Sept. 1948," *Selected Letters of William Faulkner*, ed. Joseph Blotner (New York: Random House, 1978), 276.

37. Job 1:21, NKJV.

38. With thanks to DMin student Linda Grenz, who first provoked these questions and reflections.

39. Quote attributed to President Harry S Truman, as referenced in *The Oxford Dictionary of Quotations,* 5th ed., ed. Elizabeth Knowles (New York: Oxford University Press, 1999), 784.

40. Lloyd John Ogilvie, *A Life Full of Surprises: Patterns of New Life from the Sermon on the Mount* (Nashville: Abingdon, 1969), 130–31.

41. One wonders how Augustine would have fared in today's climate: Augustine was a libertine; he had promiscuous sex with all sorts of women, even got one pregnant, then left her.

42. Daniel J. Solove, *The Future of Reputation: Gossip, Rumor, and Privacy on the Internet* (New Haven, CT: Yale University Press, 2007), 11.

43. Quoted in S. Milius, "Perils of Migration: New Evidence That Bats Stalk Birds," *Science News,* February 17, 2007, 102, http://findarticles.com/p/articles/mi _m1200/is_7_171/ai_n27171462.

44. Arabella Katherine Hankey, "I Love to Tell the Story," 1869. Public Domain.

45. Ignazio Silone, *And He Hid Himself: A Play in Four Acts,* trans. Darina Tranquilli (New York: Harper & Row, 1946), vi.

Chapter 9

The chapter epigraph is quoted in David Whyte, *The Heart Aroused: Poetry and the Preservation of the Soul in Corporate America* (New York: Currency/Doubleday, 1996), 162.

1. Matthew Arnold, "The Study of Poetry," in *Essays, English and American: With Introductions and Notes* (New York: P. F. Collier, 1910), 65–86.

2. John Ruskin, "Of Many Things," vol. 3. of *Modern Painters* (New York: Merrill & Baker, 1873), 2:331. (Note: Vol. 3–4 are published in vol. 2 of this edition. See also v. 3, pt. 4, ch. 16, sect. 28.)

3. Wallace Stevens, *Collected Poetry and Prose* (New York: Library of America, 1997), 901.

4. Repeated refrain from Henry Wadsworth Longfellow, "The Song of Hiawatha," in *The Poetical Works of Henry Wadsworth Longfellow* (London: George Routledge, 1867), 228–88, that is, 235, 251, 277, 286.

5. A few years ago the leaders of the world (presidents, prime ministers, statespersons) were asked to select their favorite poems for a book benefitting world peace. One wonders if such a project would be conceivable ten years from now, especially a project where some of these leaders contributed original poems of their own. Tony Blair, Ariel Sharon, and Gerhard Schroder were some of the contributors to *World Leaders' Favourite Poems: A Book of Peace,* comp. Mehmet Basci (Cardigan, Wales: Parthian, 2008).

6. The phrase is that of Sebastian Barker in "Off with the Shackles of Certitude," *The Tablet,* January 1, 2011, 24, but the thesis is that of Malcolm Guite, *Faith, Hope and Poetry: Theology and the Poetic Imagination* (Burlington, VT: Ashgate, 2010).

7. Emily Dickinson, "Apparently with No Surprise," in *The Poems of Emily Dickinson*, ed. R. W. Franklin (Cambridge, MA: Belknap, 1999), 603.

8. The first quote is from Robert Frost, "The Figure a Poem Makes," in *The Collected Prose of Robert Frost*, ed. Mark Richardson (Boston: Harvard University Press, 2007), 133. The second quote (with hyphens added) is from "The Road Not Taken," in *The Road Not Taken and Other Poems*, ed. Stanley Appelbaum (New York: Dover, 1993), 1.

9. Geoffrey Hill, *The Triumph of Love* (Boston: Houghton Mifflin, 1998), 46.

10. Of course, there always are exceptions that prove the rule, but even these exceptions are becoming scarcer. One of the exceptions is Craig Oldenburg, who wrote "A Prayer for When We Limit God" (used here by permission) during his doctoral studies with me:

> Dear God beyond my personal design
> I may attempt to lock Your eminence into my mind
> But I understand this image is not You
> Only what a finite imagination will construe
> So please love me more than one can know
> Especially when so predisposed
> To think too small, too narrow, too brief
> In the isolation of my own predictable beliefs
> Surprise me then, if You will, at times
> That I might comprehend You out of my mind.
> Amen

Here is a poem (used here by permission) from another doctoral student, Timothy Orton, called "The Mysting":

> The mysty rain, a veil that, sheer, unfolds
> In soft gray silkiness, and lavender,
> Comes falling with the slightest sound,
> Caressing in its cool embrace.
> In droplets barely felt or heard,
> With graceful presence and restraint,
> To quench and moisten all that lives,
> And dignified in what it gives to those.
> How so, that some cannot abide this calm,
> And rail against the cloak of silver, falling,
> Sadness cries from depths unseen,
> Unsettled soul, this sadness would betray.
> And whispering, the myst responds in subtle joy.

A mirror, this, reflects what lies within.
For some, the pain is all that can be seen or heard,
The mysting more like tears than not.
But sadness, thought by most a grief,
The myst brings forth in silent shroud,
To test the fabric of the heart; to see
If joy and sadness, hand-in-hand, can go.
And like the warp and woof, our lives are woven,
Not from joy alone, but sadness also,
Like the mysting, tears can be
From sadness, or from joy.
For me, the mysty rain, all thick and rich,
And filled with mystery and awe,
Is sad, but lovely, dark, and deep;
Softly speaks of Him who made it so.

11. The source of this quotation is unknown.
12. Eugene H. Peterson, *The Contemplative Pastor* (Grand Rapids: Eerdmans, 1993), 44.
13. Peterson, *The Contemplative Pastor,* 44. Peterson concludes his essay with this summons: "Isn't it odd that pastors, who are responsible for interpreting the Scriptures, so much of which come in the form of poetry, have so little interest in poetry? It is a crippling defect and must be remedied. The Christian communities as a whole must rediscover poetry, and the pastors must lead them. Poetry is essential to the pastoral vocation because poetry is original speech" (45).
14. Martin Luther, "Preface to the Revelation of St. John," 1522, in *Word and Sacrament,* ed. E. Theodore Bachman, *Luther's Works,* vol. 35 (Philadelphia: Fortress, 1960), 398.
15. The full story is found in Roderick MacFarquhar and Michael Schoenhals, *Mao's Last Revolution* (Cambridge, MA: Harvard University Press, 2006), 119.
16. Martin Luther to Eoban Hess, 29 March 1523, in *Luther's Correspondence and Other Contemporary Letters,* trans. and ed. Preserved Smith and Charles M. Jacobs (Philadelphia: Lutheran Publication Society, 1918), 2:176–77.
17. D. H. Lawrence, "Song of a Man Who Has Come Through," in *The Complete Poems,* ed. Vivian de Sola Pinto and Warren Roberts (London: Penguin, 1993), 250.
18. Quoted in a report of his visit to New York by Milton Bracker, "Nobel Prize Poet Assays U.S.," *New York Times,* May 14, 1960, 47.
19. Hayden Carruth, *The Voice That Is Great Within Us: American Poetry of the Twentieth Century* (New York: Bantam, 1971).

20. Gerard Manly Hopkins, "God's Grandeur," in *Poems and Prose* (New York: Penguin, 1981), 27.

21. Ephesians 2:10 (translation by Jerrell Jobe). Used with the author's permission. See his blog at http://growdeep.blogspot.com/2005/06/god-tailor.html.

22. Van Gogh to Emile Bernard, *The Complete Letters of Vincent van Gogh* (Greenwich, CT: New York Graphic Society, 1959), 3:496, emphasis added.

23. John Boucher, *Licensed Insanities: Religions and Belief in God in the Contemporary World* (London: Darton, Longman and Todd, 1987), 7.

24. "There's a little gold in our age," English professor William Logan wrote, but there's also "more than enough bronze, a valley of lead, and as in all ages a mountain of tin" (William Logan, *The Undiscovered Country: Poetry in the Age of Tin* [New York: Columbia University Press, 2005], 1).

25. Billy Collins, "Introduction: Seventy-Five Needles in the Haystack of Poetry," in Billy Collins and David Lehman, *The Best American Poetry, 2006* (New York: Simon & Schuster, 2006), xv. Collins's exact words: "I count myself among those whose lives would be sorely impoverished without the dependable availability of the remaining 17 percent."

26. Need help writing that first line of poetry? For a while a website helped you: artofwritingzine.com. This Poetry Generator produced the first line for you. All you had to do was click on the "Create" button. Unfortunately, the site has been taken down.

27. For more about his hut, see Adam Sharr, *Heidegger's Hut* (Cambridge, MA: MIT Press, 2006). In January 2011 I made a pilgrimage to Heidegger's Hut, and to the little front stoop where he did so much of his poetry reading.

28. Wallace Stevens, "Sunday Morning," in *The Collected Poems of Wallace Stevens* (New York: Random House, 1990), 66–71.

29. Robert Frost, "The Figure a Poem Makes," *The Collected Prose of Robert Frost,* ed. Mark Richardson (Cambridge, MA: Harvard University Press, 2007), 132.

30. These I consider to be the greatest poets of the last half of the twentieth century.

31. Plutarch, "Whether Military or Intellectual Exploits Have Brought Athens More Fame," in *Essays,* trans. Robin Waterfield (New York: Penguin, 1992), 148.

32. If I remember correctly, Aristotle said something along these lines. It may be where Aristotle wrote: "The historian relates what happened, the poet what might happen" (Aristotle, *On Poetry and Style,* trans. G. M. A. Grube [Indianapolis, IN: Hackett, 1958], 18).

33. Charles Simic, in *The Best of the Best American Poetry, 1988–1997,* ed. Harold Bloom and David Lehman (New York: Simon and Schuster, 1998), 353.

34. Meister Eckhart, quoted in Roderick MacIver, *Meditations on Nature, Meditations on Silence* (Berkeley: North Atlantic Books, 2009), 61.

35. Revelation 8:1, KJV.

36. Ezra Pound, "The Constant Preaching to the Mob," in *The Literary Essays of*

Ezra Pound (New York: New Directions, 1968), 64. Originally published in *Poetry: A Magazine of Verse* 8:3 (June 1916): 145.

37. Søren Kierkegaard, "Diapsalmata," in *Either/Or: A Fragment of Life,* ed. Alastair Hanney (New York: Penguin, 1992), 43.

38. Wallace Stegner, "Ansel Adams and the Search for Perfection," in *One Way to Spell Man* (Garden City, NY: Doubleday, 1982), 159.

39. Gustave Flaubert, *Letters,* Selected, with an Introduction by Richard Rumbold, trans. J. M. Cohen (London: Weidenfeld & Nicholson, 1950), 81.

40. Howard Nemerov, "To the Congress of the United States, Entering Its Third Century," in *Trying Conclusions: New and Selected Poems, 1961–1991* (Chicago: University of Chicago Press, 1991), 143.

41. John Bayley, "State of the Nation: American Poetry," in *Selected Essays* (New York: Cambridge University Press, 1984), 8.

42. Peterson, *The Contemplative Pastor,* 46.

43. Marcel Proust, "Swann Explained by Proust," in *Against Sainte-Beuve and Other Essays* (New York: Penguin, 1988), 236.

44. Seamus Heaney, quoted in Michael Glover, "Transforming the Ordinary," *The Tablet,* December 25, 2010, 31. It also is attributed to Emily Dickinson, quoted in Michael Glover, "The Books Interview John Ashbery: A Blue Rinse for the Language," *The Independent,* November 13, 1999, www.independent.co.uk /arts-entertainment/the-books-interview-john-ashbery-a-blue-rinse-for-the -language-1125605.html.

45. See Nicholas Carr's book *The Shallows: What the Internet Is Doing to Our Brains* (New York: Norton, 2010).

46. Anne Lamott quotes "my Jesuit friend Father Tom," in *Plan B: Further Thoughts on Faith* (New York: Riverhead, 2005), 256–67. The phrase also can be attributed to John H. Westerhoff, *Living Faithfully as a Prayer Book People* (Harrisburg, PA: Morehouse, 2004), 76.

47. See Esther De Waal, *Living with Contradiction: An Introduction to Benedictine Spirituality* (Harrisburg, PA: Morehouse, 1997), esp. 22–23; and Howard Nemerov, *Figures of Thought: Speculations on the Meaning of Poetry & Other Essays* (Boston: David R. Godine, 1978), 10.

48. Opening line of Samuel Beckett's "Humanistic Quietism," a review of Thomas McGreevy's *Poems,* first printed in *Dublin Magazine* 9, July/September 1934, 79. The full quote is: "All prayer, as discriminated from the various paradigms of prosody, is prayer." Reprinted in *Disjecta: Miscellaneous Writings and a Dramatic Fragment,* ed. Ruby Cohn (New York: Grove, 1984), 68.

49. Robert Louis Stevenson, "Better Acquaintance," chap. 8 in *Ebb Tide* in *The Novels and Tales of Robert Louis Stevenson* (New York: Charles Scribner's Sons, 1895), 11:333.

50. Quoted in Philip D. Beidler, *Re-Writing America: Vietnam Authors in Their Generation* (Athens, GA: University of Georgia Press, 1991), 151.

51. Geoffrey Hill, *The Triumph of Love* (Boston: Houghton Mifflin, 1998), 26.

52. See http://imagejournal.org/page/journal/editorial-statements/whos-afraid -of-geoffrey-hill.

53. Geoffrey Hill, "On Reading *Crowds and Power*," in *A Treatise of Civil Power* (New Haven: Yale University Press, 2007), 47.

54. Jonathan Barnes, quoted in Anthony Grafton, *Worlds Made by Words: Scholarship and Community in the Modern World* (Cambridge: Harvard University Press, 2009), 322. See also Jonathan Barnes, "Bagpipe Music," *Topoi* 25, September 2006, 18.

55. Wallace Stevens, *The Contemplated Spouse: The Letters of Wallace Stevens to Elsie,* ed. J. Donald Blount (Columbia, SC: University of South Carolina Press, 2006), 40.

56. Concluding lines of R. S. Thomas, "Don't Ask Me," *Residues* (Highgreen, Northumberland, UK: Bloodaxe, 2002), 69.

57. Denis Donoghue, *Emily Dickinson* (Minneapolis: University of Minnesota Press, 1969), 5.

58. Morton Kelsey, *Encounter with God: A Theology of Christian Experience* (Minneapolis: Bethany Fellowship, 1972), 58, 44, 139.

59. David Martin, "Fundamentally," *TLS,* May 21, 2010, 10.

60. Ralph Waldo Emerson, *Emerson in His Journal,* ed. Joel Porte (Cambridge, MA: Belknap Press of Harvard University Press, 1982), 45.

61. The phrase comes from Tom Mole and his book *Byron's Romantic Celebrity.* We feed our hunger for celebrity culture and gossip by "snacking" on updates during the day. Forty-four percent of the time when USAmericans are visiting celebrity websites like omg!, TMZ, People.com, Usmagazine.com, or TheInsider, it is during work hours.

62. John Ashbery, "A Poem of Unrest," in *Notes from Air: Selected Later Poems* (New York: Ecco, 2007), 157.

63. Someone like Meghan O'Rourke, "The Instruction Manual: How to Read John Ashbery," *Slate,* March 9, 2005, www.slate.com/id/2114565.

64. Robert M. Hutchins, quoted in *Dictionary of Quotations in Communications,* ed. Lilless McPherson Shilling and Linda K. Fuller (Westport, CT: Greenwood, 1997), 235.

65. This is quoted in Max D. Isaacson, "After You Get Where You're Going, Where Will It Be," *Vital Speeches of the Day,* January 1, 1978, 204.

66. For a modern edition, see "The Defense of Poesy," in *Sir Philip Sidney: Selected Prose and Poetry,* ed. Robert Kimbrough, 2nd ed. (Madison, WI: University of Wisconsin Press, 1983), 102–60.

67. Richard Rorty, "The Fire of Life," *Poetry,* November 18, 2007; reprinted in *The Rorty Reader,* ed. Christopher J. Voparil and Richard J. Bernstein (Malden, MA: Wiley-Blackwell, 2010), 520–21. Quotes on 521.

68. Anne Boleyn had a copy of William Tyndales's English New Testament (1534) and it still survives in the British Museum, according to "Queen Anne and Tyndale," in J. Stephen Lang, *1,001 More Things You Always Wanted to Know About the Bible* (Nashville: Thomas Nelson, 2001), Item 241.
69. The committee was headed up by Alexander Jones, and essentially was a French project by the (Catholic) School of Biblical Studies in Jerusalem.
70. *The Book of Jonah,* trans. J. R. R. Tolkien (London: Darton, Longman and Todd, 2009). See also The Tolkien Library, "The Book of Jonah," www .tolkienlibrary.com/press/888-Book_of_Jonah_Translated_by_Tolkien.php.
71. Rachel Naomi Remen, *My Grandfather's Blessings: Stories of Strength, Refuge, and Belonging* (New York: Riverhead, 2001).
72. Thanks to Teri Hyrkas for this reference.
73. Mary Colwell, "Call of the Wild," *The Tablet,* March 7, 2009, 10. For an earlier version, see "Future of the Amazon a Catholic Issue Says Leading Lay Activist," *ARC News & Resources,* January 23, 2009, www.arcworld.org/news .asp?pageID=289.

Chapter 10

The chapter epigraph is taken from Desiderius Erasmus, *Adages of Erasmus,* sel. William Watson Barker (Toronto, ON: University of Toronto Press, 2001), 146.

1. It took twenty years to go from a 5-megahertz processing chip to a 500-megahertz chip; but we went from 500 megahertz to one gigahertz in only eight months.
2. Justin is a college kid from Howard Chapman's church who wants to be a weatherman. He is interning at the local TV weather station this summer. Here was his post on Twitter: "Just had a first. Homeless person calling on a cellphone to find out when the rain will start."
3. For this statistic see Frank Bures, "Can You Hear Us Now? Why Technology Is Africa's Latest Greatest Poverty Fighter," *Utne Reader,* March/April 2011, 11, www.utne.com/Science-Technology/Technology-Cell-Phones-Africa-Poverty -Fighter.aspx?page=2.
4. Virginia Woolf, "Mr. Bennett and Mrs. Brown," in *The Captain's Death Bed and Other Essays* (London: Hogarth, 1950), 96.
5. In 1905, only 5 percent of urban USAmerican dwellings had electricity. By 1930, more than 90 percent did.
6. Youth marketing expert Joanne McKinney, quoted in Noah Rubin Brier, "Coming of Age," *American Demographics,* November 2004, 18.
7. In 1978, 50 percent of sixteen-year-olds and 75 percent of seventeen-year-olds had a driver's license. In 2008, 31 percent of sixteen-year-olds and 49 percent of seventeen-year-olds had one. Ford is trying to lure TGIFers with Sync, an automotive technology that is voice activated. It rivals Xbox or PlayStation or Nintendo.

8. Even if they don't know the name of the company, Rovio Mobile. For more on this, go to www.rovio.com/index.php?page=company. Rovio Mobile is, along with other innovative companies, the new hope of Finland's economic future. For more on gaming developments, see Tom Chatfield, *Fun Inc.: Why Gaming Will Dominate the Twenty-First Century* (New York: Pegasus, 2010), esp. chap. 11: "Future Inc.?" 209–45.

9. Margaret Lyons, "Videogames vs. Movies: A Leader Emerges…and We Applaud?" *Pop Watch,* May 21, 2009, http://popwatch.ew.com/2009/05/21/more-people-pla.

10. Ninety percent of Western adolescents play video games.

11. There are now Barbie Video Girl dolls and Barbie Video games. See www.ibisworld.com. A 2008 NPD market research study revealed that video games are not just for teen boys, blowing the conventional wisdom out the window. For more on this, see "Girl Power: Understanding This Important Consumer Segment," www.npd.com/lps/PDF_SpecialReports/Girls_Topical.pdf.

12. According to a 2009 report by the Entertainment Software Association. See their "Essential Facts about the Computer and Video Game Industry: 2009 Sales, Demographics and Usage Data," www.theesa.com/facts/pdfs/ESA_EF_2009.pdf.

13. Cognitive scientists from the University of Rochester report their findings in an upcoming study in the journal *Current Biology.* Authors Daphne Bavelier, Alexandre Pouget, and C. Shawn Green tested dozens of eighteen- to twenty-five-year-olds who were not skilled video game players. They split the subjects into two groups. One group played fifty hours of the fast-paced action video games "Call of Duty 2" and "Unreal Tournament," and the other group played fifty hours of the slow-moving strategy game "The Sims 2." After the training period, all of the subjects were asked to make quick decisions in several tasks. The action-game players were up to 25 percent faster at coming to a conclusion and answered just as many questions correctly as their strategy-game playing peers. See also Steven Johnson, *Everything Bad Is Good for You* (New York: Penguin, 2006).

14. Chatfield, *Fun Inc.,* 69. For discussion of differing views on the relation between violent games and violence in society, see Chatfield, 65–71. For a discussion on games and the military, see Chatfield, 187–97.

15. Jane McGonigal, "Gaming Can Make a Better World," February 10, 2010. From a video: http://dotsub.com/view/87e58675-24ba-408b-abbe-97718a3b17b5. and a transcript: http://dotsub.com/view/87e58675-24ba-408b-abbe-97718a3b17b5/viewTranscript/eng.

16. See Peter Burrows and Caroline Dye, "They Still Believe in Steve," *Bloomberg Businessweek,* 26 July–1 August, 2010, 34. Also, Peter Burrows, "Steve Jobs, Apple Get a Vote of Confidence after Antenae-gate," www.businessweek.com

/magazine/content/10_31/b4189034703517.htm?chan=magazine+channel
_news+-+technology.

17. Other nonrhyming English words? *Purple, month, silver, depth, pint, breadth, warmth, bilge, film, and wolf.*

18. The most popular fruit in Japan? The orange. In Canada, France, Germany, China, it is the apple. In the UK, Russia, Brazil, Mexico, and Iceland, it's the banana.

19. See Michael Oakeshott, *Experience and Its Modes* (New York: Cambridge University Press, 1933; repr. 1985), 313; and Alasdair MacIntyre, *After Virtue* (Notre Dame, IN: University of Notre Dame Press, 2007), 204. For John Cobb's critique of the disciplinary organization of knowledge, see his *Transforming Christianity and the World: A Way Beyond Absolutism and Relativism* (Maryknoll, NY: Orbis, 1999), 98–99, 112. This is discussed more fully in Herman Daly and John B. Cobb, *For the Common Good: Redirecting the Economy Toward Community, the Environment, and a Sustainable Future* (Boston: Beacon, 1989).

20. Donald Barthelme, "See the Moon," *Unspeakable Practices, Unnatural Acts* (New York: Farrar, Straus and Giroux, 1968), 157.

21. Owen Barfield, *History, Guilt, and Habit* (Middletown, CT: Wesleyan University Press, 1979), xix.

22. Zygmunt Bauman, *Liquid Love: On the Frailty of Human Bonds* (New York: Wiley-Blackwell, 2003), 64. The quote within the quote is from Michael Schluter and David Lee, *The R Factor* (London: Hodder & Staughton, 1993), 37.

23. For more on this idea, see Konstantin Stanislavski, *Building a Character,* trans. Elizabeth Reynolds Hopgood (New York: Routledge, 1936, 2003). Stanislavski argues for the "ensemble principle"—the interaction between our sense of our unique identity with the collective life that shapes and directs it. "Collective creative effort is the root of our kind of art. That requires ensemble acting and whoever mars that ensemble is committing a crime not only against his comrades but also against the very art of which he is the servant" (284).

24. Charles A. Lindbergh, "Entry for Sunday, 2 July 1939" in *The Wartime Journals of Charles A. Lindbergh* (New York: Harcourt, Brace, Jovanovich, 1970), 222. How can we be both free and bound? (Have someone read the lyrics to the hymn "Make Me a Captive, Lord," George Matheson, "Make Me a Captive, Lord," 1890, Public Domain, www.cyberhymnal.org/htm/m/a/makecapt.htm.

Chapter 11

The chapter epigraph is taken from Harry Mulisch, quoted in Cees Nooteboom, "A Bigger Puzzle" (a tribute to Harry Mulisch), *TLS: Times Literary Supplement,* November 12, 2010, 17.

1. Sylvia Lettice Thrupp, "Editorial from the First Issue of *Comparative Studies in Society and History,*" reprinted in *Society and History: Essays* (Ann Arbor, MI: University of Michigan Press, 1977), 329.

2. The metaphor comparing ecosystems to Persian carpets is adopted and adapted from David Quammen, as referenced in Caroline Fraser, *Rewilding the World: Dispatches from the Conservation Revolution* (New York: Macmillan, 2010), 23. For the original quote see David Quammen, *The Song of the Dodo: Island Biogeography in an Age of Extinctions* (New York: Simon & Schuster, 1997), 11.

3. So argues Sri Lanken theologian Tissa Balasuriya in *Planetary Theology* (Maryknoll, NY: Orbis, 1984), 193.

4. This phrase is in Tom Gegax, *Winning in the Game of Life* (New York: Harmony, 1999), 277. It is also referred to in several later books, but the first place I ever heard it was from Sandra Hay.

5. The phrase can be traced to the sixteenth century. It was used by William James in *Grace for Grace: Letters of Rev. William James* (New York: Dodd & Mead, 1874), 79–80. "Self-esteem" became popular as a psychological movement after the publication of *The Principles of Psychology* (Chicago: Macmillan, 1890).

6. This phrase was coined in a 1966 episode of *Star Trek* and adopted by Adam Sternbergh, "Up with Grups," *New York Magazine,* March 26, 2006, 24.

7. Michael Bywater, *Big Babies: Or, Why Can't We Just Grow Up?* (London: Granta, 2007), 127. Bywater further maintains that you can have a full-grown body and be a full-grown baby.

8. A. McKechnie [M'Kechnie], *Sugar Candy for Spoiled Husbands, or The Wife at Home. Also Sugar Plums for Big Babies* (Bingley, England: J. Harrison and Son, 1865).

9. For more on this idea, see George William Rutler, *The Seven Ages of Man: Meditations on the Last Words of Christ* (San Francisco: Ignatius, 1991), 142.

10. Robert A. Orsi, "2+2=Five, or the Quest for an Abundant Empiricism," *Spiritus* 6 (2006), 115, 113–21.

11. Wilfred Owen, "Dulce et Decorum Est," in *The Complete Poems and Fragments,* ed. Jo Stallworthy (New York: Norton, 1983), 1:140.

12. Louis MacNeice, "Snow" (second stanza), in *Collected Poems* (New York: Oxford University Press, 1967), 30.

13. Isaac Rosenberg, *Isaac Rosenberg,* ed. Vivien Noakes (New York: Oxford University Press, 2009), 106.

14. Isaac Rosenberg, "To Gordon Bottomley, 19 August 1916," in *Isaac Rosenberg,* 312.

15. D. H. Lawrence, "Morality and the Novel," in *Selected Literary Criticism,* ed. Anthony Beal (New York: Heinemann, 1955), 110.

16. Albert Einstein, quoted in Ram Dass and Paul Gorman, "The Listening Mind," *The Wisdom of Listening,* ed. Mark Brady (Boston: Wisdom Publications, 2003), 112.

17. Iain McGilchrist, *The Master and His Emissary: The Divided Brain and the Making of the Western World* (New Haven: Yale University Press, 2009), 93.

18. Quoted in Carl E. Braaten, *The Whole Counsel of God* (Philadelphia: Fortress, 1974), 20. Excerpted from Plato's *Apology of Socrates.*

19. Socrates, quoted in Braaten, *The Whole Counsel of God,* 20.

20. Max Beerbohm, "Dandies and Dandies," in *The Works of Max Beerbohm, with a Biography by John Lane* (New York: Dodd, Mead, 1922), 23.

21. See "Transcript of President Barack Obama's Commencement Address at Hampton University, www.wtkr.com/news/wtkr-obama-hampton-address -transcript,0,7478536.story.

Chapter 12

The chapter epigraph is taken from Max Frisch, *Homo Faber* (Boston: Houghton Mifflin, 1959), 178.

1. Isaiah 4:5, MSG.

2. See Hebrews 12:1.

3. Matthew 3:11, KJV.

4. Lucy Larcom, "Three Old Saws," *Friend's Intelligencer: A Religious and Family Journal* 25 (1868): 108. Also in *The Poetical Works of Lucy Larcom* (Boston: Houghton Mifflin, 1884), 57.

5. See Mark 14:67; Luke 22:56.

6. 1 Samuel 15:3, KJV.

7. George Clooney, quoted in James Rocci, "Toronto Notebook: George Clooney's Rectal Exam on Facebook?" www.eonline.com/uberblog/b143930_toronto _notebook_george_clooneys_rectal.html, as referenced in *Bloomberg Businessweek,* 07–13 March 2011, 83.

8. For more on the ways in which the world is getting more amazingly flat, see Thomas L. Friedman, *The World Is Flat: A Brief History of the Twenty-First Century* (New York: Farrar, Straus and Giroux, 2005).

9. At the time of writing, Facebook's user base is 517 million. See "The World's Global Media Habits in a Word? More," *Advertising Age,* February 14, 2011, 5.

10. Along with text messages, tweetstreams, podcasts, Flickr, YouTube, BitTorrent, Bebo, blogging, microblogging, and others.

11. "Part A: Mobile Subscribers; Global Mobile Handset and Smartphone Market Share; World's Top Five Operators," Global Mobile Statistics 2011, Mobithinking, http://mobithinking.com/mobile-marketing-tools/latest-mobile -stats#subscribers.

12. Kevin Kelly, *What Technology Wants* (New York: Viking, 2010), 286–87.

13. Mark Pesce, "Hyperpolitics (American Style)," from an address presented at the Personal Democracy Forum, June 24, 2008, www.edge.org/3rd_culture /pesce08/pesce08_index.html.

14. Jean-Paul Sartre, *No Exit,* in *No Exit and Three Other Plays* (New York: Vintage, 1989), 45.

15. Robin Dunbar, *How Many Friends Does One Person Need? Dunbar's Number and Other Evolutionary Quirks* (Cambridge, MA: Harvard University Press, 2010).

16. Posting of "Here Comes the Sun," http://blog.gideonaddington.com. This blog and URL are no longer available. See also www.youtube.com /watch?v=H2XCgcxsvTg.

17. These are 2007 USAmerican statistics from the American Foundation for Suicide Prevention, "National Statistics," www.afsp.org/index.cfm?fuseaction =home.viewpage&page_id=050fea9f-b064-4092-b1135c3a70de1fda.

18. In a scholarly study of suicide notes by Baylor University professor M. David Rudd, these four themes dominate the letters. As reported in "Matters of Life and Death," *Baylor Magazine,* July/August 2003, www.baylor.edu/alumni /magazine/0201/news.php?action=story&story=7547.

19. Mark Zuckerberg, quoted in Adam L. Penenberg, "How Much Are You Worth on Facebook?" *Fast Company,* October 2009, 57, www.fastcompany.com /magazine/139/loop-de-loop.html.

20. Anne Jackson, quoted from her comments made during a panel conversation at The Oaks. The author also was a participant in the panel.

21. For more on this, see Mark Simon, *Facial Expressions: A Visual Reference for Artists* (New York: Watson-Guptill, 2005).

22. Sherry Turkle, *Alone Together: Why We Expect More from Technology and Less from Each Other* (New York: Basic, 2011), 160.

23. For more on this, see the research results from Ruder Finn Public Relations, www.ruderfinn.com.

Chapter 13

The chapter epigraph is taken from William James, "Memory," in *Talks to Teachers on Psychology and to Students on Some of Life's Ideals* (New York: Henry Holt, 1914), 143.

1. Martin Luther, quoted in Jürgen Moltmann, *The Crucified God: The Cross of Christ as the Foundation* (Minneapolis: Fortress, 1993), 7. The Latin phrase is from Martin Luther, "Opertiones in Psalmos: Psalmus Quintus V," in *Werke* (Weimar: Hermann Böhlau, 1892), 5:179.

2. See Psalm 118:22; Acts 4:11.

3. Mary Douglas, *Thinking in Circles: An Essay on Ring Composition* (New Haven: Yale University Press, 2007).

4. For my elaboration of this idea, see Leonard Sweet, *The Gospel According to Starbucks: Living with a Grande Passion* (Colorado Springs, CO: WaterBrook, 2007), 38–40.

5. Marvin J. Cetron and Owen Davies, "Trends Now Changing the World, Technology, the Workplace, Management, and Institutions," *Futurist*, March/April 2001, 42.

6. Rowan Williams, *On Christian Theology* (Malden, MA: Blackwell, 2000), 132.

7. See Shane Hipps, interview by Lee Stone, "Your Disembodied Digital Mind," *Relevant*, September/October 2009, 80, www.mygazines.com/issue/2432/81.

8. Blaise Pascal, *Pensées*, trans. A. J. Krailsheimer (New York: Penguin, 1993), 105.

9. If there were no TGIF, there would have been no Egypt Revolution, says thirty-year-old Google executive Wael Ghonim. One of the greatest mistakes of Mubarak's regime was blocking Facebook. Sixty percent of the population of Egypt is younger than thirty.

10. Al Neuharth, "Facebook and Twitter Now Are Our Triggers," *USA Today*, February 25, 2011, 11A, www.usatoday.com/news/opinion/forum/2011-02 -25-column25_ST_N.htm. For a dissenting voice, a voice I feel was proven wrong by events six months later, see Malcolm Gladwell's dismissal of TGIF social networks as weak facilitators in "Small Change: Why the Revolution Will Not Be Tweeted," *New Yorker*, October 2010, www.newyorker.com /reporting/2010/10/04/101004fa_fact_gladwell.

11. "After Mubarak: The Autumn of the Patriarchs," *The Economist*, February 17, 2011, 48, www.economist.com/node/18186984?story_id=E1_TRTRGJRQ.

12. Alfred North Whitehead, *Science and the Modern World* (New York: Cambridge University Press, 2011), 120.

13. Matt Ridley, "When Ideas Have Sex," *The Rational Optimist: How Prosperity Evolves* (New York: Harper, 2010), 6.

14. For more on this idea, see Gino Segré, *Faust in Copenhagen: A Struggle for the Soul of Physics* (New York: Penguin, 2007).

15. Martin Luther, quoted in Robert E. A. Lee, *Martin Luther: The Reformation Years: Based on the Film "Martin Luther"* (Minneapolis: Augsburg, 1967), 64.

16. One scholar even contends about Paul that "no other intellect contributed as much to making us who we are." See Sarah Ruden, "Preface: Who Was Paul," *Paul Among the People: The Apostle Reinterpreted and Reimagined in His Own Time* (New York: Pantheon, 2010), xix.

17. For the lack of individual human agency in fiction, see Jan-Dirk Müller, *Rules for the Endgame: The World of the Nibelungenlied*, trans. William T. Whobrey (Baltimore, MD: Johns Hopkins University Press, 2007).

18. John Locke, *An Essay Concerning Human Understanding* (London: T. Tegg, 1836), 226–27.

19. Jean Jacques Rousseau, *Confessions* (Herfordshire: Wordsworth, 1996), 3.

20. See the suggestive comments of Rabbi Joshua Boettiger, "The Word Is on Fire," *Parabola*, Spring 2011, 64.

21. This view is reiterated by Barbara Ehrenrich in *Dancing in the Streets: A History of Collective Joy* (New York: Metropolitan, 2007), where she argues that the

decline of carnivals, other public festivals, and religious celebrations facilitated people's retreat into self-absorption and the privacy of the home.

22. Ayn Rand, quoted in Jennifer Burns, *Goddess of the Market: Ayn Rand and the American Right* (New York: Oxford University Press, 2009), 65.

23. Thomas Merton, "Hagia Sophia" in *The Collected Poems of Thomas Merton* (New York: New Directions, 1977), 363.

24. This phrase is repeated on at least five different occasions between 1957 and 1968, by Martin Luther King Jr. The most well-known version is found in "Letter from Birmingham City Jail," April 16, 1963. See also *A Testament of Hope: The Essential Writings and Speeches of Martin Luther King, Jr.,* ed. James M. Washington (New York: HarperCollins, 1991), 290. For other occasions see pages 138, 210, 254, 269.

25. Matthew 25:40, NKJV.

26. Thomas Merton, *New Seeds of Contemplation* (New York: New Directions, 1961), 72.

27. James Surowiecki, *The Wisdom of Crowds: Why the Many Are Smarter Than the Few and How Collective Wisdom Shapes Business, Economics, Societies, and Nations* (New York: Anchor, 2004).

28. So says Pew Internet and American Life Survey, as reported in Arnold Brown, "Relationships, Community, and Identity in the New Virtual Society," *The Futurist,* March/April 2011, 29–34, http://proquest.umi.com/pqdweb /nosession?passwd=welcome&session=0&ver=1&did=2261520521&userid =MKN4NFBBNG&uipw=AA2003&rqt=309&vinst=PROD&fmt=3&startp age=-1&vname=PQD&exp=09-24-2008&deli=1&scaling=FULL&vtype=PQ D&uurl=USPW%3DAA2003&cert=vAcG8PU0bf%2FaDRHkOsj09A0ikzJZ G%2BZ7LjSegKLhvc380mplbBOj1DZv554hd2xLSGcVMOtfkG7fS%2FiX3 Ju2zmnObgnt0PmE&y=15&req=1&x=42&mtd=1&TS=1298057830&client Id=1974.

29. Jaron Lanier, quoted in "Virtual Reality," *Mondo 2000: A User's Guide to the New Edge,* ed. Rudy Rucker, R. U. Sirius, and Queen Mu (New York: HarperCollins, 1992), 257–59.

30. Jaron Lanier, *You Are Not a Gadget: A Manifesto* (New York: A. A. Knopf, 2010), 4. For other Lanier quotes see "hive mind," 4; "fake friendship" and "just bait," 54; "digital Maoism," 79.

31. Lisa Miller also contended that "Young people want to 'consume' their spirituality the way they do their news or their music. They want to dip and dabble, the way they browse Facebook." See Lisa Miller, "My Take: How Technology Could Bring Down the Church," CNN BeliefBlog, http://religion.blogs.cnn.com/2011/05/15 /my-take-how-technology-could-bring-down-the-church. See also Lisa Miller, "How Technology Could Bring Down the Church," *Urban Christian News,* May 16, 2011, www.urbanchristiannews.com/ucn/2011/05/how-technology-could -bring-down-the-church-by-lisa-miller.html.

32. Henry Adams, *The Education of Henry Adams: An Autobiography* (Boston: Houghton Mifflin, 1918), 7.

33. Paper, http://paper.li.

34. One of many places this story is told is Bob Fenster, *Twisted Tales from the Wacky Side of Life* (Kansas City, MO: Andrews McMeel, 2006), 137.

35. Ludwig Wittgenstein, *Notebooks 1914–1916*, ed. G. H. von Wright and G. E. M. Amscombe, 2nd ed. (Chicago: University of Chicago Press, 1979), 57.

36. See Kathleen Parker, "A Way Out of the Chaos," *Chicago Tribune*, September 14, 2005, http://articles.chicagotribune.com/2005-09-14/news/0509140006 _1_school-buses-negligent-deamonte-love.

37. Henry David Thoreau, quoted in Gerald Kennedy, *My Third Reader's Notebook* (Nashville: Abingdon, 1974), 94.

38. Clive Thompson, "Your Outboard Brain Knows All," *Wired*, September 25, 2007, www.wired.com/techbiz/people/magazine/15-10/st_thompson.

39. Shane Hipps, *Flickering Pixels: How Technology Shapes Your Faith* (Grand Rapids: Zondervan, 2009), 14.

40. Shane Hipps, "What's [Actually] On Your Mind?" *Relevant Magazine*, September/October 2010, 74.

41. Hipps, "What's [Actually] On Your Mind?" 73.

42. Nicholas Carr, *The Shallows: What the Internet Is Doing to Our Brains* (New York: Norton, 2011), 12.

43. The quotes are from Patrick Tucker, "What the Internet Is Doing to Our Brains," [review of *The Shallows*], *Futurist*, July/August 2010, www.wfs.org /Jul-Aug2010/Carr.htm. Tucker goes on: "He is limited in terms of his capacity for original thought.... He communicates constantly but only in sparse bursts. He can think with great speed but cannot know anything with certainty. He cannot conceive of hard-won knowledge yet is isolated in his hastily reached convictions."

44. The work that journalists produced was called not literature but "columns," or in French newspapers *feuilleton*, which could be translated "talk of the town."

45. Quoting Nadine, a character in Simone de Beauvoir, *The Mandarins* (New York: Norton, 1999), 186. People don't pay attention to literature like they used to. Or even recognize it when they see it. Sharply minted phrases, or dazzling stylistic play, get dismissed as so much interference or unwelcome excess. We seem to be losing an exquisite feeling for words, where the sound and music of the sentences matter almost as much as the thoughts and storyline. Complex thoughts sometimes require complex sentences of theological heft and carefully calibrated stylishness.

46. Joan Ball, in a statement written specifically for this book at the request of the author.

47. John Newton, "The Kite; or Pride Must Have a Fall," in John Cecil, *The Works of the Rev. John Newton...to Which Are Previxed, Memoirs of His Life* (Philadelphia: Uriah Hunt, 1839), 2:207. Public Domain.

48. Margaret Visser, *The Geometry of Love: Space, Time, Mystery, and Meaning in an Ordinary Church* (New York: Penguin, 2002), 45–46.

49. John Habgood, quoted in Mary Loudon, *Revelations: The Clergy Questioned* (London: H. Hamilton, 1994), 16.

50. Philip Hill, *The Church of the Third Millennium* (Carlisle, England: Paternoster, 1999), 3.

51. See www.huffingtonpost.com/2010/03/05/couple-let-baby-starve-to_n_487287 .html.

52. Shane Hipps, quoted in Lee Stone, "Disembodied Mind: Shane Hipps, Author of *Flickering Pixels* Talks about Technology and How It's Shaping Your Faith," *Relevant*, September/October 2009, 80, www.relevantmagazine.com/magazine /magazine-archive/18015-septoct-2009-wilco. See also Shane Hipps, *Flickering Pixels: How Technology Shapes Your Faith* (Grand Rapids: Zondervan, 2009).

53. Hipps, quoted in Stone, "Your Disembodied Digital Mind," 80, www.relevant magazine.com/magazine/magazine-archive/18015-septoct-2009-wilco. See also Hipps, *Flickering Pixels*.

54. Jesse Rice, *The Church of Facebook: How the Hyperconnected Are Redefining Community* (Colorado Springs, CO: David C. Cook, 2009), 170–71.

Chapter 14

Regarding the chapter epigraph, Juliette Lewis recites this line in Woody Allen's "Husbands and Wives" (1992); see Woody Allen, *Woody Allen on Woody Allen: In Conversation with Stig Björkman*, rev. ed. (London: Faber and Faber, 2004), 90.

1. Pliny, *The Natural History of Pliny*, trans. John Bostock and H. T. Riley (London: Henry G. Bohn, 1856), 4:197.

2. For more on this idea, see Leonard Sweet, *Nudge* (Colorado Springs, CO: David C. Cook, 2010).

Appendix

1. Amazingly, playbills advertising plays to be performed each day did not even mention the author's names until around 1700. For more on this, see Peter Holland, "As It Likes You," *TLS: Times Literary Supplement*, August 13, 2010, 11.

2. Austen Ivereigh, "Lessons from the Vulnerable, [review of Jean Vanier, *Our Life Together*]," *The Tablet*, December 11, 2008, www.thetablet.co.uk /review/424.

3. Ivereigh, "Lessons from the Vulnerable," *The Tablet*.

4. See 2 Corinthians 12:9.

Also Available from Leonard Sweet!

In *What Matters Most,* Leonard Sweet explains why we are often more interested in winning religious arguments than in following the Servant of humanity. As Sweet helps us find a biblical balance with active obedience in our correct beliefs, he brings us back to the Person whom God created us to know intimately.

Real Church in a Social-Network World distills the insights and analysis of Leonard Sweet in an eBook exclusive. Drawn from three of Sweet's most paradigm-shifting books (*What Matters Most, The Three Hardest Words,* and *The Gospel According to Starbucks*), this topical sampler delivers the best of Sweet's future-oriented look at Christian faith.

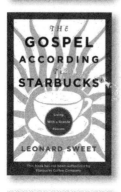

The doors are open and the coffee is brewing. God is serving the refreshing antidote to an unsatisfying, arms-length spiritual life and he won't even make you stand in line. Let Leonard Sweet show you how the passion that Starbucks® has for creating an irresistible experience can connect you with God's stirring experience of faith.

Popular culture has ruined love's reputation by redefining it first as romance, and then as lust. But it's not just the meaning of the word *love* that causes so much confusion. To fully understand love, we also need to find out who we are in God's eyes and whom we are commanded to love. Following Jesus can be described as the daily practice of all three words: *I. Love. You.* There is nothing more rewarding, and nothing more risky.

Read sample chapters @ WaterBrookMultnomah.com